# First World War
## and Army of Occupation
# War Diary
## France, Belgium and Germany

48 DIVISION
145 Infantry Brigade
Gloucestershire Regiment
1/5th Battalion (Territorial)
1 March 1915 - 31 October 1917

WO95/2763/1

Published by

The Naval & Military Press Ltd

Unit 10 Ridgewood Industrial Park,

Uckfield, East Sussex,

TN22 5QE England

Tel: +44 (0) 1825 749494

www.naval-military-press.com

www.nmarchive.com

*This diary has been reprinted in facsimile from the original. Any imperfections are inevitably reproduced and the quality may fall short of modern type and cartographic standards.*

**© Crown Copyright**

**Images reproduced by permission of The National Archives, London, England, 2015.**

# Contents

| Document type | Place/Title | Date From | Date To |
|---|---|---|---|
| Heading | WO95/2763/1 1/5 Battalion Gloucestershire Regiment. | | |
| Heading | 48th Division 145th Infy Bde 1-5th Bn Gloster Regt Mar 1915-1917 Oct To Italy | | |
| Heading | 145th Inf. Bde. 48th Div. Battn. disembarked Boulogne from England 29.3.15 1/5th Battn. The Gloucestershire Regiment. March 1915 1 Aug 18 | | |
| Heading | War Diary of 1/5th Bn. Gloucestershire Regiment (Territorial Force) From 1st March 1915 To 31st March 1915 1/1st South Midland Infantry Brigade. | | |
| War Diary | Chelmsford | 01/03/1915 | 29/03/1915 |
| War Diary | Folxeston | 29/03/1915 | 29/03/1915 |
| War Diary | Boulogne | 29/03/1915 | 30/03/1915 |
| War Diary | Steenvorde | 30/03/1915 | 01/04/1915 |
| Heading | 145th Inf. Bde. 48th Div. 1/5th Battn. The Gloucestershire Regiment. April 1915 | | |
| Heading | War Diary of 1/5th Battn-Gloucestershire Regiment. (Territorial Force). From 1st April 1915. To 30th April, 1915 | | |
| War Diary | Steenvorde | 01/04/1915 | 04/04/1915 |
| War Diary | Meteren | 04/04/1915 | 04/04/1915 |
| War Diary | Ploegsteert | 08/04/1915 | 12/04/1915 |
| War Diary | Steenwerck | 12/04/1915 | 15/04/1915 |
| War Diary | Neuve Eglise | 15/04/1915 | 15/04/1915 |
| War Diary | Ploegsteert Wood | 15/04/1915 | 19/04/1915 |
| War Diary | Romarin Nr Nieppe | 20/04/1915 | 23/04/1915 |
| War Diary | Ploegsteert Wood | 24/04/1915 | 27/04/1915 |
| War Diary | Ploegsteert | 28/04/1915 | 28/04/1915 |
| War Diary | Romarin | 29/04/1915 | 30/04/1915 |
| Heading | 145th Inf. Bde. 48th Div. 1/5th Battn. The Gloucestershire Regiment. May 1915 | | |
| War Diary | Romarin | 01/05/1915 | 01/05/1915 |
| War Diary | Ploegsteert Wood | 01/05/1915 | 05/05/1915 |
| War Diary | Romarin | 06/05/1915 | 10/05/1915 |
| War Diary | Ploegsteert Wood | 11/05/1915 | 14/05/1915 |
| War Diary | Romarin | 15/05/1915 | 18/05/1915 |
| War Diary | Ploegsteert Wood | 19/05/1915 | 22/05/1915 |
| War Diary | Romarin | 23/05/1915 | 26/05/1915 |
| War Diary | Ploegsteert Wood | 27/05/1915 | 30/05/1915 |
| War Diary | Romarin | 31/05/1915 | 31/05/1915 |
| Heading | 145th Inf. Bde. 48th Div. 1/5th Battn. The Gloucestershire Regiment. June 1915 | | |
| Heading | War Diary of 1/5th Battalion-Gloucestershire Regiment. From 1st June, 1915. To 30th June, 1915 (Volume 4) | | |
| War Diary | Romarin | 01/06/1915 | 03/06/1915 |
| War Diary | Ploegsteert Wood | 04/06/1915 | 07/06/1915 |
| War Diary | Romarin | 07/06/1915 | 11/06/1915 |
| War Diary | La Plus Douve Farm Wulverghen | 11/06/1915 | 11/06/1915 |
| War Diary | La Plus Douve | 12/06/1915 | 15/06/1915 |
| War Diary | Courte Dreve Farm | 16/06/1915 | 17/06/1915 |
| War Diary | Courte Dreve Farm Ploegsteert | 19/06/1915 | 19/06/1915 |

| | | | |
|---|---|---|---|
| War Diary | Pont De Nieppe | 20/06/1915 | 24/06/1915 |
| War Diary | Bailleul | 25/06/1915 | 25/06/1915 |
| War Diary | Vieux Berquin | 26/06/1915 | 26/06/1915 |
| War Diary | Gonnehem | 27/06/1915 | 27/06/1915 |
| War Diary | Allouagne | 27/06/1915 | 30/06/1915 |
| Heading | 145th Inf. Bde. 48th Div. 1/5th Battn. The Gloucestershire Regiment. July 1915 | | |
| Heading | War Diary of 1/5th Battalion-Gloucestershire Regiment from 1st July, 1915 to 31st July, 1915 (Volume 5) | | |
| War Diary | Allouagne | 01/07/1915 | 12/07/1915 |
| War Diary | Noeux Les Mines | 13/07/1915 | 16/07/1915 |
| War Diary | Ames | 17/07/1915 | 18/07/1915 |
| War Diary | Sarton | 19/07/1915 | 19/07/1915 |
| War Diary | Bayencourt | 20/07/1915 | 20/07/1915 |
| War Diary | Hebuterne | 20/07/1915 | 24/07/1915 |
| War Diary | Bayoncourt | 25/07/1915 | 28/07/1915 |
| War Diary | Sailly Au Bois | 28/07/1915 | 28/07/1915 |
| War Diary | Hebuterne | 29/07/1915 | 31/07/1915 |
| Heading | 145th Inf. Bde. 48th Div. 1/5th Battn. The Gloucestershire Regiment. August 1915 | | |
| War Diary | Hebuterne | 01/08/1915 | 21/08/1915 |
| War Diary | Sailly Aux Bois | 22/08/1915 | 23/08/1915 |
| War Diary | Sailly | 25/08/1915 | 26/08/1915 |
| War Diary | Hebuterne | 26/08/1915 | 31/08/1915 |
| Miscellaneous | Diving | | |
| Heading | 145th Inf. Bde. 48th Div. 1/5th Battn. The Gloucestershire Regiment. September 1915 | | |
| Heading | War Diary of 1/5th Battalion-Gloucestershire Regiment. From 1st September, 1915. To 30th September, 1915. Volume VII. | | |
| War Diary | Hebuterne | 01/09/1915 | 05/09/1915 |
| War Diary | Sailly | 06/09/1915 | 08/09/1915 |
| War Diary | Bus | 09/09/1915 | 17/09/1915 |
| War Diary | Hebuterne | 17/09/1915 | 29/09/1915 |
| War Diary | Bus | 30/09/1915 | 30/09/1915 |
| Heading | 145th Inf. Bde. 48th Div. 1/5th Battn. The Gloucestershire Regiment. October 1915 | | |
| Heading | War Diary of 1/5th Battalion-Gloucestershire Regiment. From 1st October, 1915. To, 31st October, 1915. Volume 8. | | |
| War Diary | Bus | 01/10/1915 | 11/10/1915 |
| War Diary | Hebuterne | 11/10/1915 | 19/10/1915 |
| War Diary | Bus | 20/10/1915 | 27/10/1915 |
| War Diary | Hebuterne | 27/10/1915 | 31/10/1915 |
| Miscellaneous | Diving | | |
| Heading | 145th Inf. Bde. 48th Div. 1/5th Battn. The Gloucestershire Regiment. November 1915 | | |
| Heading | War Diary of 1/5th Battalion-Gloucestershire Regiment. From 1st November, 1915. To 30th November, 1915. Volume IX. | | |
| War Diary | Hebuterne | 01/11/1915 | 04/11/1915 |
| War Diary | Bus | 04/11/1915 | 12/11/1915 |
| War Diary | Hebuterne | 13/11/1915 | 20/11/1915 |
| War Diary | Bus | 21/11/1915 | 28/11/1915 |
| War Diary | Hebuterne | 28/11/1915 | 30/11/1915 |

| Type | Location | From | To |
|---|---|---|---|
| Heading | 145th Inf. Bde. 48th Div. 1/5th Battn. The Gloucestershire Regiment. December 1915 | | |
| Heading | War Diary of 1/5th Battalion-Gloucestershire Regiment. From 1st December, 1915. To 31st December, 1915 (Volume 10) | | |
| War Diary | Hebuterne | 01/12/1915 | 06/12/1915 |
| War Diary | Bus | 07/12/1915 | 14/12/1915 |
| War Diary | Hebuterne | 14/12/1915 | 22/12/1915 |
| War Diary | Bus | 23/12/1915 | 28/12/1915 |
| War Diary | Hebuterne | 28/12/1915 | 31/12/1915 |
| Heading | 145th Brigade. 48th Division. 1/5th Battalion Gloucestershire Regiment January 1916 | | |
| War Diary | Hebuterne | 01/01/1916 | 03/01/1916 |
| War Diary | Bus | 04/01/1916 | 09/01/1916 |
| War Diary | Hebuterne | 10/01/1916 | 15/01/1916 |
| War Diary | Bus | 16/01/1916 | 21/01/1916 |
| War Diary | Hebuterne | 21/01/1916 | 27/01/1916 |
| War Diary | Bus | 28/01/1916 | 31/01/1916 |
| Heading | 145th Brigade. 48th Division. 1/5th Battalion Gloucestershire Regiment February 1916 | | |
| War Diary | Bus | 01/02/1916 | 02/02/1916 |
| War Diary | Hebuterne | 02/02/1916 | 19/02/1916 |
| War Diary | Courcelles-Sailly | 20/02/1916 | 22/02/1916 |
| War Diary | Hebuterne | 23/02/1916 | 29/02/1916 |
| Heading | 145th Brigade. 48th Division. 1/5th Battalion Gloucestershire Regiment March 1916 | | |
| Miscellaneous | The A.G. Base. | 31/08/1916 | 31/08/1916 |
| War Diary | Hebuterne | 01/03/1916 | 02/03/1916 |
| War Diary | Sailly | 03/03/1916 | 06/03/1916 |
| War Diary | Hebuterne | 07/03/1916 | 14/03/1916 |
| War Diary | Sailly | 15/03/1916 | 18/03/1916 |
| War Diary | Hebuterne | 19/03/1916 | 26/03/1916 |
| War Diary | Sailly | 27/03/1916 | 31/03/1916 |
| War Diary | Hebuterne | 30/03/1916 | 31/03/1916 |
| Heading | 145th Brigade. 48th Division. 1/5th Battalion Gloucestershire Regiment April 1916 | | |
| Miscellaneous | To The Officer i/c 'A.' Gs. Office at the Base. | 04/05/1916 | 04/05/1916 |
| War Diary | Hebuterne | 01/04/1916 | 04/04/1916 |
| War Diary | Sailly | 05/04/1916 | 05/04/1916 |
| War Diary | Covin Sailly | 06/04/1916 | 09/04/1916 |
| War Diary | Couin Sailly | 10/04/1916 | 12/04/1916 |
| War Diary | Hebuterne | 12/04/1916 | 20/04/1916 |
| War Diary | Couin Sailly | 21/04/1916 | 21/04/1916 |
| War Diary | Sailly | 22/04/1916 | 30/04/1916 |
| Heading | 145th Brigade. 48th Division. 1/5th Battalion Gloucestershire Regiment May 1916 | | |
| Miscellaneous | D.a.g. Bn Echelon. G.H.Q. | 02/06/1916 | 02/06/1916 |
| War Diary | Sailly | 01/05/1916 | 01/05/1916 |
| War Diary | Hebuterne | 02/05/1916 | 10/05/1916 |
| War Diary | Coigneux | 11/05/1916 | 14/05/1916 |
| War Diary | Authie | 15/05/1916 | 17/05/1916 |
| War Diary | Beauval | 18/05/1916 | 31/05/1916 |
| War Diary | Coulonvillers | 31/05/1916 | 31/05/1916 |
| Heading | 145th Brigade. 48th Division. 1/5th Battalion Gloucestershire Regiment June 1916 | | |
| War Diary | Coulonvillers | 01/06/1916 | 04/06/1916 |

| | | | |
|---|---|---|---|
| War Diary | Gapennes | 05/06/1916 | 09/06/1916 |
| War Diary | Outrebois | 10/06/1916 | 10/06/1916 |
| War Diary | Coigneux | 11/06/1916 | 12/06/1916 |
| War Diary | Hebuterne | 12/06/1916 | 16/06/1916 |
| War Diary | Sailly (Dell) | 17/06/1916 | 18/06/1916 |
| War Diary | Sailly (The Dell) | 19/06/1916 | 22/06/1916 |
| War Diary | Couin | 23/06/1916 | 29/06/1916 |
| War Diary | 57a 6-1 | 30/06/1916 | 30/06/1916 |
| Heading | 145th Inf. Bde. 48th Div. 1/5th Battn. The Gloucestershire Regiment. July 1916 | | |
| War Diary | Couin J 7a 61 | 01/07/1916 | 01/07/1916 |
| War Diary | Mailly-Maillet | 02/07/1916 | 03/07/1916 |
| War Diary | Couin | 04/07/1916 | 04/07/1916 |
| War Diary | Hebuterne | 04/07/1916 | 10/07/1916 |
| War Diary | Sailly Au Bois (Dell) | 11/07/1916 | 12/07/1916 |
| War Diary | Hebuterne | 13/07/1916 | 16/07/1916 |
| War Diary | Couin | 17/07/1916 | 17/07/1916 |
| War Diary | Bouzincourt | 18/07/1916 | 19/07/1916 |
| War Diary | Ovillers La Boisselle | 20/07/1916 | 23/07/1916 |
| War Diary | Bivouac East of Albert W 29 B9-4 | 24/07/1916 | 26/07/1916 |
| War Diary | Lealvillers | 27/07/1916 | 28/07/1916 |
| War Diary | Beauval | 29/07/1916 | 29/07/1916 |
| War Diary | Cramont | 30/07/1916 | 31/07/1916 |
| Heading | 145th Brigade. 48th Division. 1/5th Battalion Gloucestershire Regiment August 1916 | | |
| Miscellaneous | Headquarters 145th Inf. Bde. | 01/09/1916 | 01/09/1916 |
| War Diary | Cramont | 01/08/1916 | 09/08/1916 |
| War Diary | Beauval | 10/08/1916 | 10/08/1916 |
| War Diary | Varennes | 11/08/1916 | 11/08/1916 |
| War Diary | Bouzincourt (Bivouac) | 12/08/1916 | 13/08/1916 |
| War Diary | Reserve Trenches W 21a (Central) | 14/08/1916 | 14/08/1916 |
| War Diary | Ovillers-La-Boisselle | 14/08/1916 | 16/08/1916 |
| War Diary | Gun Pits W 24 A 34 | 17/08/1916 | 18/08/1916 |
| War Diary | Support Trenches | 19/08/1916 | 19/08/1916 |
| War Diary | Bouzincourt (Bivouac) V 12c 67 | 20/08/1916 | 21/08/1916 |
| War Diary | Bouzincourt V 12c 67 | 22/08/1916 | 23/08/1916 |
| War Diary | Donnets Post | 24/08/1916 | 25/08/1916 |
| War Diary | Trenches R 31 D 81 to X 8 A 0.5 | 25/08/1916 | 26/08/1916 |
| War Diary | Trenches | 27/08/1916 | 28/08/1916 |
| War Diary | Bouzincourt Bivouac | 29/08/1916 | 29/08/1916 |
| War Diary | Bus-Les-Artois | 30/08/1916 | 31/08/1916 |
| Heading | 145th Brigade. 48th Division. 1/5th Battalion Gloucestershire Regiment September 1916 | | |
| War Diary | Bus-Les-Artois | 01/09/1916 | 08/09/1916 |
| War Diary | Trenches Near Beaumont Hamel | 08/09/1916 | 10/09/1916 |
| War Diary | Bois De Warnimont | 11/09/1916 | 11/09/1916 |
| War Diary | Beauval | 12/09/1916 | 17/09/1916 |
| War Diary | Beauval to Vacquerie to Gorges. | 18/09/1916 | 18/09/1916 |
| War Diary | Vacquerie & Gorges | 19/09/1916 | 29/09/1916 |
| War Diary | Humbercourt | 30/09/1916 | 30/09/1916 |
| Heading | 145th Brigade. 48th Division. 1/5th Battalion Gloucestershire Regiment October 1916 | | |
| War Diary | Humbercourt & Warlincourt | 01/10/1916 | 01/10/1916 |
| War Diary | Warlincourt | 02/10/1916 | 06/10/1916 |
| War Diary | Henu | 07/10/1916 | 07/10/1916 |
| War Diary | Warlincourt | 08/10/1916 | 09/10/1916 |

| | | | |
|---|---|---|---|
| War Diary | Henu | 10/10/1916 | 14/10/1916 |
| War Diary | Hebuterne | 14/10/1916 | 16/10/1916 |
| War Diary | Henu | 16/10/1916 | 19/10/1916 |
| War Diary | Warlincourt | 19/10/1916 | 20/10/1916 |
| War Diary | Humbercourt | 20/10/1916 | 21/10/1916 |
| War Diary | Humbercourt Beauval | 22/10/1916 | 22/10/1916 |
| War Diary | Beauval Talmas | 23/10/1916 | 23/10/1916 |
| War Diary | Talmas Behencourt | 24/10/1916 | 24/10/1916 |
| War Diary | Behencourt | 25/10/1916 | 31/10/1916 |
| Heading | 145th Brigade. 48th Division. 1/5th Battalion Gloucestershire Regiment November 1916 | | |
| War Diary | Contalmaison | 01/11/1916 | 01/11/1916 |
| War Diary | Trenches N.W. Le Sars | 02/11/1916 | 02/11/1916 |
| War Diary | Le Sars | 03/11/1916 | 04/11/1916 |
| War Diary | M 27a 16 Martinpuica | 05/11/1916 | 05/11/1916 |
| War Diary | Martinpuich. | 06/11/1916 | 06/11/1916 |
| War Diary | X 27a. 8.2 | 07/11/1916 | 09/11/1916 |
| War Diary | Shelter Wood X 22c 2.7 | 10/11/1916 | 10/11/1916 |
| War Diary | Shelter Wood | 11/11/1916 | 14/11/1916 |
| War Diary | Trenches Le Sars | 14/11/1916 | 16/11/1916 |
| War Diary | Martinpuich. | 17/11/1916 | 18/11/1916 |
| War Diary | Trenches Le Sars | 19/11/1916 | 20/11/1916 |
| War Diary | Middle Wood Camp | 21/11/1916 | 30/11/1916 |
| Map | Le Sars To Irles And Grevillers | | |
| Heading | 145th Brigade. 48th Division. 1/5th Battalion Gloucestershire Regiment December 1916 | | |
| War Diary | Trenches Le Sars | 01/12/1916 | 03/12/1916 |
| War Diary | Shelter Wood Camp North | 04/12/1916 | 08/12/1916 |
| War Diary | Middle Wood Camp | 09/12/1916 | 12/12/1916 |
| War Diary | Scotts Redoubt Camp South | 13/12/1916 | 13/12/1916 |
| War Diary | Le Sars Trenches | 14/12/1916 | 15/12/1916 |
| War Diary | Villa Camp | 16/12/1916 | 16/12/1916 |
| War Diary | Becourt Camp A | 17/12/1916 | 28/12/1916 |
| War Diary | Bresle | 29/12/1916 | 31/12/1916 |
| Heading | 1/5th Bn Gloucestershire Regiment War Diary Vol XXII 1st Jan 1917 to 31st Jany 1917 January 1917 Vol 23 | | |
| War Diary | Bresle | 01/01/1917 | 09/01/1917 |
| War Diary | Merelessart | 10/01/1917 | 29/01/1917 |
| War Diary | Hamel | 30/01/1917 | 31/01/1917 |
| Heading | War Diary of 1/5th Battalion Gloucestershire Regiment From February 1st 1917 to February 28th 1917 Vol 24 | | |
| War Diary | Hamel | 01/02/1917 | 02/02/1917 |
| War Diary | Marly Froissy | 03/02/1917 | 03/02/1917 |
| War Diary | Marly | 04/02/1917 | 06/02/1917 |
| War Diary | Marly Support Trenches S. of Biaches | 07/02/1917 | 07/02/1917 |
| War Diary | (La. Maisonette) In Trenches. | 08/02/1917 | 08/02/1917 |
| War Diary | Front Line Trenches | 09/02/1917 | 11/02/1917 |
| War Diary | In Trenches | 12/02/1917 | 12/02/1917 |
| War Diary | In Trenches 20 Sophie Tr | 13/02/1917 | 13/02/1917 |
| War Diary | Sophie Tr | 14/02/1917 | 16/02/1917 |
| War Diary | Sophie Tr Marly Camp | 17/02/1917 | 17/02/1917 |
| War Diary | Marly | 18/02/1917 | 23/02/1917 |
| War Diary | Marly Sophie Tr | 24/02/1917 | 24/02/1917 |
| War Diary | Sophie Tr Front Line | 25/02/1917 | 25/02/1917 |
| War Diary | In Trenches | 26/02/1917 | 27/02/1917 |

| | | | |
|---|---|---|---|
| War Diary | Support | 28/02/1917 | 28/02/1917 |
| Heading | War Diary of 1/5th Gloucestershire Regiment from 1st March To 31st March 1917 Volume IX | | |
| War Diary | Support Achille Wood 0.5a 89 | 01/03/1917 | 01/03/1917 |
| War Diary | In Trenches | 02/03/1917 | 02/03/1917 |
| War Diary | In Trenches Caddy | 03/03/1917 | 03/03/1917 |
| War Diary | Cappy | 04/03/1917 | 07/03/1917 |
| War Diary | Achillewood | 07/03/1917 | 10/03/1917 |
| War Diary | Achillewood to Trenches | 11/03/1917 | 11/03/1917 |
| War Diary | Trenches | 12/03/1917 | 12/03/1917 |
| War Diary | Trenches Cappy | 13/03/1917 | 13/03/1917 |
| War Diary | Cappy | 14/03/1917 | 17/03/1917 |
| War Diary | Trenches. | 17/03/1917 | 17/03/1917 |
| War Diary | Cappy | 18/03/1917 | 19/03/1917 |
| War Diary | Cappy Peronne | 20/03/1917 | 20/03/1917 |
| War Diary | Peronne | 21/03/1917 | 21/03/1917 |
| War Diary | Peronne Cartigny | 22/03/1917 | 22/03/1917 |
| War Diary | Cartigny | 23/03/1917 | 23/03/1917 |
| War Diary | Cartigny Bouvincourt | 24/03/1917 | 24/03/1917 |
| War Diary | Bouvincourt | 25/03/1917 | 26/03/1917 |
| War Diary | Bouvincourt Cartigny | 27/03/1917 | 27/03/1917 |
| War Diary | Cartigny | 28/03/1917 | 29/03/1917 |
| War Diary | Doignt | 29/03/1917 | 30/03/1917 |
| War Diary | Doignt Tincourt | 31/03/1917 | 31/03/1917 |
| Heading | 1/5th Battn. Gloucestershire Regiment War Diary Volume XXV | | |
| War Diary | Tincourt | 01/04/1917 | 01/04/1917 |
| War Diary | Bivouac Camp K7b 33 | 02/04/1917 | 02/04/1917 |
| War Diary | Epehy | 03/04/1917 | 03/04/1917 |
| War Diary | Villers Faucon | 04/04/1917 | 04/04/1917 |
| War Diary | Lempire | 05/04/1917 | 05/04/1917 |
| War Diary | Villers Faucon | 06/04/1917 | 06/04/1917 |
| War Diary | Bivouacs E 29b. 8.7 Nr Seemelie | 06/04/1917 | 06/04/1917 |
| War Diary | Hamel | 07/04/1917 | 12/04/1917 |
| War Diary | Lempire Positions | 13/04/1917 | 14/04/1917 |
| War Diary | Camp S of Bn Emelie | 15/04/1917 | 17/04/1917 |
| War Diary | To Lempire Tombois Farm. to Camp Ry Cutting Camp | 18/04/1917 | 24/04/1917 |
| War Diary | To Tombois Farm Positions | 25/04/1917 | 25/04/1917 |
| War Diary | To Camp. near St Emelie | 26/04/1917 | 27/04/1917 |
| War Diary | To Tombois Farm Positions. | 28/04/1917 | 28/04/1917 |
| War Diary | To Tincourt | 29/04/1917 | 30/04/1917 |
| Map | Position Taken By Battalion On Night 18 March 1917 | | |
| Heading | 1/5th Bn. Gloucestershire Regt War Diary Vol. XXVI May 1917 | | |
| War Diary | Cartigny | 01/05/1917 | 01/05/1917 |
| War Diary | Camp Le Mesnil | 02/05/1917 | 11/05/1917 |
| War Diary | Camp Combles | 12/05/1917 | 12/05/1917 |
| War Diary | Camp Bancourt | 13/05/1917 | 13/05/1917 |
| War Diary | Support Line Beaumetz | 14/05/1917 | 17/05/1917 |
| War Diary | Demicourt | 18/05/1917 | 21/05/1917 |
| War Diary | Demicourt to W of Hermies | 22/05/1917 | 22/05/1917 |
| War Diary | Bivouacs | 23/05/1917 | 26/05/1917 |
| War Diary | Camp Velu Wood | 27/05/1917 | 28/05/1917 |
| War Diary | To Front Line Hermies | 28/05/1917 | 31/05/1917 |
| Heading | 1/5th Bn. Gloucestershire Regiment War Diary. Vol. XXVII June 1917 | | |

| | | | |
|---|---|---|---|
| War Diary | Hermies | 01/06/1917 | 03/06/1917 |
| War Diary | Beaumetz | 04/06/1917 | 08/06/1917 |
| War Diary | Hermies | 09/06/1917 | 15/06/1917 |
| War Diary | Velu Wood | 16/06/1917 | 21/06/1917 |
| War Diary | Hermies | 22/06/1917 | 27/06/1917 |
| War Diary | Beaumetz | 28/06/1917 | 30/06/1917 |
| Heading | War Diary of 1/5th Battalion Gloster Regiment Volume XXVIII From 1st July 1917 to 31st July 1917 | | |
| War Diary | Hermies | 01/07/1917 | 02/07/1917 |
| War Diary | Fremicourt | 03/07/1917 | 03/07/1917 |
| War Diary | Bihucourt | 04/07/1917 | 04/07/1917 |
| War Diary | Bellacourt | 05/07/1917 | 20/07/1917 |
| War Diary | Pommier | 21/07/1917 | 22/07/1917 |
| War Diary | Houtkerque | 23/07/1917 | 29/07/1917 |
| War Diary | St Jan Ter Biezen | 31/07/1917 | 31/07/1917 |
| War Diary | Houtkerque | 30/07/1917 | 30/07/1917 |
| War Diary | St. Jan Ter Biezen | 31/07/1917 | 31/07/1917 |
| Heading | 1/5th Bn. Gloucester Regiment War Diary. Volume XXIX August 1917 | | |
| War Diary | St Jan Ter Biezen | 01/08/1917 | 01/08/1917 |
| War Diary | St Jan Ter Biezen | 01/08/1917 | 03/08/1917 |
| War Diary | Vlamertinghe | 04/08/1917 | 04/08/1917 |
| War Diary | Ypres | 05/08/1917 | 07/08/1917 |
| War Diary | Vlamertinghe | 08/08/1917 | 14/08/1917 |
| War Diary | Ypres | 15/08/1917 | 15/08/1917 |
| War Diary | St Julien | 16/08/1917 | 17/08/1917 |
| War Diary | Vlamertinge | 18/08/1917 | 26/08/1917 |
| War Diary | Reigersburg | 27/08/1917 | 27/08/1917 |
| War Diary | St Julien | 28/08/1917 | 28/08/1917 |
| War Diary | Dambre Camp | 29/08/1917 | 29/08/1917 |
| War Diary | St. Janster-Biezen | 30/08/1917 | 31/08/1917 |
| Heading | 1/5th Bn. Gloucestershire Regt. War Diary Volume XXIX September 1917 | | |
| War Diary | Roads Camp | 01/09/1917 | 01/09/1917 |
| War Diary | St Jan Ter Biezen | 02/09/1917 | 13/09/1917 |
| War Diary | Roads Camp | 14/09/1917 | 16/09/1917 |
| War Diary | Licques Area | 17/09/1917 | 24/09/1917 |
| War Diary | Bonningues | 25/09/1917 | 25/09/1917 |
| War Diary | Reigersburg | 26/09/1917 | 26/09/1917 |
| War Diary | Canal Bank | 27/09/1917 | 30/09/1917 |
| Heading | 1/5th Bn. Gloucestershire. Regt. War Diary Vol. XXI October 1917 | | |
| War Diary | Canal Bank | 01/10/1917 | 02/10/1917 |
| War Diary | Reigersburg | 03/10/1917 | 08/10/1917 |
| War Diary | Dambre Camp | 09/10/1917 | 12/10/1917 |
| War Diary | St Janster Biezen | 13/10/1917 | 14/10/1917 |
| War Diary | Camblain L'Abbe | 15/10/1917 | 18/10/1917 |
| War Diary | Villers Au Bois | 19/10/1917 | 31/10/1917 |
| Heading | WO95/2763 5 Parts | | |
| Map | | | |
| Map | WO95/2763 5 Parts | | |
| Map | | | |
| Heading | WO95/2763 5 Parts | | |
| Map | Trench Map 62c. S.W. | | |
| Map | | | |

WO95/2763/1

1/5 Battalion Gloucestershire Regiment

48TH DIVISION
145TH INFY BDE

1-5TH BN GLOSTER REGT

MAR 1915-~~AUG 1918~~
1917 OCT

TO ITALY

145th Inf.Bde.
48th Div.

Battn. disembarked
Boulogne from
England 29.3.15.

1/5th BATTN. THE GLOUCESTERSHIRE REGIMENT.

M A R C H

1915

Aug '18

CONFIDENTIAL

WAR DIARY
of
1/5th Bn GLOUCESTERSHIRE
REGIMENT
(TERRITORIAL FORCE)

From 1st March 1915

To 31st March 1915

1/1st SOUTH MIDLAND INFANTRY
BRIGADE

# WAR DIARY
## or
## INTELLIGENCE SUMMARY.

*(Erase heading not required.)*

Army Form C. 2118.

Instructions regarding War Diaries and Intelligence Summaries are contained in F. S. Regs., Part II. and the Staff Manual respectively. Title pages will be prepared in manuscript.

| Place | Date | Hour | Summary of Events and Information | Remarks and references to Appendices |
|---|---|---|---|---|
| CHELMSFORD | 1/3/15 | | 1st to 7th inclusive Training | |
| " | 8/3/15 | | Captain & Adjutant V.N. JOHNSON proceeded to the War Front to be attached for Instruction to the Army in the Field for 3 days | 1D |
| " | 12/3/15 | | Captain & Adjutant V.N. JOHNSON returned from FRANCE | 1D |
| " | 13/3/15 | | Received orders to prepare for Foreign Service | 1D |
| " | 14/3/15 4 pm | | Incidents in Deficiencies rendered to D.O.O. | 1D |
| " | 15/3/15 to 27/3/15 | | Inspections & Training | 1D |

[signature]

Army Form C. 2118.

# WAR DIARY
## or
## INTELLIGENCE SUMMARY.
*(Erase heading not required.)*

Instructions regarding War Diaries and Intelligence Summaries are contained in F. S. Regs., Part II. and the Staff Manual respectively. Title pages will be prepared in manuscript.

| Place | Date | Hour | Summary of Events and Information | Remarks and references to Appendices |
|---|---|---|---|---|
| CHELMSFORD | 29/3/15 | | Web Equipment received & issued. New Army Pattern Boots received. Harness etc received | (1) |
| " | 21/3/15 | | | (1) |
| " | 26/3/15 | | Battalion completely equipped, with exception of 2 Machine Guns & 2 trumpet bugles | (1) |
| | | | | etc |

Army Form C. 2118.

# WAR DIARY
## or
## INTELLIGENCE SUMMARY.

1/5th/Pr GLOUCESTERSHIRE REGT

(Erase heading not required.)

| Place | Date | Hour | Summary of Events and Information | Remarks and references to Appendices |
|---|---|---|---|---|
| CHELMSFORD | 27/3/15 | 7am | Received orders that the following will entrain to join the Expeditionary Force 1st Line Transport and Train Machine Gun Section Sergt Shoemaker Orderly Room Sergt Ammunition Sergt  Total Officers 2 Other Ranks 82 Horses 58 entrain waggon 21 Train to leave CHELMSFORD Goods yard at 3.35 am 28/3/15 | |
| | | 9.30pm | Received Time Table for trains to move the personnel of the Battalion | |

[signature]

# WAR DIARY
## INTELLIGENCE SUMMARY

Army Form C. 2118.

| Place | Date | Hour | Summary of Events and Information | Remarks and references to Appendices |
|---|---|---|---|---|
| CHELMSFORD | 28/3/15 | 2 am | Lieut G.J. LISTER Transport Officer & 2/Lt E.C. ONDER machine Gun officer Armour Sergt Major SAIERS, orderly Room Sergt HILL Sergt Shoe-maker HINCH, Transport Sergt JONES 81 N.C.O. & men, 10 mules, 23 Vehicles entrained for SOUTHAMPTON | |
| " | 29/3/15 | 3-30 pm | Arrived SOUTHAMPTON Embarked in S.S. ARCHITECT for HAVRE Arrived HAVRE | |

# WAR DIARY
## INTELLIGENCE SUMMARY

| Place | Date | Hour | Summary of Events and Information | Remarks and references to Appendices |
|---|---|---|---|---|
| CHELMSFORD | 29/3/15 | 5 p.m. | 1st Train.  Head Quarters (less Machine gun) A and B Companies entrained 1 p.m. FOLKESTONE. Strength:- 176 Officers & 58 other ranks. List of officers:- Lt Col J H COLLETT (Commanding) Major J F TARRANT (2nd in Command) Capt V N JOHNSON (Adjutant) Capt R CARRUTHERS-LITTLE Commdg B Coy Capt G F COLLETT  " A Coy Lieut R C SUMNER  " W FREAM Capt R.S.D. STUART YC Supplies (Reynolds) 2 Lt T. H. MOORE 2 Lt J.P. WINTERBOTHAM 2 Lt E.F.R. BARNETT Yr Qr Mr C. F. FOOTE 2 Lt C.S. NASON  Lieut F.H. SPRAGUE (RAMC) 2 Lt H.S. KING  L⁴ Class Chaplain F.C. HELM 2 Lt L.W. MOORE | |

# WAR DIARY
## INTELLIGENCE SUMMARY

Army Form C. 2118.

| Place | Date | Hour | Summary of Events and Information | Remarks and references to Appendices |
|---|---|---|---|---|
| CHELMSFORD | 24/6/15 | 5.30pm | 2nd Train  C and D Coys + Signallers entrain for FOLKESTONE.  Strength 11 officers 458 other Ranks, 9 Bicycles  List of officers:  Major N H WALLER   Comdg C Coy  Capt H HARVE          "    D Coy  Capt F N COLE          Capt Viscount CAMPDEN  2/Lt R M F COOKE  "   F E FRANCILLON  "   H P SNOWDEN  2/Lt H&C GUISE  2/Lt C W WINTERBOTHAM  2/Lt W VAUGHAN  2/Lt G HAWKINS | 19 |

Army Form C. 2118.

# WAR DIARY
## or
## INTELLIGENCE SUMMARY.
*(Erase heading not required.)*

Instructions regarding War Diaries and Intelligence Summaries are contained in F. S. Regs., Part II. and the Staff Manual respectively. Title pages will be prepared in manuscript.

| Place | Date | Hour | Summary of Events and Information | Remarks and references to Appendices |
|---|---|---|---|---|
| FOLKESTONE | 29/3/15 | 9pm | Battalion embarked in S.S. INVICTA for BOULOGNE. Strength 28 Officers, 916 other Ranks | |
| BOULOGNE | | 11pm | Arrival BOULOGNE and disembarked | |
| | | 11.30pm | Marched to Rest Camp (2½ miles) | |
| " | 30/3/15 | 12.30am | Arrival at Rest Camp | |
| | | 9am | Marched to PONT de BRIQUE Station (3 miles) | |
| | | 10.55am | Entrained in Cattle Trucks (42 in a truck) in Train from HAVRE which was bringing up Transport & details. | |
| | | 11.5am | Train leaves for ST OMER and CASSEL | |
| | | 3.16pm | Arrive CASSEL & detrain | |

1577 Wt. W10791/1773 500,000 1/15 D. D. & L. A.D.S.S./Forms/C. 2118.

**Army Form C. 2118.**

# WAR DIARY
## or
## INTELLIGENCE SUMMARY.
*(Erase heading not required.)*

| Place | Date | Hour | Summary of Events and Information | Remarks and references to Appendices |
|---|---|---|---|---|
| STEENVOORDE | 30/3/15 | 4.15 pm | March to STEENVOORDE and Billet Battalion Billet in Farms EAST of Town. Head Quarters at 66 Rue de POPERINGHE East Company in distrint 5 or 6 Farms, each form can accommodate 30 to 50 men. Inter-communication between H.Q. & Company is carried out by cycle orderlies, between company & Platoon by Runners. Men sleep in Barns or Sheds provided by the Farmer. Eggs & milk are plentiful. Water is drawn out daily in Battalion Water Carts. The only complaint down here from CHELMSFORD was from Rothy Michael. Weather. Sunshine by day. Frost by night. | |

# WAR DIARY
## or
## INTELLIGENCE SUMMARY.

*Army Form C. 2118.*

(Erase heading not required.)

| Place | Date | Hour | Summary of Events and Information | Remarks and references to Appendices |
|---|---|---|---|---|
| STEENVOORDE | 31/3/15 | | Company Returns. Inspection Iron Rations with Biscuits Weather. Smoking. Front at myr [?] | |
| | until 1st 1/4/15 | | | |

145th Inf.Bde.
48th Div.

1/5th BATTN. THE GLOUCESTERSHIRE REGIMENT.

A P R I L

1 9 1 5

CONFIDENTIAL.

# WAR DIARY

## OF

### 1/5TH BATTN - GLOUCESTERSHIRE REGIMENT.
### (TERRITORIAL FORCE).

From    1st April, 1915.

To      30th April, 1915.

Army Form C. 2118.

# WAR DIARY
## or
## INTELLIGENCE SUMMARY.
*(Erase heading not required.)*

1/5th Gloucestershire Regt (T.F.)

April

| Place | Date | Hour | Summary of Events and Information | Remarks and references to Appendices |
|---|---|---|---|---|
| STEENVOORDE | 1/4/15 | | Company Training. Rations: Bully Beef & Biscuit. Weather: Sunshine | |
| | 2/4/15 | 11 am | Genl SMITH-DORIEN commanding II Army inspected the Brigade. Capt H.C. BLAIR - SESSIONS returned from special work at BOULOGNE | |
| | | 6 pm | 1 Heavy Draught Horse fell dead whilst Bttn was returning to D Company. Rations: Frozen Meat & Bread; Vegetables brought locally | |
| | | 8 pm | Commenced Raining | |

Army Form C. 2118.

# WAR DIARY
## or
## INTELLIGENCE SUMMARY.
(Erase heading not required.)

Instructions regarding War Diaries and Intelligence Summaries are contained in F. S. Regs., Part II. and the Staff Manual respectively. Title pages will be prepared in manuscript.

| Place | Date | Hour | Summary of Events and Information | Remarks and references to Appendices |
|---|---|---|---|---|
| STEENVOORDE | 3/4/15 | | Work in Billets. Return from Rest, Brest, Bacon. Emmmm and work. Weather: Raining | |
| | | 4.15pm | Received orders that the Brigade will move tomorrow | |
| | | 4pm | | |
| | | 9pm | Pte BATCHELOR D Coy taken to hospital at HAZEBROUCK with Pleurisy | |
| | 4/4/15 | 8.30am | Billeting Party, Capt H.C.B. SESSIONS & 3 Signallers proceed to FLÊTRE to meet Staff Captain | |
| | | 1.30pm | Battalion marched in Brigade to Via EECKE - CAESTRE - FLÊTRE to Billets in Farms 1 mile SOUTH of METEREN (8½ mile march). One Park Army Sfob (left at M. DEQUEKERE's Farm) Strength 30 Officers 996 Other ranks | |
| METEREN | | 11.30pm | Head Quarters at M. V. DERYCKE'S Farm Arrived in Billeting area. | |

Army Form C. 2118.

# WAR DIARY
## or
## INTELLIGENCE SUMMARY.
(Erase heading not required.)

Instructions regarding War Diaries and Intelligence Summaries are contained in F. S. Regs., Part II. and the Staff Manual respectively. Title pages will be prepared in manuscript.

| Place | Date | Hour | Summary of Events and Information | Remarks and references to Appendices |
|---|---|---|---|---|
| METEREN | 5/4/15 | | Easter Monday. Rained all day. Inspection of Iron in Billets Ration, Belly Beef, Biscuits, Bacon Potatoes | |
| " | 6/4/15 | | Fine bright morn. Rained afternoon. Battalion Route march. Route :- VIEUX BERQUIN – MONT de MERRIS – STRAZEELE. | |
| " | " | 2-30pm | Received orders that Brigade will move to Billets EAST of BAILLEUL on 7/4/15 | |

| Place | Date | Hour | Summary of Events and Information | Remarks and references to Appendices |
|---|---|---|---|---|
| METEREN | 4/24/15 | 2:30 p.m. | Marched in Brigade to PLOEGSTEERT via BAILLEUL - NIEPPE - LE BIZET. Left our transport lines at M. Victor Thibaert's Farm with Battalion. | |
| | | 6:15 p.m. | Arrived at PLOEGSTEERT & went into billets. Head Qrs at The Brewery & mid South of PLOEGSTEERT. Battalion attached to 11th Infantry Brigade for instruction in Trench Warfare. Transport in Farm Mr RABOT | 10 |

# WAR DIARY
## or
## INTELLIGENCE SUMMARY.

Army Form C. 2118.

(Erase heading not required.)

| Place | Date | Hour | Summary of Events and Information | Remarks and references to Appendices |
|---|---|---|---|---|
| PLOEGSTEERT | 8/4/15 | | Morning & Afternoon. Working Parties with R.E. in PLOEGSTEERT WOOD. | |
| | | 5 pm | No 9 Platoon went to LONDON RIFLE BRIGADE Trenches in PLOEGSTEERT WOOD | |
| | | 7.30 p | No 10 " " " | |
| | | 7.30 p | A Company " 1/Bn SOMERSET L.I. Trenches at ST YVES | |
| | | | All the above move up in light Kit. Battalion they go to, In Instruction in Trench routine. In 24 hours. | |
| | | | GERMAN Trenches vary from 30 yds to 200" distance from our trenches | |
| | | | GERMANS shelled our Artillery situated SOUTH-WEST & EAST of our Head Quarters. Some shells dropping within 200 yds of the same. | |
| | | | Weather. April showers. | |

Army Form C. 2118.

# WAR DIARY
## or
## INTELLIGENCE SUMMARY.
(Erase heading not required.)

Instructions regarding War Diaries and Intelligence Summaries are contained in F. S. Regs., Part II. and the Staff Manual respectively. Title pages will be prepared in manuscript.

| Place | Date | Hour | Summary of Events and Information | Remarks and references to Appendices |
|---|---|---|---|---|
| PLOEGSTEERT | 9/4/15 | 9 am | Morning Patrol (Nos 9 & 10 Company) 9 am to 5 pm worked on R.E. in POLYGON WOOD | |
| | | 10 am | A Company & No 9 & 10 Platoon (C Coy) in Trenches | |
| | | | No 381 Sergt LLOYD C Coy slightly wounded in hand by enemy sniper | |
| | | 10.35am | No 1614 Pte LEE E Coy wounded bullet in left eye | |
| | | 3 am | Driver Horne died in Billets | |
| | | 11.30pm | Great gallantry which in EAST LANCS REAR Trenches – man leaning through a loophole when it was shattered by a bullet from German sniper. His chin was slightly cut by broken glass. | [?] |
| | | 9.45 pm | D Company & Nos 11 & 12 Platoon (C Coy) went into Trenches in relief of A Company & No 9 & 10 Platoon for maintenance in trench position. | Chs |
| | | 10.24 am | | |
| | | | Weather: Fine | |

1577  Wt. W10791/1773  500,000  1/15  D. D. & L.  A.D.S.S./Forms/C. 2118.

# WAR DIARY
## or
## INTELLIGENCE SUMMARY.

Army Form C. 2118.

| Place | Date | Hour | Summary of Events and Information | Remarks and references to Appendices |
|---|---|---|---|---|
| PLOEGSTEERT | 10/4/15 | | Enemy shelled Battalion area on H.Q. area. D Company + No 11 & 12 Platoons (C Coy) in Trenches. Remainder of Battalion working parties with R.E. B Company went into Trenches with SOMERSET & relieved by D Company for instruction in trench warfare in front, posting for 24 hours. | b |
| | | 7.45 p.m | Weather: Fine | |

# WAR DIARY
or
## INTELLIGENCE SUMMARY.
(Erase heading not required.)

Army Form C. 2118.

Instructions regarding War Diaries and Intelligence Summaries are contained in F.S. Regs., Part II. and the Staff Manual respectively. Title pages will be prepared in manuscript.

| Place | Date | Hour | Summary of Events and Information | Remarks and references to Appendices |
|---|---|---|---|---|
| PLOEGSTEERT | 11/4/15 | | Sunday. B Company in Trenches. A & C Companies find working parties for R.E. in PLOEGSTEERT WOOD | |
| | | 9.30 am | Received orders that Brigade will move tomorrow 12/4/15 to Billets between STEENWERCK and NOOTE BOOM. B Company return to Billets from Trenches | |
| PLOEGSTEERT | 12/4/15 | 8-45 am | Battalion Fives Brigade Battalion marched via STEENWERCK via ROMARIN – RABOT – STEENWERCK STATION | |
| STEENWERCK | | 11-30 am | Battalion arrived at Billets Consisting of Farms situated 1 mile to 1½ mile NORTH EAST of STEENWERCK Head Quarters in HENRI WAULOREY's FARM | |
| | | | Strength Officers 30 Other Ranks 986 | |

Army Form C. 2118.

# WAR DIARY
## or
## INTELLIGENCE SUMMARY.
(Erase heading not required.)

Instructions regarding War Diaries and Intelligence Summaries are contained in F. S. Regs., Part II and the Staff Manual respectively. Title pages will be prepared in manuscript.

| Place | Date | Hour | Summary of Events and Information | Remarks and references to Appendices |
|---|---|---|---|---|
| STEENWERCK | 13/4/15 | | Inspection by Corps Commander. 8 Officers & 2 Sergts attend Instruction in Bomb throwing at Pont de Nieppe. Skirmishing & musketry Parades. Matten Finn | (1) |
| STEENWERCK | 14/4/15 | | Company Parades. Bngnt Exercise, Bomb throwing. 8 Officers & 2 Sergts attend Instruction in Bomb throwing at Pont de Nieppe. Remainder return to Huts and had own Parades at St IVES on night of 15/4/15. Two sich horses left at Farm. | (1) |
| | | 9 am | 2/Lieut COLLETT and 4 Officers proceed to PLOEGSTEERT WOOD | |
| STEENWERCK | 15/4/15 | 9.30 am | Marched to Huts 1¼ miles SOUTH of NEUVE EGLISE via LA CRÈCHE. Remained in Full Order Kits until 6 pm | (2) |
| NEUVE EGLISE | | 6 pm | Marched to PLOEGSTEERT WOOD via ROMARIN & PLOEGSTEERT. Transport & Q.M. Stores Billeted 600 yds EAST of ROMARIN in FARM. | (1) |
| | | 7 pm | A and C Coys arrive at PLOEGSTEERT WOOD | (1) |

Army Form C. 2118.

# WAR DIARY
## or
## INTELLIGENCE SUMMARY.
(Erase heading not required.)

| Place | Date | Hour | Summary of Events and Information | Remarks and references to Appendices |
|---|---|---|---|---|
| PLOEGSTEERT WOOD | 15/4/15 | 7-20 pm | B & D & machine guns at entrance to WOOD. The Battalion took over the Trenches held by TRIPLE BRIGADE. Disposition of Companies etc. Head Quarters at SOMERSET HOUSE. Situated in centre of PLOEGSTEERT WOOD. A Company Right Trench. Situated SOUTH EAST of ST IVES on ST IVES—LE GHEER ROAD (Cmd Capt A FOULK) Right Comd Lieut W FREAM pro right. No 2 Platoon Comd Lieut W FREAM 2/Lt C F R BARNETT Centre No 3 " " Lieut W R E SUMNER. Left No 1 " " 2/Lt H S KING In Support No 4 " " In HULLS BURNT FARM and THREE HUNS FARM. In Support No 5 & Platoon Comd 2/Lt T H MOORE No 6 " " 2/Lt J P WINTERBOTHAM No 7 " " 2/Lt C S NASON No 8 " " 2/Lt L W MOORE B Company (Cmd Capt R C LITTLE) | |

**Army Form C. 2118.**

# WAR DIARY
## or
## INTELLIGENCE SUMMARY.
*(Erase heading not required.)*

| Place | Date | Hour | Summary of Events and Information | Remarks and references to Appendices |
|---|---|---|---|---|
| PLOEGSTEERT WOOD | 15/4/15 | | Distribution of Battalion. Continued C Company (No 3 Trench) No 9 Platoon (under Lieut R COOKE) in Support (Comd Major N H WALKER) in Dugouts in ROTTEN ROW (Capt F. E. OLE) No 10 Platoon (Cooke) 2/Lt C WINTERBOTHAM in Trench PROWSE POINT and pratry (South Way Garden Butts) No 11 Platoon (Winter) 2/Lt H&C GUISE in Trench in GARDEN. No 12 Platoon (Cooke) Capt F. E. COLE in Trench on Right of GARDEN with Lt. Col. Pratt in Garden was run Kent. No 13 Platoon Cmde Lieut H P SNOWDEN on Left " 14 " " " " Left Centre " 15 " " " " Right Centre " 16 " " " " Right D Coy (No 2 Trench) (Comd Capt H H AGUE) (2nd in Capt Lieutenant CAPRDDEN) Machine Guns (2 Lieut E CONDER) Platoon No 11 A Coy, No 11 Goon with D Coy, No 15 Goon with ACoy The 4 Guns kept support in ST YVES. | 19 |

# WAR DIARY
## *or*
## INTELLIGENCE SUMMARY.
*(Erase heading not required.)*

Army Form C. 2118.

| Place | Date | Hour | Summary of Events and Information | Remarks and references to Appendices |
|---|---|---|---|---|
| PLOEGSTEERT WOOD | 15/4/15 | 10.30 p.m. | Finished taking over Trenches etc at ST YVES | |
| | | 11.30 p.m. | HULLS BURNT FARM set on fire by Enemy Flare. Weather Fine. One Horse died at STEENWERCK Strength 30 Officers 984 other Ranks | |
| PLOEGSTEERT WOOD | 16/4/15 | | In Trenches. Quiet day. Sniping Brisk | |
| | | | Strength 30 Officers 982 other Ranks. | |
| " | 17/4/15 | | In Trenches. Quiet day. Sniping Brisk. 2nd Lieut Trench in front of ST YVES Lengthened & Communication Improved | |
| | | 6 pm | M2345 Pte C W GIDDINGS D Coy accidentally wounded (slight) The 4th Bn WORCESTER REGT took our trenches on our Right from LONDON RIFLE BRIGADE | |
| | | 7 pm | The 4th OXFORD LIGHT INFANTRY took over our LEFT Trench and neighboring Trenches | |

# WAR DIARY or INTELLIGENCE SUMMARY

Army Form C. 2118.

| Place | Date | Hour | Summary of Events and Information | Remarks and references to Appendices |
|---|---|---|---|---|
| PLOEGSTEERT WOOD | 17/4/15 | 8 pm | No 10 Platoon relieved by BEDFORD L.I. Moves into BROWNE BUTTS No 4 " " Took over MAXIM FARM from 7th WORCESTER REGT Garrison 1 S/t 10 men. The BUCKS BATTALION took up BURNT WOOD and CORNER GAP Strength : 36 Officers 983 other Ranks. Casualties Pte GIDDING C.W. slight wound (H.B.) | (5) W |
| " | 18/4/15 | | In T trenches. No chances in situation. B.M.R. from sniper contusion (casualties: Pte HOWELL H.B. (A Coy) | W |
| " | 19/4/15 | 3.30 pm | In trenches. No change in situation. Enemy shelled our Right Trench at 3.30 pm. Sniping more brisk and very accurate by enemy 2/Lt C.F.R. BARNETT killed at 5.30 pm. Shot by enemy sniper in head Pte G.E. Johnson (O Coy) Wounded accidentally whilst returning from Patrol duty. 12345 GODDARD (O Coy) wounded in head 2/Lt BARNETT Buried in PLOEGSTEERT WOOD Cemetery | W |
| | | 9 pm | Battalion relieved by BUCKS Battalion marched to ROMARIN and | |
| | | 8 pm | Billeted. Lieut LISTER to Hospital at BAILLEUL. | W |

# WAR DIARY or INTELLIGENCE SUMMARY

Army Form C. 2118.

| Place | Date | Hour | Summary of Events and Information | Remarks and references to Appendices |
|---|---|---|---|---|
| ROMARIN NIEPPE | 20/4/15 | | Rest Day. A Coy went to Baths in PONT de NIEPPE. Weather Fine. Strength. 28 Officers Other Ranks | |
| " | 21/4/15 | | Church Parade morning + Afternoon. ROUTE MARCH by Companies 10 am to 11am. Weather Fine. Horse died at STEENWERCK. | (9) |
| " | 22/4/15 | | Parades Morning + Afternoon | (9) |
| " | 23/4/15 | 8 am | B Coy went to Baths in PONT de NIEPPE. Battalion took over JOVES Trenches from BUCKS BATTALION. A Coy No I (Right) Trench. B Coy In Support C Coy No II (Centre) Trench D Coy No III (LEFT) Trench | (9) |
| | | 8 pm | Received another MAXIM gun from A.O.D. Strength 28 Officers 943 Other Ranks | |

**WAR DIARY**
or
**INTELLIGENCE SUMMARY.**

*(Erase heading not required.)*

Army Form C. 2118.

| Place | Date | Hour | Summary of Events and Information | Remarks and references to Appendices |
|---|---|---|---|---|
| PLOEGSTEERT WOOD | 24/4/15 | 1.50 p.m. | In Trenches. Quiet day. Sniping. Burial at farm. Pte H. TIMMS (D Coy) Accidently shot through whilst cleaning Rifle. Wound slight. | W |
|  |  | 6.45 p.m. | Pte C PHILLIPS wounded in arm by German sniper. Received 4 Field Troop from K Farm from A.D.D. | W |
|  |  |  | Strength 28 officers 970 | |
|  | 25/4/15 |  | In Trenches. Quiet day. | |
|  |  |  | Casualties. Pte A Lt KINGSCOTE (A Coy) accidently shot in foot (slight wound) | W |
|  | 26/4/15 |  | In Trenches. Quiet day. | |
|  |  |  | Casualties. Pte J PHILLIPS (A Coy) cut face. Pte E R CUMMINS (D Coy) shot in Head at 7.15. died 8.30 pm | W |
|  |  |  | 2/Lt A SEABRIGHT (13 Coy) wounded Right Arm serious | W |
|  |  |  | Received message from BRIGADIER GEN McCLINTOCK expressing his appreciation of the manner in which reconnoitring patrols carried out by the Battalion | (App. 4) |

# WAR DIARY or INTELLIGENCE SUMMARY

Army Form C. 2118.

| Place | Date | Hour | Summary of Events and Information | Remarks and references to Appendices |
|---|---|---|---|---|
| PLOEGSTEERT Wood | 27/4/15 | 8.30 p | Quiet day. Battalion relieved by BUCKS BATTALION 3rd Battalion formed BRIGADE RESERVE and two 2 Companies in PLOEGSTEERT WOOD in Huts and 2 Companies in PLOEGSTEERT in Billets | D |
| PLOEGSTEERT | 28/4/15 | 3 pm | Battalion moved to ROMARIN into Billets In Divisional Reserve. C and D Coys went to Baths at PONT de NIEPPE. Working Party of B and D Coys Worked on 2nd Line Trenches 8.15pm to 1.15am | R |
| ROMARIN | 29/4/15 | | In Billets. Church Parade. The BISHOP of PRETORIA preached. Working Party A and C Coys worked on 2nd Line Trenches 9pm to 1am | D |
| ROMARIN | 30/4/15 | | In Billets Working Party of B & D Coy worked on 2nd line Trenches 8.15pm to 12.30am Strength 29 Officers 962 other Ranks | W |

145th Inf.Bde.
48th Div.

1/5th BATTN. THE GLOUCESTERSHIRE REGIMENT.

M A Y

1915

# WAR DIARY
## or
## INTELLIGENCE SUMMARY.

Army Form C. 2118.

| Place | Date | Hour | Summary of Events and Information | Remarks and references to Appendices |
|---|---|---|---|---|
| ROMARIN | 1/5/15 | | On Billets until 6 pm. 3 Coys of GERMAN Meadows brokes out | |
| PLOEGSTEERT WOOD | | 6 pm | Battalion took over ST IVES Trenches from 13 UKS BATTALION with 1 Platoon in support. A Coy Right Trench B Coy Centre Trench C Coy Left Trench and B small trench of GRENADE BUTTS and Comm GAP D Coy In Support 3 Platoons in ST YVES and 1 Platoon in cottages in MUDLANE. No Casualties. Sniping by both sides brisk | |
| PLOEGSTEERT WOOD | 2/5/15 | | In Trenches. Trenches received numerous Rifle Trench As 33 both As 36 Left 35+36 Quiet day. Offensive Patrol gave information about Enemy snipers Position No Casualties | |

# WAR DIARY
## or
## INTELLIGENCE SUMMARY

Army Form C. 2118.

| Place | Date | Hour | Summary of Events and Information | Remarks and references to Appendices |
|---|---|---|---|---|
| PHOEBSTEERT WOOD | 3/5/15 | | In Trenches (ST YVES) Fired Indirect Fire at 4pm & 10pm On Enemys FARM with Maxim Gun | |
| | 4/5/15 | | Quiet day. Casualty Pte BRANIFORD A Coy Intermittent In Trenches (ST YVES) Quiet day. Enemy snipers & Maxim Guns fire heavily during night. Enemy in Trenches opposite C Coy call out the following remarks. "Shoot up GLOUCESTERS" "ENGLAND kaput" "murren ENGLAND". Killed Whilst on Working Party Casualties Pte MORLEY | |
| " | 5/5/15 | 8pm | In Trenches (ST YVES) Quiet day Battalion is relieved by 1 BUCKS BATALION and moves Dumment Recoux at ROMARIN | |
| ROMARIN | 6/5/15 | | In Billets A & B Coys went to Baths at PONT du NIEPPE. C Coy found working Party at PHOEBSTEERT WOOD | |

Army Form C. 2118.

# WAR DIARY
## or
## INTELLIGENCE SUMMARY.
(Erase heading not required.)

| Place | Date | Hour | Summary of Events and Information | Remarks and references to Appendices |
|---|---|---|---|---|
| ROMARIN | 6/5/15 | | Continued | |
| | | 5.30 pm | 2/Lieut H.B.C. GUISE whilst instructing his Platoon Grenadiers accidently exploded a Trench Grenade which killed himself and Pte BATES and wounded 6 others seriously | W |
| ROMARIN | 7/5/15 | | 2/Lieut H.B.C. GUISE and Pte BATES were Buried in PLOEGSTEERT WOOD. A B & C Coys found working Parties for evening operations in PLOEGSTEERT WOOD | W |
| ROMARIN | 8/5/15 | 10.45 pm | Capt R.S.D. STUART is appointed Brigade Grenadier Officer. Lieut W. FREAM is appointed Battalion Grenadier Officer. Vice 2/Lt H.B.C. GUISE. Battalion ordered to stand in readiness to move out in two hours notice | W |

Army Form C. 2118.

# WAR DIARY
## or
## INTELLIGENCE SUMMARY.
*(Erase heading not required.)*

Instructions regarding War Diaries and Intelligence Summaries are contained in F. S. Regs., Part II. and the Staff Manual respectively. Title pages will be prepared in manuscript.

| Place | Date | Hour | Summary of Events and Information | Remarks and references to Appendices |
|---|---|---|---|---|
| | 8/5/15 | | Continued from 4 am 9/5/15 to 6 am 10/5/15 | A |
| ROMARIN | 9/5/15 | | Nothing unusual occurred. In Billets | A |
| ROMARIN | 10/5/15 | 9 am | C Compy went to hand it Pont de NIEPPE. B Coy found working parts at HYDE PARK CORNER | |
| | | 1 pm | D Coy Washed at PONT de NIEPPE Capt H HAGUE taken to hospital for operation | |
| | | 8 pm | Battalion relieved BUCK'S BATTALION in ST YVES TRENCHES A Coy Right Trench with 1 Platoon in support in HYDE PARK CORNER FARM, THREE HUNS and MAXIMS B Coy On Support 3 Platoons in ST YVES, 1 in HUD LANE C Coy LEFT Trench a x Breastworks D Coy Centre Trench | A |

# WAR DIARY
## or
## INTELLIGENCE SUMMARY.
(Erase heading not required.)

Army Form C. 2118.

| Place | Date | Hour | Summary of Events and Information | Remarks and references to Appendices |
|---|---|---|---|---|
| PLOEGSTEERT WOOD | 11/5/15 | | In Trenches at ST YVES. Quiet Day. Strength 27 Officers 951 others Ranks | 2) |
| " | 12/5/15 | 2-30am | PAROLE C Coy Wounded in head and died at ROMARIN. Buried at SOMERSET HOUSE Cemetery PLOEGSTEERT WOOD | 3) |
| | | 6-30am | Pte F. HOBBS C Coy wounded in head | |
| " | 13/5/15 | | In Trenches at ST YVES | |
| | | 3-30pm | Enemy Shelled C Coy Trenches | |
| | | 5-45pm | Enemy shelled C & D Coy Trenches. Two men killed (D Coy) | |
| | | 5-30pm | Two men shot by Enemy machine Gun (D Coy) | |
| | | | Casualties :— Sergt H.H. MORGAN C Coy Killed. Pte T. FRANKLIN, Pte J. ASTON, Pte C.H. ROMANS, Pte H. MIDDLEDITCH all D Coy Killed. All Buried in Battalion Cemetery PLOEGSTEERT WOOD | 3) |

# WAR DIARY
## or
## INTELLIGENCE SUMMARY.
(Erase heading not required.)

Army Form C. 2118.

| Place | Date | Hour | Summary of Events and Information | Remarks and references to Appendices |
|---|---|---|---|---|
| PLOEGSTEERT WOOD | 14/5/15 | 8pm | In Trenches at ST YVES. Battalion relieved by Bucks Battalion and (two?) Divisional Reserve. Billets at ROMARIN. Strength 29 Officers 946 Other Ranks | 1/ |
| ROMARIN | 15/5/15 | | In Billets at ROMARIN. A and C Coy found working parties for rear defences in PLOEGSTEERT WOOD | 1/ |
| " | 16/5/15 | | In Billets. Rain | 1/ |
| " | 17/5/15 | | In Billets. Rain | 1/ |
| " | 18/5/15 | 8pm | In Billets. 300 yds on working party in PLOEGSTEERT WOOD. Battalion relieved BUCKS BATTALION in ST YVES Trenches. A Coy Right (No33 Trench) B Coy Centre (No34 Trench) C Coy Left (No35+36 Trench) D Coy in support ST YVES. | 1/ |

Army Form C. 2118.

# WAR DIARY
or
## INTELLIGENCE SUMMARY.
(Erase heading not required.)

Instructions regarding War Diaries and Intelligence Summaries are contained in F. S. Regs., Part II. and the Staff Manual respectively. Title pages will be prepared in manuscript.

| Place | Date | Hour | Summary of Events and Information | Remarks and references to Appendices |
|---|---|---|---|---|
| PLOEGSTEERT WOOD | 19/5/15 | | In Trenches at St YVES. Quiet day. Casualties | |
| " | 20/5/15 | | Accidental wound Capt R West 7/S. Wilts Regt Pte J Falkener 24 Pte A Hodgson 24 Wound In Trenches at St Yves Quiet day. Casualties B Coy Pte Butler Sheveter Moxie to new Batt [?]n Pte J.W. [?] Snider to [?] Fort Hood | A A |
| " | 21/5/15 | | In Trenches at St Yves. Moral H[?] from [?] Sgt W. Heath and Pte J. Sleeman Killed Casualties Sgt W. Heath and Pte J. Sleeman killed | A |
| " | 22/5/15 | 8pm | In Trenches at St Yves Butcher Roboins [?] Bucks Landsirn sent billet at Romarin to [?] Reserve | A |

1577 Wt. W10791/1773 500,000 1/15 D. D. & L. A.D.S.S./Forms/C. 2118

# WAR DIARY
## or
## INTELLIGENCE SUMMARY.

Army Form C. 2118.

| Place | Date | Hour | Summary of Events and Information | Remarks and references to Appendices |
|---|---|---|---|---|
| ROMARIN | 23/5/15 | | In Billets. A & B Coys. worked at PONT DE NIEPPE. 300 men on working party to PLOEGSTEERT WOOD. Strength 27 officers 932 other ranks | (1) |
| ROMARIN | 24/5/15 | | In Billets | (2) |
| ROMARIN | 25/5/15 | | In Billets. C & D Coys worked at PONT DE NIEPPE | (2) |
| ROMARIN | 26/5/15 | 6 p.m. | In Billets. Ball 6 p.m. Battalion relieved BUCKS Battalion in ST YVES Trenches. A Coy No 33 Trench, B Coy Support, C Coy No 35 & 36 Trench, D Coy 34 Trench. Strength 27 officers 935 other ranks. Casualties No 2751 Pte T.B. CURTIS and 3433/4 Pte MAYBY wounded, No 2356 Pte E. COVERAGE D Coy severely wounded in head. | (3) (4) |

# WAR DIARY or INTELLIGENCE SUMMARY

Army Form C. 2118.

| Place | Date | Hour | Summary of Events and Information | Remarks and references to Appendices |
|---|---|---|---|---|
| PLOEGSTEERT WOOD | 27/5/15 | | In Trenches at ST YVES. Quiet day. Pte Chandler, Pte G. REDMOND (C Coy) wounded. | |
| PLOEGSTEERT WOOD | 28/5/15 | | In Trenches at ST YVES. Pte H.J. YEATES (C Coy) wounded. Quiet day. Pte T. HALL (A Coy) wounded. Pte GOULHARD killed at ROMARIN churchyard from fragment of British Grenade exploded at PLOEGSTEERT WOOD. | |
| PLOEGSTEERT WOOD | 29/5/15 | | In Trenches at ST YVES. Quiet day. Pte W. MACE (C Coy) wounded. | |
| PLOEGSTEERT WOOD | 30/5/15 | 8pm | In Trenches at ST YVES - until 5pm. Pte ADAMS wounded. Relieved by BUFFS BATTALION and billeted in ROMARIN. [Owing DIVISIONAL RESERVE]. Trench Strength [Coy] A 27 officers 929 other ranks. | |
| ROMARIN | 31/5/15 | | In billets. B, C & D Coys found working parties. | |

145th Inf.Bde.
48th Div.

1/5th BATTN. THE GLOUCESTERSHIRE REGIMENT.

J U N E

1 9 1 5

CONFIDENTIAL.

WAR DIARY

of

1/5TH BATTALION - GLOUCESTERSHIRE REGIMENT.

------------------------------

From 1st June, 1915.　　　　To 30th June, 1915.

(Volume 4).

*[signature]* Lt-Colonel.
Comdg 1/5th Gloucester Regiment.

# WAR DIARY
## or
## INTELLIGENCE SUMMARY.
(Erase heading not required.)

Army Form C. 2118.

Regiment: 1/5th GLOUCESTERSHIRE

| Place | Date | Hour | Summary of Events and Information | Remarks and references to Appendices |
|---|---|---|---|---|
| ROMARIN | 1/6/15 | | Battalion in Billets as Divisional Reserve. Strength 27 Officers 928 other ranks. A.B. & C Coy. Front working parties | 10 |
| ROMARIN | 2/6/15 | | In Billets. 2Lt C.W.N. PUCKERIDGE and 2Lt D.G. DURRANT Joined from ENGLAND A & B A.D. Coys Front working parties. A & B Coys work at PONT de NIEPPE | 11 |
| ROMARIN | 3/6/15 | 4pm | In Billets until 6pm. Battalion returned Ruins Battalion to St YVES Trenches. A Coy 33 Trench, B Coy 34 Trench, C Coy 35/36 Trench 10 Coy in support at St YVES. Strength 29 officers 920 other ranks | 12 |
| PLOEGSTEERT WOOD | 4/6/15 | | In Trenches St YVES. Quiet day. A.Sub.Lieut. PEABLACK C Coy, Pt L. TURNER B Coy. G.K. Slightly wounded | 17 |

# WAR DIARY
## or
## INTELLIGENCE SUMMARY.
*(Erase heading not required.)*

Army Form C. 2118.

| Place | Date | Hour | Summary of Events and Information | Remarks and references to Appendices |
|---|---|---|---|---|
| PLOEGSTEERT WOOD | 5/6/15 | | In Trenches at ST YVES. Quiet day. Casualties Pte W.Hs. INGLES Acy B{ } wounded Pte L REAY Acy B{ } | |
| " | 6/6/15 | 10-20am | In Trenches at ST YVES. Mine exploded on Right of A Coy by R.E. A.2 Brigade & Machine Gunners opened rapid Long Range fire on M. Emma & Route in Rear of Enemy trenches. On Germans firing red & red & green lights. Pte A HAWKINS A Coy KILLED PTE H KING D Coy Enemy shelled PLOEGSTEERT wounded & ST YVES | |
| " | 7/6/15 | 10-45am 9.20pm | In Trenches at ST YVES. Mines 7 hm MOBS. Battalion relieved. Battalion Billetted at ROMARIN in Divisional Reserve Pte 1 H.T. THOMPSON D Coy Killed in ST YVES Pte P SYMONS A Coy Buried at Cemetery in wood | |
| ROMARIN | | | | |

# WAR DIARY
## or
## INTELLIGENCE SUMMARY.

*(Erase heading not required.)*

Army Form C. 2118.

| Place | Date | Hour | Summary of Events and Information | Remarks and references to Appendices |
|---|---|---|---|---|
| ROMARIN | 8/6/15 | | In Billets as during Previous | 20 |
| ROMARIN | | | 3rd 1/4 Bn DURRANT joined Battalion from 2nd/5th Battalion Strength 30 Officers 911 other Ranks | 10 |
| " | 9/6/15 | | In Billets | 10 |
| " | 10/6/15 | 6pm | In Billets. The G.O.C. and the Division (General R. FANSHAWE) inspected the Battalion | 10 |
| " | 11/6/15 | 9pm | In Billets. until 9pm Battalion took over from 7th/13th WARWICKS 1200 yds SOUTH-WEST of MESSINES Dispositions A Coy Trenches 64 & 65. B Coy Trenches 66, 67 & 68 C Coy " 69, 70, & 71. D Coy " 72 & 73 |  |
| LA PLUS DOUVE FARM | | | | |
| WULVERGHEM | | | Battalion HQ at LA PLUS DOUVE FARM | 10 |

# WAR DIARY
## or
## INTELLIGENCE SUMMARY.
(Erase heading not required.)

Army Form C. 2118.

| Place | Date | Hour | Summary of Events and Information | Remarks and references to Appendices |
|---|---|---|---|---|
| LA PLUS | 12/6/15 | | In Trenches | |
| DOUVE Fm | | | Casualties. 2nd Lt. L.W. ORGAN slightly wounded (A Coy). Strength 30 Officers 921 Other Ranks | |
| " | 13/6/15 | | In Trenches | |
| " | 14/6/15 | | In Trenches. H¼ & A Coy 9th Essex Regt attached to Battalion for instruction in trenches. 80. Lt Col LEWES & Capt SPOONER (A.M.) | |
| " | 15/6/15 | 10 pm | In Trenches. 2 men ESSEX and one boy killed by shell. Battalion relieved by BUCKS and 1 Coy Brigade Reserve in Billets at COURTE DREVE FARM and Farm nearby | |
| COURTE DREVE FARM | 16/6/15 | | In Billets. Strength 30 Officers 919 Other Ranks | |
| | 17/6/15 | | In Billets | |

# WAR DIARY
## or
## INTELLIGENCE SUMMARY.

Army Form C. 2118.

| Place | Date | Hour | Summary of Events and Information | Remarks and references to Appendices |
|---|---|---|---|---|
| POURTE DREVE FARM PROESTEERT | 18/6/15 | | In Billets | (1) |
| | 19/6/15 | | Battalion moved into Divisional Reserve, & took over Billets at PONT DE NIEPPE. One Company in Schools near goods station ARMENTIERES. Two Companies at H.Q. PONT DE NIEPPE and 1 Coy at NIEPPE | (1) |
| PONT DE NIEPPE | 20/6/15 | | In Billets. A Coy moved from billets near Goods Stn ARMENTIERES and took over billets at OOSTHOVE FARM. Confessions and Communions at ADJUTANT (Captain Johnson) who acts as Brigade Major. Strength 30 Officers 918 other ranks. | (1) |
| | 21/6/15 22 | | In Billets | (1) |
| | 22/6/15 | | In Billets. Major WALKER and 8 other ranks went to England on leave for 6 days. | (1) |
| | 23/6/15 | | In Billets. The Battalion was warned to be ready to turn out on the "Alarm" at half an hour notice. Strength 30 Officers 914 other ranks. | (1) |

Army Form C. 2118.

# WAR DIARY
## or
## INTELLIGENCE SUMMARY.
(Erase heading not required.)

Instructions regarding War Diaries and Intelligence Summaries are contained in F. S. Regs., Part II. and the Staff Manual respectively. Title pages will be prepared in manuscript.

| Place | Date | Hour | Summary of Events and Information | Remarks and references to Appendices |
|---|---|---|---|---|
| PONT DE NIEPPE | 24/6/15 | 8 pm | In Billets until 8 pm. Battalion marches (in Brigade) to BAILLEUL and Billets | // |
| BAILLEUL | 25/6/15 | 9 pm | In Billets until 9 pm. Battalion marches (in Brigade) to VIEUX BERQUIN and Billets | // |
| ~~BAILL~~ VIEUX BERQUIN | 26/6/15 | 9 pm | In Billets until 8-30 pm. Battalion marches (in Brigade group) to Billets. The Division joins IV Corps. Marching via VIER-HOUCK - MERVILLE - CALONNE - ROBECK nr GONNEHEM. Capt and Adjutant V N JOHNSON returns to the Battalion. Battalion arrives and Billets in Farm at CENSE LA VALLÉE west of GONNEHEM | // |
| GONNEHEM | 27/6/15 | 1-30 am | | // |
| GONNEHEM | 28th | 6 pm | Battalion leaves GONNEHEM and marches to Billets in ALLOUAGNE | // |
| ALLOUAGNE | | 8 pm | Battalion settled in Billets | // |

Army Form C. 2118.

# WAR DIARY
## or
## INTELLIGENCE SUMMARY.
(Erase heading not required.)

Instructions regarding War Diaries and Intelligence Summaries are contained in F. S. Regs., Part II. and the Staff Manual respectively. Title pages will be prepared in manuscript.

| Place | Date | Hour | Summary of Events and Information | Remarks and references to Appendices |
|---|---|---|---|---|
| ALLOUAGNE | 28/6/15 | | In billets in Corps Reserve | (1) |
| ALLOUAGNE | 29/6/15 | | In billets | (1) |
| ALLOUAGNE | 30/6/15 | | In billets | (1) |

145th Inf.Bde.
48th Div.

**1/5th BATTN. THE GLOUCESTERSHIRE REGIMENT.**

J U L Y

1 9 1 5

C O N F I D E N T I A L.

WAR DIARY

of

1/5TH BATTALION - GLOUCESTERSHIRE REGIMENT

from 1st July, 1915        to 31st July, 1915.


(Volume 5.)


*[signature]*
Lt. COLONEL
COMDG. 5TH BN. GLOUCESTER REGT.

Army Form C. 2118.

# WAR DIARY
## or
## INTELLIGENCE SUMMARY.

1/5th Gloucestershire Regt

| Place | Date | Hour | Summary of Events and Information | Remarks and references to Appendices |
|---|---|---|---|---|
| ALLOUAGNE | 1/7/15 | | In Billets in IV Corps Reserve. Strength Officers 30, Other ranks 909 | |
| " | 2/7/15 | | In Billets. Capt F.W. COLE goes to HAVRE to command Brigade Reinforcements. | |
| " | 3/7/15 | | In Billets. War Establishment of other ranks is reduced to 800. | |
| " | 4/7/15 | | LIEUT W. FREAM appointed Commander of Brigade Grenadier Corps. Sergt BISHOP and 30 other ranks form Brigade Grenadier Corps. Capt R.S.D. STUART appointed to Command 1st Brigade Trench Mortar Battery of 145th Brigade | |
| " | 5/7/15 | | In Billets | |
| " | 6/7/15 | | In Billets | |
| " | 7/7/15 | | In Billets. 2nd Col J.H. COLLETT, Capt N.H. WALLER & Capt G.F. COLLETT attend Divisional Tactical Exercise | |

**Army Form C. 2118.**

# WAR DIARY
## or
## INTELLIGENCE SUMMARY.
(Erase heading not required.)

| Place | Date | Hour | Summary of Events and Information | Remarks and references to Appendices |
|---|---|---|---|---|
| ALLOUAGNE | 8/7/15 | | LORD KITCHENER, Secretary of State for War, went to 1st Army. The Supreme Lineal Road between LILLERS & CHOQUES | |
| " | 9/7/15 | | In Billets. Capt H.C.B.SESSIONS went to MAZINGARBE to see Trenches occupied by 2/4th LONDON Battalion with a view to our taking over same | |
| " | 10/7/15 | | In Billets. Capt H.C.B. SESSIONS returned from MAZINGARBE | |
| " | 11/7/15 | | In Billets. | |
| " | 12/7/15 | 4pm | In Billets until 4pm at ALLOUAGNE. Battalion marched (in Brigade) to NOEUX LES MINES and Bivouaced in Field. Strength Officers 28 other Ranks 903. Accidental explosion of Hand Grenade at School of Instruction in Brigade Grenadiers ALLOUAGNE wounded 3 men 4/Lt G.N.HENSLEY, Pte IKE WHITE D Coy & Pte C HEBB C Coy. NCOs & men of Brigade Grenadiers by Report Battalion | |

**Army Form C. 2118.**

# WAR DIARY
## or
## INTELLIGENCE SUMMARY.
*(Erase heading not required.)*

Instructions regarding War Diaries and Intelligence Summaries are contained in F. S. Regs., Part II. and the Staff Manual respectively. Title pages will be prepared in manuscript.

| Place | Date | Hour | Summary of Events and Information | Remarks and references to Appendices |
|---|---|---|---|---|
| NOEUX LES MINES | 13/7/15 | 10 am | Received orders that Battalion would not now relieve 24th LONDON Regt. Brigade is detailed to dig 2nd line Trenches near SAILLY LABOURSE instead of taking over trenches | (1) |
| " | 14/7/15 | 7 am | Battalion finds working party of 400 for digging 2nd line Trenches | |
| | | 4-30 pm | Battalion moved to Bivouacs at DISTILLERIE ½ mile South West of NOEUX LES MINES. Reached bivouacs | |
| | | 11 pm | Battalion found working party of 350 for digging 2nd line Trenches 1½ miles East of NOEUX LES MINES | (2) |
| " | 15/7/15 | 8 am | Battalion found working party of 350 for digging Trenches East of NOEUX LES MINES | (3) |

1577 Wt. W10791/1773 500,000 1/15 D. D. & L. A.D.S.S./Forms/C. 2118.

Army Form C. 2118.

# WAR DIARY
## or
## INTELLIGENCE SUMMARY.
*(Erase heading not required.)*

| Place | Date | Hour | Summary of Events and Information | Remarks and references to Appendices |
|---|---|---|---|---|
| NOEUX LES MINES | 16/7/15 | 7.30 a.m. | Battalion found working party of 350 for digging trenches at SAILLY LABOURSE | (1) |
|  |  | 9.15 p.m. | Battalion marched (in Brigade) to AMES and Billeted. Very wet. |  |
| AMES | 17/7/15 | 3.30 a.m. | Battalion arrives at AMES Strength Officers 28 Other ranks 892 2/Lt K.F. DURRANT goes to Mezerolles from School for Course of Instruction | (2) |
| AMES | 18/7/15 | 4.15 a.m. | Battalion marches to BERQUET from and entrains for DOULLENS | (3) |
|  |  | 3.20 p.m. | Arrives DOULLENS station and detrains |  |
|  |  | 4.35 p.m. | Leaves DOULLENS Station & marches to SARTON Remains from new 7th CORPS of new 3rd Army. Battalion marches to Billets in BAYENCOURT |  |
| SARTON | 19/7/15 | 4.30 p.m. | Battalion marches to Billets in BAYENCOURT | (4) |
| BAYENCOURT | 20/7/15 | 7 p.m. | Battalion marches to HEBUTERNE and takes over trenches from 1st Battalion of 3rd Regiment French army | (5) |

Army Form C. 2118.

# WAR DIARY
or
## INTELLIGENCE SUMMARY.
*(Erase heading not required.)*

Instructions regarding War Diaries and Intelligence Summaries are contained in F. S. Regs., Part II. and the Staff Manual respectively. Title pages will be prepared in manuscript.

| Place | Date | Hour | Summary of Events and Information | Remarks and references to Appendices |
|---|---|---|---|---|
| HEBUTERNE | 20/7/15 | | Disposition of Battalion in trenches. A Coy (Capt COLLETT) Right Trench with Right on BUCQUOY Rd. B Coy (Capt CARUTHERS-LITTLE) Centre Trench C Coy (Major N.H. WALLER) Left Trench opposite BOIS de BOMMECOURT D Coy (Capt WISE CAMPDEN) Reserve in Redoubt in HEBUTERNE On our Left is 294th French Infantry On our Right is 4th OXFORDS The 32nd Regt ARTILLERIE (French) supports our sector. Lieut Col JAHAN commdg 93rd Regiment French Army commands whole sector. Capt V.N. JOHNSON is attached to him as LIASON officer. Strength 28 Officers 886 Other Ranks | |
| HEBUTERNE | 21/7/15 | | In Trenches | |
| HEBUTERNE | 22/7/15 | 5 pm | In Trenches Lt Col JAHAN hands over command of HEBUTERNE to Gen M CLINTOCK | |

Army Form C. 2118.

# WAR DIARY
## or
## INTELLIGENCE SUMMARY.
(Erase heading not required.)

Instructions regarding War Diaries and Intelligence Summaries are contained in F.S. Regs., Part II. and the Staff Manual respectively. Title pages will be prepared in manuscript.

| Place | Date | Hour | Summary of Events and Information | Remarks and references to Appendices |
|---|---|---|---|---|
| HEBUTERNE | 23/7/15 | | In Trenches. Quiet day | W |
| HEBUTERNE | 24/7/15 | 9 pm | In Trenches until 9 pm. No casualties during Tour. Battalion handed over Trenches to BUCKS Battn and marched to Billets in BAYENCOURT and SAILLY au BOIS to form Brigade Reserve. Distribution:- H.Q., A & B Coys & Machine Gun Section at BAYENCOURT C & D Coys at SAILLY au BOIS | W |
| BAYENCOURT | 25/7/15 | | In Billets | W |
| BAYENCOURT | 26/7/15 | | In Billets | W |
| BAYENCOURT | 27/7/15 | | In Billets. Capt R.H.F. COOKE taken to hospital | W |

1577 Wt. W10791/1773 500,000 1/15 D. D. & L. A.D.S.S./Forms/C. 2118.

# WAR DIARY
## or
## INTELLIGENCE SUMMARY.
*(Erase heading not required.)*

Army Form C. 2118.

| Place | Date | Hour | Summary of Events and Information | Remarks and references to Appendices |
|---|---|---|---|---|
| RAVENCOURT | 28/4/15 | 12 noon | In Billets until 12 noon H.Qrs & A & B Coys marched to SAILLY and Bivouaced until 8 p.m. | 1) |
| SAILLY au BOIS | | 8 pm | Battalion marched to HEBUTERNE and took over trenches from BUCKS Battalion. Disposition  A Coy  Right Trench  B Coy  Centre Trench  D Coy  Left Trench  C Coy  Reserve  H'Qrs in dugout in rear of Centre Coy. CAPT A.T. MITCHELSON, Lieut L.J. CLAYTON and 2ⁿᵈ Lt G.E. RATCLIFF joined Battalion for first time from England. Strength 31 officers 894 other Ranks. | 1) |

Army Form C. 2118.

# WAR DIARY
## or
## INTELLIGENCE SUMMARY.
*(Erase heading not required.)*

Instructions regarding War Diaries and Intelligence Summaries are contained in F. S. Regs., Part II. and the Staff Manual respectively. Title pages will be prepared in manuscript.

| Place | Date | Hour | Summary of Events and Information | Remarks and references to Appendices |
|---|---|---|---|---|
| HEBUTERNE | 29/7/15 | | In Trenches. No casualties | 4 |
| " | 30/7/15 | | In Trenches. No casualties | 5 |
| " | 31/7/15 | | In Trenches. No casualties. Seven Time Expired men who have signed on to serve until end of war, go on one month's leave. | 6 |

145th Inf.Bde.
48th Div.

1/5th BATTN. THE GLOUCESTERSHIRE REGIMENT.

A U G U S T

1 9 1 5

Army Form C. 2118.

# WAR DIARY
or
## INTELLIGENCE SUMMARY.
(Erase heading not required.)

Instructions regarding War Diaries and Intelligence Summaries are contained in F. S. Regs., Part II. and the Staff Manual respectively. Title pages will be prepared in manuscript.

| Place | Date | Hour | Summary of Events and Information | Remarks and references to Appendices |
|---|---|---|---|---|
| MEBOYANE | 1/8/15 | | Battalion in Trenches. | B |
| | 2/8/15 | | Battalion in Trenches. PTE H.T. ENG. SHARP (wounded). Strength of other ranks 870 | |
| " | 3/8/15 | | Battalion in Trenches. Patrol consisting of CORPL R.E. KNIGHT, L/CPL F.W. HARVEY, PTES. W. TIMMS, A.E. SAMPSON, A.H. WINTLE, WINTER-MEGRAN, L/C K.A. ROBERTSON, LEWIS HAMMOND met an enemy patrol of 5 men killing 3 and and wounding one. CORPL R.E. KNIGHT and L/CPL F.W. HARVEY have been recommended for distinguished conduct in the field. Quiet day. Battalion in Trenches. | |
| " | 4/8/15 | | | B |
| " | 5/8/15 | 9 p.m. | Battalion relieved by BUCKS and go into billets in Brigade Reserve with 13 x 0 Coys 1 mining th Garrison of the KEEP | |

# WAR DIARY or INTELLIGENCE SUMMARY

Army Form C. 2118.

| Place | Date | Hour | Summary of Events and Information | Remarks and references to Appendices |
|---|---|---|---|---|
| HEBUTERNE | 5/8/15 | | (Continued) Strength Officers 31 Other Ranks 840 Capt. & Adj. V.N. JOHNSON & Capt. CARRUTHERS - LITTLE & 12 other ranks to ENGLAND | (1) |
| " | 6/8/15 to 12/8/15 | | In Billets. Fined working parties each day & night in defences of village. | (1) |
| " | 13/8/15 | | Battalion moved north to P. Marston Line | |
| " | 13/8/15 | 8 pm | Battalion took over Trenches (Sector K) from BUCKS VOLS. B Coy Right Infantry. D Coy Left Infantry. A Coy Local Reserve Rue de BUCQUOY C Coy Local Reserve Rue de FONCQUEVILLERS Officers 30 Other Ranks 846 | (1) |
| " | 14/8/15 | | In Trenches. Rum. Situation Quiet | (1) |
| " | 15/8/15 | | In Trenches. Rum. Situation Quiet | (1) |

# WAR DIARY or INTELLIGENCE SUMMARY

Army Form C. 2118.

| Place | Date | Hour | Summary of Events and Information | Remarks and references to Appendices |
|---|---|---|---|---|
| HEBUTERNE | 16/8/15 | | In Trenches. Run. Situation Quiet. Intermittent Shelling | |
| " | 17/8/15 | | 2/Lt. HAWKINS crawled out in daylight & reconnoitred enemy's Sap S.W. of ROMMECOURT WOOD & was wounded whilst on daylight Patrol reconnoitring Enemy's Sap S.W. of BOIS de ROMMECOURT. Patrol found good information. A Coy relieved B Coy and E Coy relieved D Coy in Trenches. In Trenches. Run. 2/Lt. G. HAWKINS D.C.M. | |
| " | 18/8/15 | | In Trenches. Run dry. Situation Quiet. Intermittent Shells | |
| " | 19/8/15 | | In Trenches. Intermittent Shelling. Dry day. Lt Col COLLETT, Capt COLLETT & VISCOUNT CAMPDEN and 18 other Ranks went to ENGLAND on leave | |
| * | 19/9/15 | | Went to ENGLAND on leave | |
| " | 20/8/15 | | Capt HERB SESSIONS went to ENGLAND on leave. Battalion in Trenches. Intermittent Shelling. Dry day | |

# WAR DIARY
## or
## INTELLIGENCE SUMMARY.

Army Form C. 2118.

| Place | Date | Hour | Summary of Events and Information | Remarks and references to Appendices |
|---|---|---|---|---|
| HEBUTERNE | 21/9/15 | | 2nd Lieut. Winter Botham & Lieut C W WINTER BOTHAM C Coy with Corpl M BAILEY & Pte T H LEGWORTHY went out on Daylight Patrol to reconnoitre HAIE en Z Fence (situated about 100 yds from enemy Trenches) & to see what enemy is seen of enemy trenches in the S.W. corner of BONCOURT WOOD. They found they could not see into the Wood as Fence was in bad repair. They thoroughly inspected the whole of the Fence & returned at 11-30 am. | 42 |
| | | 8pm | 2/Lt A C R WELSH joined Battalion from 2/5th Battn. 10 O.R.s made posted to D Coy. Battalion relieved by BUCKS BATTALION and marched to Billets in SAILLY-AUX-BOIS. 1/1st Bucks Brigade Reserve. Strength 31 Officers 867 other ranks | 1 |
| SAILLY AUX BOIS | 22/8/15 | | In Billets. Day & hot. | |

Army Form C. 2118.

# WAR DIARY
## or
## INTELLIGENCE SUMMARY.
(Erase heading not required.)

| Place | Date | Hour | Summary of Events and Information | Remarks and references to Appendices |
|---|---|---|---|---|
| SAILLY AUX BOIS | 23/9/15 | | In Billets. Bn. at rest. Enemy shelled Villages throughout the morning | (1) |
| SAILLY | 24/9/15 | | In Billets. Bn. at rest. Battalion in general notes ready between an 1st September | (1) |
| SAILLY | 25/9/15 | | In Billets. Bn. at rest. Battalion under orders to take over trenches from 4th & 8th WARWICKS on 26/9/15 | (1) |
| SAILLY HEBUTERNE | 26/9/15 2/pm | | Battalion takes over trenches 24 to 28 inclusive from 7th WARWICKS & 8th WARWICKS and trenches 29 to ½ 32 inclusive from 7th WARWICKS. These trenches are situated SOUTH EAST of HEBUTERNE about 1500 yards from the centre of the Village. Trenches 31 & 32 are in support. Trenches and Battn. Head Qrs. are in front of the line captured by the FRENCH in JUNE. Position is from enemy line from 500 ys on Right to 450 x on Left of line. Posts to 450 x on Left of line between own trench and theirs, numbering | (1) |

**Army Form C. 2118.**

# WAR DIARY
## *or*
## INTELLIGENCE SUMMARY.
*(Erase heading not required.)*

| Place | Date | Hour | Summary of Events and Information | Remarks and references to Appendices |
|---|---|---|---|---|
| HEBUTERNE | 26/8/15 | | Disposition | |

Hd Qrs 400 yds NORTH of TOUTVENT FARM in Communication Trench PU 140.

Right Company 2 Platoons in Trenches 31 and 32
2 Platoons in Local Support in Trench JEAN BART y DOMINIQUE

Centre Company 3 Platoons in Trenches 29 and 30
1 Platoon in Local Support in Trench JEAN BART

Left Company 2½ Platoons in Trenches 24 to 28 inclusive
1½ " in Support in BUGEAUD.

Reserve Company 3 Platoons in Dugouts in DUGESCLIN
1 " in Billets in HEBUTERNE

Qr Mr Stores in HEBUTERNE Transport at COIGNEAUX

# WAR DIARY
## or
## INTELLIGENCE SUMMARY.
*(Erase heading not required.)*

Army Form C. 2118.

| Place | Date | Hour | Summary of Events and Information | Remarks and references to Appendices |
|---|---|---|---|---|
| HEBUTERNE | 26/8/15 | | Battalion in trenches as follows:— A Coy Reserve Coy, B Coy Centre Coy, C Coy Right Coy, D Coy Left Coy | |
| " | 27/8/15 | | Weather Bright Hot. Strength 31 Officers 962 Other Ranks. No 2382 Corpl RE KNIGHT and No Corpl F W HARVEY are awarded the Distinguished Conduct MEDAL for consistent good patrolling on front line. Quiet day. Enemy put 50 shells along our line. No damage. Snipping & machine gun fire brisk at night. C.Coy 11th WARWICKS attached to 6th Battalion for instruction in Trench Warfare from 27th to 5th Sept. They arrived and go into billets in HEBUTERNE Village at 8.30pm | W) D) W) |

Army Form C. 2118.

# WAR DIARY
or
## INTELLIGENCE SUMMARY.
*(Erase heading not required.)*

| Place | Date | Hour | Summary of Events and Information | Remarks and references to Appendices |
|---|---|---|---|---|
| HEBUTERNE | 28/8/15 | | In Trenches. Quiet day. Wet. No casualties | |
| | | 3pm | C Coy 11th WARWICKS go into trenches for individual instruction in Trench duties | |
| " | 29/8/15 | | In Trenches. Quiet day. No casualties. No casualties | |
| " | 30/8/15 | | In Trenches. Quiet day. Any & Urmidy. In Trenches. | |
| | | 3pm | C Coy 11th WARWICKS go into trenches to complete platoon returning from/completion. In Trenches. Considerable shelling of our trenches, slight damage. On night of 30th Lieut T.H. MOORE and 4 men patrolled in front of 29 Trench and found enemy saying pits 200 yds from our trench. Patrol surprised in a matter opened fire on by enemy and their entrenching tools left in the pits. Pte R.N. LEWIS & Coy slightly wounded by splinter of shell. | |
| " | 31/7/15 | 11am | Battalion is relieved by 4th OXFORDS and moves into billets in HEBUTERNE Village. A Coy from Reserve Reserve and | |

**Army Form C. 2118.**

# WAR DIARY
*or*
# INTELLIGENCE SUMMARY.
(Erase heading not required.)

| Place | Date | Hour | Summary of Events and Information | Remarks and references to Appendices |
|---|---|---|---|---|
| HEBUTERNE | 31/9/15 | | Continued:- B & D Coys from the garrison of HEBUTERNE KEEP. MAJOR J.F. TARRANT takes over command of the KEEP | (1) |

145th Inf.Bde.
48th Div.

1/5th BATTN. THE GLOUCESTERSHIRE REGIMENT.

S E P T E M B E R

1 9 1 5

CONFIDENTIAL.

# WAR DIARY
## OF
## 1/5TH BATTALION - GLOUCESTERSHIRE REGIMENT.

---

From 1st September, 1915.    To 30th September, 1915.

Volume VII.

Lt-Colonel.
Comdg 1/5th Gloucester Regiment.

Army Form C. 2118.

# WAR DIARY
## or
## INTELLIGENCE SUMMARY.
*(Erase heading not required.)*

Instructions regarding War Diaries and Intelligence Summaries are contained in F. S. Regs., Part II. and the Staff Manual respectively. Title pages will be prepared in manuscript.

SEPTEMBER 1915

| Place | Date | Hour | Summary of Events and Information | Remarks and references to Appendices |
|---|---|---|---|---|
| HEBUTERNE | 1/9/15 | | Battalion in Billets in HEBUTERNE KEEP. Employed on R.E. working parties. Strength 30 Officers 861 other ranks. Weather wet. Capt. F.W. COLE returned to the Battalion from the Entrenching Battalion. | W |
| " | 2/9/15 | | In Billets. R.E. working parties. Weather showery. | W |
| " | 3/9/15 | | In Billets. Weather showery | W |
| " | 4/9/15 | | In Billets. Weather dry. | W |
| " | 5/9/15 | | Battalion moved to Billets in SAILLY in Divisional Reserve. Strength Officers 31 other Ranks 852. In Billets | W |
| SAILLY | 6/9/15 | | In Billets. | W |
| " | 7/9/15 | | In Billets. Capt & adj V.N. JOHNSON takes over duties of Brigade Major temporarily. Capt. H.C.B. JESSIONS acts as adjutant | W |

1577 Wt. W10791/1773 500,000 1/15 D. D. & L. A.D.S.S./Forms/C. 2118.

Army Form C. 2118.

# WAR DIARY
## or
## INTELLIGENCE SUMMARY.
(Erase heading not required.)

| Place | Date | Hour | Summary of Events and Information | Remarks and references to Appendices |
|---|---|---|---|---|
| SAILLY | 8/9/15 | 11 am | Battalion marched to BUS les ARTOIS | 10 |
| | | | Strong MR | |
| BUS | 9/9/15 | | In Billets. Muster. Fire Ant. | |
| " | 10/9/15 | | " Billets " " " | 10 |
| " | 11/9/15 | | " Billets " " " | 10 |
| " | 12/9/15 | | " Billets " " " | 10 |
| " | 13/9/15 | | " Billets " " " | 10 |
| " | 14/9/15 | | " Billets " " " Grenadier class returned to Battalion 5 pm. | 10 |
| " | 15/9/15 | | " Billets Capt & Adj V.N. JOHNSON return & resume duties | 10 |
| " | 16/9/15 | | " Billets Muster. Fire Ant. | 10 |
| " | 17/9/15 | 9 am | Battalion leaves BUS and takes over trenches 19 to 25. (situated between PUISIEUX Rd and SERRE Rd) HEBUTERNE. Preparation. Left sub-sector Trenches 19 to 22 (incl.) C Coy (2nd Lay WALLER) " " " 22 to 25 Comy of 8th HAMPSHIRE 4½. (attached for instruction) Right | |

Army Form C. 2118.

# WAR DIARY
## or
## INTELLIGENCE SUMMARY.
(Erase heading not required.)

Instructions regarding War Diaries and Intelligence Summaries are contained in F. S. Regs., Part II. and the Staff Manual respectively. Title pages will be prepared in manuscript.

| Place | Date | Hour | Summary of Events and Information | Remarks and references to Appendices |
|---|---|---|---|---|
| HEBUTERNE | 17/9/15 | | B. Cy (Capt R.E. LITTLE) in the Sypres in support <br> A Cy (Capt G.F. COLLETT) in Billets in HEBUTERNE <br> D Cy (Lieut H.P. NOWDEN) in Billets in Th KEEP in BDE Reserve <br> Casualties per PRESTON. Situation Quiet - Weather Fine | |
| HEBUTERNE | 18/9/15 | | A Cy relieve 8th Bn SHROPSHIRE L.I. Cy in Trenches <br> Situation normal - Casualties nil - Weather Fine - <br> Intermittent shelling by both sides. | |
| HEBUTERNE | 19/9/15 | | Situation normal - Intermittent shelling - Casualties nil - Weather Fine <br> Capt F.E. FRANCILLON returns from leave & takes command of D Cy. | |
| HEBUTERNE | 20/9/15 | | Situation normal - Casualties nil - Weather Fine <br> Enemy shelling. | |
| HEBUTERNE | 21/9/15 | | Situation normal - Enemy shelling - Casualties nil - Weather Fine | |
| " | 22/9/15 | | Situation normal - Enemy shelling - Casualties L/Cpl MS. BROWN wounded by shell splinter - Weather Fine - Strength Officers 31 Other Ranks 828 <br> B Cy relieve A Cy - D Cy relieve C Cy in trenches. | |

1577  Wt.W10791/1773  500,000  1/15  D.D. & L.  A.D.S.S./Forms/C. 2118.

# WAR DIARY
## or
## INTELLIGENCE SUMMARY.
(Erase heading not required.)

Army Form C. 2118.

| Place | Date | Hour | Summary of Events and Information | Remarks and references to Appendices |
|---|---|---|---|---|
| HEBUTERNE | 23-9/15 | | Situation unchanged - Patrols went out in the night 22nd-23rd to reconnoitre a French Post West of TEN BROTHER Trench NEBUTERNE - PUISIEUX Rd. Petrol found trench not held by enemy. In daytime Patrol went by sniper CORPL BAILLEY C. Coy found 6 GERMAN BOMBS & brought it in. SERGT KNIGHT A Coy with CORPL HARRIS went out in daylight Patrol to within 10 yds of enemy wire, found a sniper hit and a hat with English writing in German. 2ND LT T.H. MOORE B Coy went out in my lyper patrol doubled own Battalion wire shelling enemy wire he brought in a GERMAN BOMB and Field Primer. Our Artillery shelled enemy trenches heavily (See week) enemy unusual inactivity — No casualties. | (1) |

D. Smyth Officer. John Rawson

Army Form C. 2118.

# WAR DIARY
## or
## INTELLIGENCE SUMMARY.
(Erase heading not required.)

Instructions regarding War Diaries and Intelligence Summaries are contained in F.S. Regs., Part II. and the Staff Manual respectively. Title pages will be prepared in manuscript.

| Place | Date | Hour | Summary of Events and Information | Remarks and references to Appendices |
|---|---|---|---|---|
| HEBUTERNE | 24/9/15 | | Situation unchanged. Our Battn. heavily shell enemy trenches and cut wire at Point 873. In front of our Right Trenches. Lt. T.H. MOORE & CORPL J.C. JACKSON B Coy crawled out & inspect the cut in enemy wire at Point 873 made by the 4.m. Patrol found the wire was completely cut in a gap of 15 yds. wide x 25 yds deep but – enemy wire much het – | |
| | | 6 pm | Two Platoons were sent to 5th Bn ROYAL SUSSEX REGT an attached to Lt Batten and take over trenches. One Platoon to D Coy the other to B Coy, with a view to clearing up Trenches if an return to Hebuterne. | |
| " | 25/9/15 | | Advance of 1st ARMY commenced North of ARRAS – Situation unchanged on our front. Our Artillery opened heavy fire on enemys trenches & wire. Corpl R.C. JACKSON and Pte A. ENOCK of B Coy crawled out to | |

| Place | Date | Hour | Summary of Events and Information | Remarks and references to Appendices |
|---|---|---|---|---|
| | | | the enemy him to see if they had moved the G of made by the artillery the day before. Patrol found wire had not been mended. — Casualties nil — Weather Wet | |
| HEBUTERNE | 26/9/15 | 11 pm | Situation unchanged — Lieut T.H. MOORE with a Patrol consisting of Sergt G.E. COOK Corpl R.C. JACKSON L/C RODWAY and 11 men of B Coy went out to ascertain if the enemy were evacuating their line. Patrol reached the enemy line and as they were moving across the front a German patrol came out and an encounter ensued in which 3 Germans were shot L/C RODWAY was hit, and Lt T.H MOORE and Corpl JACKSON went to bring him away when 2nd Lt H MOORE, whilst lifting him, were also shot. The Patrol returned and returned to our lines except Lt T.H. MOORE and L/Cpl RODWAY and Pte BINGHAM. The latter was not seen to fall. Casualties Lt T.H MOORE & Officer L/Cpl RODWAY Returned killed Pte BINGHAM missing | |

# WAR DIARY or INTELLIGENCE SUMMARY

Army Form C. 2118.

| Place | Date | Hour | Summary of Events and Information | Remarks and references to Appendices |
|---|---|---|---|---|
| HEBUTERNE | 27/9/15 | | Situation unchanged. A Patrol consisting of Corpl R.C. JACKSON and Pte ENOCK went round out in daylight to the scene of the Patrol fight of last night to see if Lt TH MOORE and 2/c RODWAY were there. Patrol found both dead | |
| | | 5.15pm | Corpl R.C. JACKSON led a patrol of 5t to try to bring in bodies of Lt TH MOORE & 2/c RODWAY. They reached the bodies and but attempts ensued them & when about to bring them in at dusk when two German patrols came out of their trench and fired at our patrol who returned without the two bodies. | W |
| | 28/9/15 | | Situation unchanged - own Patrols active during daylight. Weather fine - Casualties nil - | W |

# WAR DIARY
## or
## INTELLIGENCE SUMMARY.

Army Form C. 2118.

| Place | Date | Hour | Summary of Events and Information | Remarks and references to Appendices |
|---|---|---|---|---|
| HEBUTERNE | 24/9/15 | 10 am | Situation unchanged – Weather wet – Grenadier Pl - Battalion is relieved by 8th Bn WORCESTER REGT and moves to Billets in BUS les ARTOIS from Division Reserve. Capt F.W. COLE takes command of D Coy vice Capt VISCOUNT CAMPDEN invalided | 1) |
| BUS | 30/9/15 | | Situation unchanged – Weather fine – Strength Officers 29, Other Ranks 833 | 1) |

145th Inf.Bde.
48th Div.

1/5th BATT. THE GLOUCESTERSHIRE REGIMENT.

O C T O B E R

1 9 1 5

CONFIDENTIAL.

# WAR DIARY

OF

1/5TH BATTALION - GLOUCESTERSHIRE REGIMENT.

From 1st October, 1915.    To, 31st October, 1915.

Volume 8.

*[signature]* Lt-Colonel.
Comdg 1/5th Gloucester Regiment.

**Army Form C. 2118.**

# WAR DIARY
## or
## INTELLIGENCE SUMMARY.
*(Erase heading not required.)*

October 1915

| Place | Date | Hour | Summary of Events and Information | Remarks and references to Appendices |
|---|---|---|---|---|
| BUS | 1/10/15 | | Situation unchanged. Weather Fine. Strength Officers 29 Other Ranks 831 | W.F. |
| " | 2/10/15 | | Situation unchanged. Weather Fine. | W.F. |
| BUS | 3/10/15 | | " " " " | W.F. |
| " | 4/10/15 | | " " Weather Wet. | |
| " | 5/10/15 | | Situation unchanged. Walter Fine. Captain and Adjutant V.N. Johnson notified of his appointment as Brigade Major of 125 Infantry Brigade. Capt + Qm V.N. Johnson left Battalion to take up duties of Brigade Major of 125 Infantry Brigade and the duties of A/Adjutant were taken over by 2nd Lieut J.R.W. Derbyshire. | S.R.W. |
| BUS | 6/10/15 | | Cards of congratulation on good work in the field from Major General Fanshawe commanding 48th Division were received by the following:- Capt + A/Qm V.N. Johnson, Capt. J.F. Collett, Sergt. E. Endref, 154 Sergt. J.W. Jewing 133 Sergt. A. Faville 392 Sergt. F. Field 2717 Sergt. R.O. Renfrew 2741 Cpl. J.W. Watkins. Walter Fine. | S.R.W. |

# WAR DIARY or INTELLIGENCE SUMMARY

Army Form C. 2118.

| Place | Date | Hour | Summary of Events and Information | Remarks and references to Appendices |
|---|---|---|---|---|
| BUS | | | October 1915 | |
| | 7/10/15 | | Field General Court martial assembled at Head Quarters. No 2513 Pte F Coleman and No 2483 Pte H Richardson charge. When on active service drunkenness. Found guilty. Sentence 2 months F.P. no 1. Sentence confirmed by Gen Wanless O'Gowan commanding 14th Infantry Bde and duly promulgated. Weather fine. | JRW |
| | 8/10/15 | | Battalion Route march and Field Yard exercise. Fine | JRW |
| " | 9/10/15 6.6pm | | Practice alarm. Fine. | JRW |
| " | 10/10/15 | | In Billets. Weather Fine | JRW |
| " | 11/10/15 9AM | | Battalion leave BUS and takes over Trenches 19 to 25 inclusive (situated between PUISIEUX Rd and SERRE Rd) East of HEBUTERNE. Disposition Left Sub sector Trenches 19 to 21 inclusive and PAS DE TIR to junction of VILLON e COY (Comd Major WALLER | |

# WAR DIARY
## INTELLIGENCE SUMMARY

Army Form C. 2118.

| Place | Date | Hour | Summary of Events and Information | Remarks and references to Appendices |
|---|---|---|---|---|
| HEBUTERNE | 11/4/15 | | Dispositions (Cont.) Right Subsector Trenches PA 9 De Tir from junction of VILLON and TM 22 to 25 inclusive A Coy (Com. Capt G.F. COLLETT) | |
| | | | D Coy (Capt COLE) in the Square in Suffold | |
| | | | B - (Capt R.E. LITTLE) in the KEEP in Bde. Reserve. | |
| | | 6 P.M. | C Coy. 10th Battn. ROYAL IRISH RIFLES attached for instruction as follows | |
| | | | No 9 Platoon R.I.R. to A Coy 5th R. | |
| | | | - 10 - - C - | |
| | | | - 11 - - D - | |
| | | | - 12 - - B - | |
| | | | Lieut. H.P. SNOWDEN with 3 N.C.Os and 22 men went to Bde. Grenade School SAILLY for course | |
| | | | Lieut. C.V.N. PUCKRIDGE detailed as Battalion Grenade Officer Fighting Strength 27 Officers 818 Other Ranks - Casualties nil - 2nd Lieut - Fine | S.P.W. |
| | | | Lieut W. Frean and 9 other ranks left on leave. Lieut H.S. KING | |
| 12/4/15 | | | left to act as instructor at Grenade School vice Lieut. W FREAH on leave. Intermittent shelling on both sides. Casualties nil. Fine | S.P.W. |

Army Form C. 2118.

# WAR DIARY
## or
## INTELLIGENCE SUMMARY.
(Erase heading not required.)

Instructions regarding War Diaries and Intelligence Summaries are contained in F. S. Regs., Part II. and the Staff Manual respectively. Title pages will be prepared in manuscript.

| Place | Date | Hour | Summary of Events and Information | Remarks and references to Appendices |
|---|---|---|---|---|
| HEBUTERNE | 13/10/15 | 2 P.M. | Inter-company relief. B Coy relieved A Coy and D Coy relieved C Coy R. IRISH RIFLES No. 12 Platoon relieved No. 9 and No. 11 relieved No. 10. (C Coy) | |
| | | 4 P.M. | 2nd Lieut. L.W MOORE and 3 men went on leave. Situation very quiet. Weather fine. Casualties nil. | 3910 |
| " | 14/10/15 | | Station quiet. Casualties nil. Enemy patrols active at night. Fine | 3910 |
| " | 15/10/15 | 2 P.M. | Inter-company relief. A Coy relieved B Coy - C Coy relieved D Coy. Situation quiet. Fine but foggy. Casualties nil. Strength 28 Officers 817 O.R. | 3910 |
| " | 16/10/15 | 5 P.M. | C Coy 10th Bn. R. Irish RIFLES occupied Tr. 19 to 21 and PAS DE TIR to junction of VILLON (Comd MAJOR PERASE) Fine but foggy. Casualties nil | 3910 |
| " | 17/10/15 | 2.15 P.M. | Enemy shelled village. Casualties - Lieut. E.W. WINTERBOTHAM R. Thigh (slight) 2611 Pte. SMITH E.W. C Coy. Back of neck 1517 Pte. SANSOM B.S L Ankle and shock all C Coy. by shell. 3318 Pte. WALKER G. L Knee 1922 Cpl. PAGE H. R. Thigh. all B Coy. by shell. | |
| " | " | 2.0 PM | Inter-company Relief - B Co. relieved A Coy - D Coy took over from C Coy. R.I.R. at 4. A.M. Weather Fine. shalom wounded. | 3910 |

Army Form C. 2118.

# WAR DIARY
## INTELLIGENCE SUMMARY.
*(Erase heading not required.)*

Instructions regarding War Diaries and Intelligence Summaries are contained in F. S. Regs., Part II. and the Staff Manual respectively. Title pages will be prepared in manuscript.

| Place | Date | Hour | Summary of Events and Information | Remarks and references to Appendices |
|---|---|---|---|---|
| HEBUTERNE | 18/10/15 | | Heavy shelling by enemy from 2.30 P.M onwards mostly on the village and replying our guns. Trenches in Section on our right and left plastered. Casualties - 14427 L/C FISHER B.W. "D" Co. wound in back by shell in Tr D'ALSACE about 9.30. A.M. Fine. Quiet at night. | JPW |
| | 19/10/15 | 9 AM | Battalion was relieved by 8th Bn. WORCESTER REGT and marched to some Billets as before at BUS. Lieut. CONDER and 9 men went on leave. 2nd Lieut K.C. DURRANT took over duties of M.G.O. Fine. Casualties - NIL. 2611 Pte SMITHEW died of wounds at 11 S.H.A. Cas. Clg STATION | JPW JPW |
| BUS | 20/10/15 | | Lieut. H.P. SNOWDEN and 3 men went on leave. Fine | JPW |
| " | 21/10/15 | | Lieut W FREAM and 9 OR returned from leave Fine | JPW |
| " | 22/10/15 | | Strength 26 Officers 812 OR. Lieut. L.W MOORE returned from leave. Fine | JPW |

Army Form C. 2118.

# WAR DIARY
## INTELLIGENCE SUMMARY.
(Erase heading not required.)

Instructions regarding War Diaries and Intelligence Summaries are contained in F.S. Regs., Part II. and the Staff Manual respectively. Title pages will be prepared in manuscript.

| Place | Date | Hour | Summary of Events and Information | Remarks and references to Appendices |
|---|---|---|---|---|
| BUS | 23/10/15 | 9 AM | Battalion Route march and practice attack. Three men returned from leave having been granted one extra days leave owing to delay in getting home. Capt. H.C.B. SESSIONS and Lieut. W. FREAM left BUS to give a course of instruction in Sniping and Grenades respectively to 107th Brigade. Lieut. H.S. KING returned from Grenade School. Weather- Fine | SRO |
| " | 24/10/15 | 10 AM | Church Parade at CHATEAU BUS. Weather Fine | SRO |
| " | 25/10/15 | | Situation unchanged. Weather wet & cold | SRO |
| " | 26/10/15 | | Situation unchanged. Fine. Lieuts C.S. NASON and H.S. KING and 11 men went on leave. | SRW |
| " | 27/10/15 | 9 AM. | Battalion leave for HEBUTERNE and takes over Trenches 19 to 25 inclusive Dispositions:- Right Subsection Trenches 22 to 25 inclusive and PAS DE TIR to junction with VILLON - A Co: (Commde Capt. G.F. COLLETT) | SRW |

Army Form C. 2118.

# WAR DIARY
## INTELLIGENCE SUMMARY.
*(Erase heading not required.)*

| Place | Date | Hour | Summary of Events and Information | Remarks and references to Appendices |
|---|---|---|---|---|
| HEBUTERNE | 27/10/15 | | Dispositions (cont) Left Subsection 19 to 21 inclusive and PAS DE TIR to junction with VILLON - C. Coy (Major WALLER) B Coy (Capt R.E. LITTLE). Platoon in SQUARE — HEBUTERNE - ROE GRANGE. 1 - Dug Out in TR. BOTHA. 2 - Dug-Outs in TR. RAGLAN. D. Coy (Capt. COLE) in KEEP (Brigade Reserve) | |
| | | 6 P.M | Strength 28 Officers 810 other Ranks. C Coy. 10th Bn ROYAL INNISKILLING FUSILIERS attached for instruction No 9 Platoon R.I.F. to C - No 10 to A Co - No 11 to B Co - No 12 to D Co. Four men Staffed and returned from Leave. Casualties Nil - Walter - Wal | T.R.W. |
| | 28/10/15 | | Situation normal. Rain. Casualties NIL. Lieut E. CONDER returned from leave | T.R.W |

**Army Form C. 2118.**

# WAR DIARY
## or
## INTELLIGENCE SUMMARY.
*(Erase heading not required.)*

| Place | Date | Hour | Summary of Events and Information | Remarks and references to Appendices |
|---|---|---|---|---|
| HEBUTERNE | 29/10/15 | 2 PM | Inter-Company Relief – B Co. & A, D Co. & C. Platoons of C Co. RIF changed over. No 11 relieved No 10 and No 12 relieved No 9. Our Artillery bombarded Trenches opposite. Dull. Casualties NIL. 15776 Pte MULLEN E. Coy R.I.F. accidentally wounded in foot. Enemy held Dull. Capt H.E.B SESSIONS returned | FWD |
| " | 30/10/15 | | Situation quiet. Lieut. H.P SNOWDEN returned from leave. Rain. Casualties No 203 Sergt HEAVEN S accidentally wounded by bayonet. Rifles 186 Enemy held. | FWD |
| " | 31/10/15 | | Inter-Company Relief – A Co. & B Co. C Co. & D Co. R.I.F. exchanged trenches. Situation normal. Casualties NIL. Drizzly Rain. Strength 28 Officers 802 Other Ranks | FWD |

145th Inf.Bde.
48th Div.

1/5th BATTN. THE GLOUCESTERSHIRE REGIMENT.

N O V E M B E R

1 9 1 5

CONFIDENTIAL.

# WAR DIARY

## OF

## 1/5TH BATTALION – GLOUCESTERSHIRE REGIMENT.

From: 1st November, 1915.   To 30th November, 1915.

Volume IX.

*[signature]* Lt-Colonel.
Comdg 1/5th Gloucester Regiment.

1st December, 1915.

# WAR DIARY
## or
## INTELLIGENCE SUMMARY.

*(Erase heading not required.)*

Army Form C. 2118.

Instructions regarding War Diaries and Intelligence Summaries are contained in F. S. Regs., Part II. and the Staff Manual respectively. Title pages will be prepared in manuscript.

| Place | Date | Hour | Summary of Events and Information | Remarks and references to Appendices |
|---|---|---|---|---|
| HEBUTERNE | 1/11/15 | 3 PM | C Co. 10th Battn R.I.F. took over trenches of ours left of S.W. sector | |
| | | 4.5 AM | No 2908 Pte SAMPSON A E C Co. was shot and killed by our sentry post on the Right of PUSIEUX ROAD in mistake for an enemy. Buried in Cemetery at K9C 9.2 (FRANCE Sheet 57D Fuis Relief 40000 at 12.30 PM. Enemy held Heavy Rain. Weather normal | SW |
| " | 2/11/15 | 8.45 AM | D Coy took over trenches from C Co. R.I.F. on their relieved. Casualties NIL | |
| | | 1.30 PM | B. relieved A Coy. Heavy Rain. Casualties NIL Lieut C.D. WINTERBOTHAM and 2nd Lieut K.G. DURRANT and 18 men went on leave | SW |
| " | 3/11/15 | | Situation normal. Rain. Casualties NIL 2nd Lieuts C.V.N. FUCKRIDGE and D.G. DURRANT and 5 men on leave | SW |
| " | 4/11/15 | 9.30 AM | Battalion was relieved by 8th Bn WORCESTER REGT and marched to ST. JOHN'S BUS. Fine. Casualties NIL Lieuts KING & NASON | |

Army Form C. 2118.

# WAR DIARY
## INTELLIGENCE SUMMARY.
(Erase heading not required.)

Instructions regarding War Diaries and Intelligence Summaries are contained in F. S. Regs., Part II. and the Staff Manual respectively. Title pages will be prepared in manuscript.

| Place | Date | Hour | Summary of Events and Information | Remarks and references to Appendices |
|---|---|---|---|---|
| BUS | 4/4/15 | | returned from leave. Casualties NIL | SRD |
| " | 5/4/15 | | In billets at BUS. Battalion Route march. Weather Fine and Cold | SRD |
| " | 6/4/15 | | In billets at BUS. Battalion Route march. Fine. Strength 28 Officers 779 OR | SRD |
| " | 7/4/15 | | Fine & cold. In Billets | SRD |
| " | 8/4/15 | | In Billets. Fine | SRD |
| " | 9/4/15 | | In Billets. Weather Dull. Major J.F. TARRANT and Capt A.T. MITCH-ESON left for leave | SRD |
| " | 10/4/15 | | Rain. Major N.W. WALLER and 2nd Lieut L.J. CLAYTON left for leave | SRD |
| " | 11/4/15 | | In Billets. Rain. Lieut. C.W. WINTERBOTHAM and 2nd Lieut K.G. DURRANT returned from leave | SRD |

Army Form C. 2118.

# WAR DIARY
## INTELLIGENCE SUMMARY.
*(Erase heading not required.)*

Instructions regarding War Diaries and Intelligence Summaries are contained in F. S. Regs., Part II. and the Staff Manual respectively. Title pages will be prepared in manuscript.

| Place | Date | Hour | Summary of Events and Information | Remarks and references to Appendices |
|---|---|---|---|---|
| BUS | 12/4/15 | 7 AM | Battalion leave for HEBUTERNE and take over trenches from 8th Bn. WORCS Regt. Dispositions:<br>Right Subsection Tr. 22 to 25 inclusive and PAS DE TIR to junction with<br>VILLON – A Coy (Capt. G.F. COLLETT in command)<br>Tr. 19 to 21 inclusive and PAS DE TIR to junction with<br>Left Subsection VILLON – D Coy (Capt. F.W. COLE in command)<br>KEEP – B Coy (Capt. R.E. LITTLE in command)<br>C Coy (Capt. R.M.F. COOKE in command)<br>Platoon in SQUARE<br>" " BOTHA<br>" " RUE GRANDE<br>2 " "<br>Weather very heavy rain. Trenches very bad and fallen in Casualties NIL. Unit on our Right 4 OXFORD & BUCKS L.I on our Left 1st R. BERKS. | |
| HEBUTERNE | 13/4/15 | | Situation quiet. Weather very wet. Lieut. WELSH & Pallot wound out from | SRW |

# WAR DIARY
## or
## INTELLIGENCE SUMMARY.
(Erase heading not required.)

Army Form C. 2118.

| Place | Date | Hour | Summary of Events and Information | Remarks and references to Appendices |
|---|---|---|---|---|
| HEBUTERNE | 13/4/15 | | T- 22 to reconnoitre new trench by enemy but were prevented by enemy fire/arty. Casualties NIL | SPW |
| " | 14/4/15 | 6 AM | Sgt P.O. THOMPSON and 3 others recalled new enemy trench and reported it as actually a trap. Casualties NIL Situation normal Cold. Inter-company Relief. B Coy. relieved A - D Coy relieved D. | SPW |
| " | 15/4/15 | | Situation normal. Casualties NIL Frost and Snow. Capt PETERS 10- Lancers Indian Army attached for Instruction. | SPW SPW |
| " | 16/4/15 | 11 AM | Inter-company relief. A Coy relieved B Coy. | SPW |
| | | 4 PM | C Coy. 13th Bn. ROYAL IRISH RIFLES attached for Instruction. Relieved E Coy. 5th GLOS. REGT Weather Cold and Frosty. Casualties NIL | SPW |
| " | 17/4/15 | | Situation normal. Casualties NIL. Cold - Snow. | SPW |
| " | 18/4/15 | 10.30 AM | Inter-company relief. B Coy relieved A. E Coy 5th G.R. relieved C. Coy 13th R.I.R. Fine cold. Casualties NIL. Enemy quiet. | SPW |

# WAR DIARY
## INTELLIGENCE SUMMARY

*(Erase heading not required.)*

Army Form C. 2118.

Instructions regarding War Diaries and Intelligence Summaries are contained in F.S. Regs., Part II. and the Staff Manual respectively. Title pages will be prepared in manuscript.

| Place | Date | Hour | Summary of Events and Information | Remarks and references to Appendices |
|---|---|---|---|---|
| HEBUTERNE | 19/11/15 | | Situation normal. Fine cold. Casualties NIL. Lt Col CROCKETT 11th Bn HAMPSHIRE Regt attached for instruction. 2nd Lt RATCLIFF went on leave | SRW |
| HEBUTERNE | 20/11/15 | | Battalion was relieved by 8th Bn WORCESTERSHIRE REGT 144th Bde (C Coy by C Coy 13th Bn R. IRISH RIFLES) and moved to Billets in BUS. Fine. casualties NIL. Strength 29 Officers 766 O.R. | SRW |
| BUS | 21/11/15 | | In Billets. Cold and Fine. No 2535 Pte MULL 133 F.S. tried by F.G. Court Martial for leaving and using a camera. Sentence 3 months imprisonment with H.L. — R.O.C.C. Cold and Fine. | SRW |
| " | 22/11/15 | | Cold and Fine. | SRW |
| " | 23/11/15 | | Frost fine | SRW |
| " | 24/11/15 | 8.30AM | Battalion Route March | SRW |

# WAR DIARY

## INTELLIGENCE SUMMARY

Army Form C. 2118.

(Erase heading not required.)

| Place | Date | Hour | Summary of Events and Information | Remarks and references to Appendices |
|---|---|---|---|---|
| BUS | 25/4/15 | | Fine. Captain G.F. COLLETT went on leave | 320 |
| " | 26/4/15 | | 2nd Lieut. A.E.R. WELSH went on leave | 320 |
| " | 27/4/15 | | Fine and cold. 2nd Lt R. MADDER joined battalion from 3rd Battalion. Battalion was posted to B Coy. Lt E.S. NASON and 20 O.R. (Grenade Sclool) | 320 |
| " | 28/4/15 | 9 AM | Battalion leaves for HEBUTERNE to relieve 3rd Bn WORCESTER REGT in firing line. B Coy (Capt R.S.E. LITTLE) Tr 22 to 25 inclusive and PAS DE TIR & Junction with VILLON. C Coy (Capt R.M.F. COOKE) Tr. 19 & 21 inclusive and PAS DE TIR & Junction with VILLON and 2 Platoons in SQUARE. D Coy (Capt F.W. COLE) KEEP A Coy (Capt L.R.E. SUHNER) 1 Platoon in SQUARE 3 Platoons in Bay Outs BOTHA and LORD RAGLAN | TYCO |

# WAR DIARY
## INTELLIGENCE SUMMARY.
*(Erase heading not required.)*

Army Form C. 2118.

| Place | Date | Hour | Summary of Events and Information | Remarks and references to Appendices |
|---|---|---|---|---|
| HEBUTERNE | 28/4/15 | | Fine roll. Casualties NIL. Had great Calm command of Grenade School SAILLY. Unit on Right 4th Oxford & Bucks LI on left 4th R BERKS. C Coy 20th Bn MANCHESTER REGT attached for instruction. | STD |
| " | 29/4/15 | | Very wet. Casualties NIL. Lt C.W. WINTERBOTHAM and 2 men patrolled from Tr. 18 to Pt. 66 on PUISIEUX ROAD at 3 P.M. rambled trees and returned at 5 P.M. | STD |
| " | 30/4/15 | 10.30 AM | Inter Company Relief - D Coy to C - A Coy to B & B Coy to A. Strength 30 Officers 708 OR Casualties NIL | STD |

145th Inf.Bde.
48th Div.

1/5th BATTN. THE GLOUCESTERSHIRE REGIMENT.

DECEMBER

1915

CONFIDENTIAL.

W A R  D I A R Y
OF
1/5TH BATTALION — GLOUCESTERSHIRE REGIMENT.

From 1st December, 1915.   To 31st December, 1915.

(Volume 10)

*J. H. Collett*
Lt-Colonel.
Comdg 1/5th Gloucester Regiment.

1st January, 1915.

Army Form C. 2118.

# WAR DIARY
# INTELLIGENCE SUMMARY.
(Erase heading not required.)

Instructions regarding War Diaries and Intelligence Summaries are contained in F. S. Regs., Part II. and the Staff Manual respectively. Title pages will be prepared in manuscript.

| Place | Date | Hour | Summary of Events and Information | Remarks and references to Appendices |
|---|---|---|---|---|
| HEBUTERNE | 1/12/15 | | Situation normal. Casualties NIL. Weather very wet | SPW |
| " | 2/12/15 | | Inter-company relief. B Coy to A – C Coy to D. Heavy rain. Casualties Nil | SPW |
| " | 3/12/15 | | Lt BALFOUR went on leave. C Coy 20th Battalion MANCHESTER REGT occupied trenches 19 to 21 inclusive and PAS DE TIR & VILLON. Heavy rain. Trenches very bad. Our Artillery fired | SPW |
| " | 4/12/15 | | Inter-company relief. A Coy to B. D Coy to C. Coy 20th MANCHESTERS Casualties NIL. Rain. Lt Col. COLLETT went on leave. Lt KING to Grande École SAILLY on instructor's course learning for only | SPW |
| " | 5/12/15 | | Situation normal. Trenches very bad. Weather fine. No 1842 Pte NASH E.H. C Coy slightly wounded by a bullet. Lieut WELSH returned from leave. | SPW |

# WAR DIARY
## INTELLIGENCE SUMMARY

Army Form C. 2118.

| Place | Date | Hour | Summary of Events and Information | Remarks and references to Appendices |
|---|---|---|---|---|
| HEBUTERNE | 6/12/15 | | Battalion relieved by 8th Bn. WORCESTER REGT and moved to BUS from Divisional Reserve. Casualties NIL. Fine | SPW |
| BUS | 7/12/15 | | Weather rain | SPW |
| " | 8/12/15 | | Showery | SPW |
| " | 9/12/15 | | Some rain. Capt. R.S.C. LITTLE and Lieut FOOTE and Lieut BALFOUR returned from leave | SPW |
| " | 10/12/15 | | Lieut BALFOUR returned from leave | SW |
| " | 11/12/15 | | Showery. Reinforcement of 25 O.R. from 1st Bn Ourselves Batn. | SW |
| " | 12/12/15 | | Fine | SPW |
| " | 13/12/15 | | Lt Col J.H COLLETT returned from leave and took over command of | |

Army Form C. 2118.

# WAR DIARY
## or
## INTELLIGENCE SUMMARY.
*(Erase heading not required.)*

| Place | Date | Hour | Summary of Events and Information | Remarks and references to Appendices |
|---|---|---|---|---|
| BUS | 13/2/15 | | 145th Brigade vice Brigadier Gen McCLINTOCK sick | SPW |
| BUS | 14/2/15 | 7AM | Battalion moved to HEBUTERNE to relieve 8th Batt. WORCESTER REGT. Dispositions:- MAP Reference Trench Map Sheet 57D N.E. 1/10,000 X 16 A + B 'A' Coy (Capt G.FOLLETT) Trenches 22-25 inclusive and PAS DE TIR & VILLON 2 Platoons by day at Bn H.Q.S. B Coy (Capt A.T. MITCHESON) KEEP C Coy (Capt R.M.F. COOKE) 2 Platoons in Shelters in RAGLAN 2 Platoons in Billets No 28 & KEEP A Coy (Capt F.E. FRANCILLON) Trenches 19-21 inclusive and PAS DE TIR & VILLON 1 Platoon in SQUARE 1 Platoon in communication trenches being 1 Platoon in Billet No 178 A Coy could not relieve till dark owing to communication trenches being waterlogged. Fine and cold. Casualties NIL. | SPW |
| | | 9PM | Patrol of about 20 Germans been near our wire in front of Tr. 25. Machine gun and Rifle were opened and some were seen. | SPW |

1577  Wt.W10791/1773  500,000  1/15  D.D.&L.  A.D.S.S./Forms/C. 2118.

# WAR DIARY
## or
## INTELLIGENCE SUMMARY.

Army Form C. 2118.

| Place | Date | Hour | Summary of Events and Information | Remarks and references to Appendices |
|---|---|---|---|---|
| HEBUTERNE | 14/4/15 | | to run back. About 10.30 PM Lieut H.S. KING and patrol searched the ground and found one corpse whom they brought in with rifle & bayonet. Infantry man of 66th Regt - name unexplained. Patrol also found tracks where wounded had been dragged back. Unit on our Right 4th OXFORD & BUCKS L.I. Unit on our Left 4 ROYAL BERKS. Capt J. PETERS 10th Lancers (attached 34th POONA Horse) returned to unit | SPW |
| " | 15/4/15 | | Situation normal. Enemy shelled SAILLY. Some rain and sleet. Curalke NIL. Lt Col. J.H. COLLETT D.S.O. 1st Bn NORFOLK REGT returned to Battalion and took over command Major H.R. DONE. & assumed command of 145th Brigade vice Brigadier General McCLINTOCK to England. | SPW |
| " | 16/4/15 | | Inter-Company Relief - C coy relieved D coy at 11 AM. B coy relieved A coy at 4.30. Very foggy. Slight rain Cur altus NIL Capt. L.R.E. SUMNER left for leave | SPW |

# WAR DIARY
## INTELLIGENCE SUMMARY

*(Erase heading not required.)*

Army Form C. 2118.

Instructions regarding War Diaries and Intelligence Summaries are contained in F. S. Regs., Part II. and the Staff Manual respectively. Title pages will be prepared in manuscript.

| Place | Date | Hour | Summary of Events and Information | Remarks and references to Appendices |
|---|---|---|---|---|
| HEBUTERNE | 17/11/15 | | Strength 30 Officers 1192 O.R. Situation normal. Lieut. V. P. WINTERBOTHAM went on leave and 2nd Lieut. K.G. DURRANT arrived. Duties of Adjutant | K.G.D. |
| " | 18/11/15 | | Inter Company Relief. D Coy relieves C Coy at 11 A.M. A Coy relieved B Coy at 4.30 P.M. Casualties Nil. 2 C.Coy 15th Bn The LIVERPOOL REGT attached for instruction. Misty and Rain during the day, fine night. | K.G.D. |
| " | 19/11/15 | | Situation normal. Weather fine. Artillery active on both sides. Casualties Nil. L/C Sergt. P.G. BISHOP wounded accidentally at Grenade School | K.G.D. |
| " | 20/11/15 | | Situation normal. Inter Company Relief. C Coy relieved D Coy at 10 A.M. B Coy relieves A Coy at 11.30 A.M. Casualties Nil. Capt R.J.C. LITTLE and Lieut FOOTE returned from leave. Misty. | K.G.D. |
| " | 21/11/15 | | Situation normal. Slight Artillery activity on both sides. Casualties Nil. Much rain - misty. | K.G.D. |

# WAR DIARY

## INTELLIGENCE SUMMARY

Army Form C. 2118.

| Place | Date | Hour | Summary of Events and Information | Remarks and references to Appendices |
|---|---|---|---|---|
| HEBUTERNE | 22/11/15 | | Battalion relieved by 6th Bn WORCESTER REGT. and moves to BUS to form Divisional Reserve. Casualties Nil. Very wet weather showery. | KSD. |
| BUS | 23/11/15 | | In billets. | KSD. |
| " | 24/11/15 | | In billets | KSD. |
| " | 25/11/15 | | " " Capt. H.E.B. SESSIONS and Lieut. SNOWDEN went on leave | KSD. |
| " | 26/11/15 | | In billets | KSD. |
| " | 27/11/15 | | In Billets. Lieut. Col. 2nd Lt & Adjt. F. WINTERBOTHAM and Capt. SUMNER returned from leave | 3740 |
| " | 28/11/15 | 7 AM | Battalion moved to HEBUTERNE to take over Section H from 8th Battalion WORCESTER REGT. Dispositions :- Map Reference Trench Map Sheet 57.d. N.E. 3+4 "A" Coy. (Capt. G.F. COLLETT) Coy in support. 4 Posts of 1:10000 K.16.A+B 2 Platoons in shelters in RAGLAN 1 Platoon in cellars N side of RUE GRANDE | 3740 |

**Army Form C. 2118.**

# WAR DIARY
## INTELLIGENCE SUMMARY.
*(Erase heading not required.)*

Instructions regarding War Diaries and Intelligence Summaries are contained in F. S. Regs., Part II. and the Staff Manual respectively. Title pages will be prepared in manuscript.

| Place | Date | Hour | Summary of Events and Information | Remarks and references to Appendices |
|---|---|---|---|---|
| HERVTERNE | 28/11/15 | | (A Coy. cont.) 1 Platoon in cellars S side of PUISIEUX ROAD B Coy (Capt R.J.C. LITTLE) Tr. 22-25 and PAS DE TIR & VILLON KEEP. 2 Platoons by day at Bn. H.Q.S. C Coy (Capt R.M.F. ROOKE) KEEP. D Coy (Capt F.W. COLE) Tr. 19 & 21 and PAS DE TIR & VILLON. Unit on our right 4th OXFORD & BUCKS. L.I. On our left 4th ROYAL BERKR Fire Casualties NIL. Situation normal. | 3RD |
| ″ | 29/11/15 | | Situation normal. Fire casualties NIL. | 3RD |
| ″ | 30/11/15 | 7.45 AM | No. 3051 Pte WASLEY A B. Coy. wounded slightly by bullet in Tr 22. Fire Situation normal. Capt. F.W. Cole and Lieut-LISTER left for leave. Left F.E. FRANCILLON took command of D Coy and heads. A.S. KING taken over duties of Transport Officer | 3RD |
| ″ | 3/12/15 | 9.30 AM | Inter-company relief. A Coy. relieved B Coy and C Coy relieved | 3RD |

Army Form C. 2118.

# WAR DIARY
## INTELLIGENCE SUMMARY
*(Erase heading not required.)*

Instructions regarding War Diaries and Intelligence Summaries are contained in F. S. Regs., Part II. and the Staff Manual respectively. Title pages will be prepared in manuscript.

| Place | Date | Hour | Summary of Events and Information | Remarks and references to Appendices |
|---|---|---|---|---|
| HEBUTERNE | 31/1/15 | | A Coy. Casualties NIL. Bombardment by our Artillery from 12 NOON and reply by enemy causing very little damage. Weather: Fine. Strength 30 Officers + 1118 O.R. | TRD |

145th Brigade.
48th Division.

----------

1/5th BATTALION

GLOUCESTERSHIRE REGIMENT

JANUARY 1 9 1 6

# WAR DIARY
## INTELLIGENCE SUMMARY

*(Erase heading not required.)*

Army Form C. 2118.

| Place | Date | Hour | Summary of Events and Information | Remarks and references to Appendices |
|---|---|---|---|---|
| HEBUTERNE | 1/1/16 | | SITUATION normal. Casualties NIL. Fine. Lt Col. J.H. COLLETT Capt. V.V.N. JOHNSON and Lt E. CONDER mentioned in dispatches London Gazette 1/1/16 | T.R.O |
| " | 2/1/16 | | Fine. Casualties NIL. Sington wound. Showery | T.R.O |
| " | 3/1/16 | 9.30 AM | Battalion relieved by 8th WORCESTERS and marched to BUS in BUS to form Divisional Reserve. Casualties NIL. Fine | T.R.O |
| BUS | 4/1/16 | | In Billets. Fine | T.R.O |
| " | 5/1/16 | | " " Fine | T.R.O |
| " | 6/1/16 | | " " Wet | T.R.O |
| " | 7/1/16 | | " " Showery. Capt. R.H.F. COOKE went on leave | T.R.O |
| " | 8/1/16 | | " " Capt. F.E. FRANCILLON went on leave | T.R.O |

# WAR DIARY
## INTELLIGENCE SUMMARY
*(Erase heading not required.)*

| Place | Date | Hour | Summary of Events and Information | Remarks and references to Appendices |
|---|---|---|---|---|
| BUS 9/1/16 | | 9.30AM | Battalion marched to HEBUTERNE and relieved 8th WORCESTERS in trenches in Section H - Trench map Sheet 57d N.E. 3 & 4 Parts of 1:10,000. Dispositions:- <br> A Coy (Capt G.F. COLLETT) Tos. 22-25 and PAS DE TIR to VILLON <br> B Coy (Capt R.J.C. LITTLE) KEEP Brigade Reserve <br> C Coy (Lieut E.W. WINTERBOTHAM) Tos 19 to 21 and PAS DE TIR to VILLON <br> D Coy (Lieut H.R. SNOWDEN) Coy in support <br> 2 Platoons in shelters in RAGLAN <br> 1 Platoon in cellars on N. side of RUE GRANDE offsite church <br> 1 Platoon in cellars on S. side of PUISIEUX ROAD <br> Unit on our Right 4th OXFORD & BUCKS L.I. On our Left 4th ROYAL BERKS. <br> Fine. Strength 30 Officers 775 O.R. Casualties NIL | BW |
| HEBUTERNE 10/1/16 | | | Situation quiet. Fine. Casualties NIL | BW |

# WAR DIARY
## or
## INTELLIGENCE SUMMARY.

*(Erase heading not required.)*

Instructions regarding War Diaries and Intelligence Summaries are contained in F. S. Regs., Part II. and the Staff Manual respectively. Title pages will be prepared in manuscript.

| Place | Date | Hour | Summary of Events and Information | Remarks and references to Appendices |
|---|---|---|---|---|
| HEBUTERNE | 11/1/16 | | Situation normal. Fine casualties NIL. Capt COLE returned from leave and took command of B Coy. | SF(1) |
| " | 12/1/16 | 10 AM | Inter-company relief. B Coy to A - D Coy to C. Casualties NIL. Fine | SF(1) |
| | | | 2nd LT N.H. GRAVES-SMITH joined from 3/5 GLOS REGT and posted to A Coy | " |
| " | 13/1/16 | 10.40 AM | Enemy Artillery Bombardment and no reply. Casualties NIL. Showers of rain | SF(1) |
| " | 14/1/16 | | Situation normal. Casualties NIL. Fine | SF(1) |
| " | 15/1/16 | 9.0 PM | Battalion were relieved by 8th Bn WORCESTERSHIRE REGT and marched to billets at BUS to form Divisional Reserve. Fine Casualties NIL | SF(1) |
| | | | Draft of 24 OR joined from Eastern Army Battalion | SF(1) |
| BUS | 16/1/16 | | Fine. In Billets. LONDON GAZETTE dated 13/1/16. Major H.N. WALLER awarded Military Cross. No 155 Sergt. A. FAVILLE and No 154 Sergt. J.C.W. JENNINGS awarded Distinguished Conduct Medal | SF(1) |
| " | 17/1/16 | | In Billets Fine | SF(1) |

# WAR DIARY
## INTELLIGENCE SUMMARY.
*(Erase heading not required.)*

| Place | Date | Hour | Summary of Events and Information | Remarks and references to Appendices |
|---|---|---|---|---|
| BUS | 18/1/16 | | In Billets. Showery | SPO |
| " | 19/1/16 | | " Fine | ZW |
| " | 20/1/16 | | " " | SPO |
| BOS | 21/1/16 | 9 AM | Battalion moved to HEBUTERNE and took over Onendlers in H section from 8th WORCS. REGT: Ref TRENCH MAP Sheet 57D NE 3&4 Part of 1:10,000 Dispositions:— <br> A Coy (Capt. G.F. COLLETT) ~~2 Platoons~~ In support <br> 1 Platoon at Bn. H.Q. Q v A <br> 2 Platoons in reserve on RUE GRANDE and POIRIEUX Road <br> B " (Capt. R.I.C. LITTLE) Tm 22-25 and PAS DE TIR & VILLON LANE <br> C " (Capt. R.H.F. COOKE). KEEP Brigade Reserve <br> D " (Capt. F.E. FRANCILLON) Tm 19-22 and PAS DE TIR & VILLON LANE <br> Unit on our right BUCKS BATTN OXFORD and BUCKS L.I. on our left 4th ROYAL BERKS | WD |

## WAR DIARY

### INTELLIGENCE SUMMARY

*(Erase heading not required.)*

Army Form C. 2118.

| Place | Date | Hour | Summary of Events and Information | Remarks and references to Appendices |
|---|---|---|---|---|
| HEBUTERNE | 21/1/16 | | Fire. Strength 29 Officers 755 O.R. Casualties NIL. Lt C.G. NASON wnd. a. base. Situation normal | SPD |
| " | 22/1/16 | | Draft of 1 Officer and 27 O.R. joined from No 1 Entrenching Battalion Lt C.G. HAWKINS & 2 Lt. H.S. KING wnd on leave. Fire. Situation normal. Casualties NIL | SPD |
| " | 23/1/16 | | Situation normal. Fire casualties NIL. CAPT H.E.B. SESSIONS took command of C Coy. | SPD |
| " | 24/1/16 | | Inter - company relief. A Coy to B - C Coy to D. Normal Fire. Casualties NIL | SPD |
| " | 25/1/16 | 2 AM | Enemy shelled wire in front of landes near FONQUEVILLERS - GOMMECOURT ROAD and fired on Coy Trenches held by WARWICK BATT". | |
| | | 6.5 AM | No 2461 Pte ADAMS E.A. Lewis gun section killed on sentry in Bay 6 Tr 25 by shell in head and was buried in Military Cemetery HEBUTERNE K9 c 9.2 Sheet 57 D. | SPD |

1577  Wt.W10791/1773  500,000  1/15  D. D. & L.  A.D.S.S./Forms/C. 2118.

# WAR DIARY
## INTELLIGENCE SUMMARY

*(Erase heading not required.)*

Army Form C. 2118.

| Place | Date | Hour | Summary of Events and Information | Remarks and references to Appendices |
|---|---|---|---|---|
| NEUVE TERNE | 25/1/16 | 10 PM | 2 Lt K.G. DURRANT with 2 N.C.O.s and 8 men left T.7. 19 at 10 PM proceeded to LONE TREE (K.17.A.2-3) and lay a faint were enemy lines. No 2562 C/Sgt G. RICKETTS and No 3129 Pte W.S. TIMMS (E Coy) proceeded to saf at K.17.a.9-3 and reconnoitred enemy wire on each side. Patrol returned at 1.15 AM. Fine. Normal. 2Lt F.R. BELL joined from 3/5 Batt. and posted to D Coy. Situation normal. Fire casualties NIL. 2Lt D.G. DURRANT and patrol went out from T.V. 23 D 10 P.M. and found no sign of the enemy. | 3PU |
| - | 26/1/16 | | | 3PU |
| - | 27/1/16 | 6.30 AM | Battalion were relieved by 8th Battn. WORCESTERSHIRE REGT and marched to billets in BUS to form Divisional Reserve. Fine. Casualties NIL. 7 P.M. Gas alarm given which turned out to be false. | 3PU |
| BUS | 28/1/16 | | In billets. Fine. 2 Lt H.W. CRUICKSHANK joined Battalion from Base. Capt and 3/5 GLOS REGT and was posted to E Coy. | 3PU |
| - | 29/1/16 | | In billets. Fine. Lt L.W. MOORE left Battalion for leave. | 3PU |

# WAR DIARY

## INTELLIGENCE SUMMARY.

Army Form C. 2118.

| Place | Date | Hour | Summary of Events and Information | Remarks and references to Appendices |
|---|---|---|---|---|
| BUS | 30/1/16 | | In billets. Fine. Battalion beaten in Association Football FANSHAWE CUP by Bucks Battalion 2-1. Lt CONDER and Lt C.W. WINTER BOTHAM left battalion for leave | SRW |
| " | 31/1/16 | | In billets. 2nd Lieut Ct wounded. Fine. Strength 32 Officers 774 OR. | SRW |

145th Brigade.
48th Division.
----------

1/5th BATTALION

GLOUCESTERSHIRE REGIMENT

FEBRUARY 1 9 1 6

# WAR DIARY
## INTELLIGENCE SUMMARY

Army Form C. 2118.

| Place | Date | Hour | Summary of Events and Information | Remarks and references to Appendices |
|---|---|---|---|---|
| BUS | 1/2/16 | - | In billets. Fine normal. Major J.F. TARRANT notified of his appointment to command 2/6th Batt. GLOS REGT. 2nd Lt W.S.H. PARKER 1st KINGS DRAGOON GUARDS attached for instruction. Lt. C.S. NASON returned from leave. | |
| BUS | 2/2/16 | | Battalion moved to HEBUTERNE and relieved 8th Bn. WORCESTERSHIRE Regt. in H Section. Ref. Trench Map Sheet 57D N.E. 3&4 Parts of 1:10,000 K1&M1B Disposition:—<br>A Coy (Capt. G.F. COLLETT) Tr. 22-25 and PAS DE TIR to VILLON LANE<br>B - (Capt. R.T.C. LITTLE) KEEP — Brigade Reserve<br>C - (Capt. H.C.B. SESSIONS) Tr. 19-21 and PAS DE TIR to VILLON LANE<br>D - (Capt. F.E. FRANCILLON) Company in support<br>1 Platoon in BETHA<br>2 - in cellars of RUE GRANDE<br>Units on our Right — 1/1 BUCKS BATTN OXFORD and BUCKS L.I.<br>Left — 4th ROYAL BERKS | |

# WAR DIARY
## INTELLIGENCE SUMMARY.
*(Erase heading not required.)*

Army Form C. 2118.

| Place | Date | Hour | Summary of Events and Information | Remarks and references to Appendices |
|---|---|---|---|---|
| HEBUTERNE | 2/2/16 | | Major J.F. TARRANT left the Battalion and Major N.H. WALLER rejoined & 2nd in command and O.C. KEEP. Fine. Casualties NIL. Normal Strength 32 Officers 777 O.R. 9 Civilian wounded. | SPW |
| " | 3/2/16 | | Fine Casualties NIL | SPW |
| " | 4/2/16 | | Lt. Col. J.H. COLLETT took over command of 1/5th Bde. vice Brig Gen DONE on leave. Major N.H. WALLER assumed command of Battalion. Normal. Casualties NIL. | SPW |
| " | 5/2/16 | | Inter-Company Relief. B Coy to A and D to C Coy. Capt. G.F. COLLETT left for leave and Capt. L.R.E. SUMNER took command of A Coy. Capt. A.T. HITCHESON also left on leave. 2 civilian wounded. Fine Casualties NIL | SPW |
| " | 6/2/16 | | Normal. Fine. Casualties NIL. 2nd Lt PUCKRIDGE went on leave | SPW |
| " | 7/2/16 | | Normal Fine Casualties 4 Shell shock. 2nd Lt G. HAWKINS | SPW |

# WARY DIARY
## or
## INTELLIGENCE SUMMARY.
*(Erase heading not required.)*

Army Form C. 2118.

| Place | Date | Hour | Summary of Events and Information | Remarks and references to Appendices |
|---|---|---|---|---|
| HEBUTERNE | 1/1/16 | | and 11 O.R. patrolled to LONE TREE | SW |
| " | 8/2/16 | | Inter-company Relief. A coy relieved B and D coy relieved C coy. went to KEEP as Brigade Reserve. B coy became Battalion Reserve. Enemy artillery very active. Casualties 2 Shell shock. Fine. Cold. | SW |
| " | 9/2/16 | | Enemy Artillery very active all day. Casualty No.10827 Pte. MIDWINTER J. C coy shot in arm by our sentry post in Sap on post 4 & 19 at about 7 p.m. Cold. Some snow. Fine | SW |
| " | 10/2/16 | | Enemy Artillery active. Casualties No 1527 Pte (L/C) SPROAT A.L. A coy wounded by shell splinter slight. Some rain. normal | SW |
| " | 11/2/16 | 5.30AM | Inter-Company Relief. B coy relieved A and D coy relieved C. Lt. WINTERBOTHAM E.W. and Lt. F. ONDER returned from leave and | SW |

# WAR DIARY
## INTELLIGENCE SUMMARY
*(Erase heading not required.)*

Army Form C. 2118.

| Place | Date | Hour | Summary of Events and Information | Remarks and references to Appendices |
|---|---|---|---|---|
| HEBUTERNE | 11/2/16 | | Rather colder over last 24hrs and Intelligence from 2nd L.E.D.G DURANT enemy artillery still active. Fine. Panelling NIL. | 3 OW |
| " | 12/2/16 | | Enemy artillery still active. Casualty No.1976 Pte (H/C) WILCOX S.J. been gun Section wounded by bullet in SERRE ROAD. Rain. B by patrolled to X rads TREE | 3 OW |
| " | 13/2/16 | | Enemy artillery active during morning. Casualty No.2728 Pte A.T. WHITE D Coy Lewis Gun Section. CAPT. R.I.C. LITTLE went on leave. To date 12/2/16 Capt. R.M.J. COOKE and C.S.M. ATTWOOD left for 3rd ARMY SCHOOL of INSTRUCTION. 2nd Lt. D.G. FROST. R.G. DURANT went on leave. To date 13/2/16. 2nd Lt. W. HAWKINS attached 2nd ROYAL DUBLIN FUSILIERS for instruction with 5thBn Infant. | asper |
| " | 14/2/16 | | Quiet. NO Enemy reply to our artillery. Casualty No.1791. Pte E.D. Price (Shrubber) A & C Companies relieved 2 Companies of 1/1 BUCKS in Q SECTOR | asper |
| " | 15/2/16 | | Enemy bombarded Foncquevillers many Light field heavy Canister NL R BERKS relieved our D Coy in H Sect. D Coy moved to support | aseen |

# WAR DIARY
## INTELLIGENCE SUMMARY

Army Form C. 2118.

| Place | Date | Hour | Summary of Events and Information | Remarks and references to Appendices |
|---|---|---|---|---|
| HEBUTERNE | 15/2/16 | | 2 platoons in VERBRANGETOUR. 2 platoons in RAGLAN. One in its | A/Gen |
| " | 16/2/16 | | Trenches very wet. D Coy relieved C Coy. Capts G.COLLETT & A.T. MITCHESON returned from leave | A/Gen wifed |
| " | 17/2/16 | | Quiet day. Enemy artillery very active at night on left Brigade on our left. B/Lt. C.V.N. PUCKRIDGE returned from leave. C Coy relieved D Coy. | A/Gen K.G.D A/Gen |
| " | 18/2/16 | | Quiet day & night. D Coy relieved C Coy. | |
| " | 19/2/16 | | Battalion relieved by 1st BUCKS BATTALION. Head Quarters and A&C Coys to COURCELLES. B&D Coys to SAILLY. Sub Battn formed DIVISIONAL RESERVE | A/Gen |
| COURCELLES & SAILLY | 20/2/16 | | In Billets | K.G.D. |
| " | 21/2/16 | | " LT. COL. J.H. COLLETT went on leave also LIEUT J.P.WINTERBOTHAM & 2/Lt L.J. CLAYTON | K.G.D. |
| " | 22/2/16 | | " CAPT. A.T. MITCHESON appointed Town Major of BUS. Draft. 131. O.R. from 4th ROYAL BERKSHIRE RGT. | K.G.D. |
| HEBUTERNE | 23/2/16 | | Battalion moved to HEBUTERNE and took over trenches from 4th ROYAL BERKSHIRE RGT. Dispositions A Coy (Capt L.R.L. SUMNER) in support 2 platoons BIRON dug outs 2 platoons cellars BUCQUOY RD. B Coy (Lieut C.S. NASON) Trenches XI — XVI inclusive C Coy (Capt N.C.B. SESSIONS) in support & 2 platoons PUISIEUX RD. 2 platoons RUE GRANDE | R.G.D |

Army Form C. 2118.

# WAR DIARY
## or
## INTELLIGENCE SUMMARY.

*(Erase heading not required.)*

| Place | Date | Hour | Summary of Events and Information | Remarks and references to Appendices |
|---|---|---|---|---|
| HEAUTERNE | 23/2/16 | | D Coy. (Capt F.N. COLE) Trenches XVII to XXI inclusive and PAS DE TIR. Situation normal. Heavy fall of snow. Unit on our Right 1/1 BUCKS BATTN OXFORD AND BUCKS L.I. — on our left. 1/4 OXFORDS. 2/LTS K.G. and D.G. DURRANT returned from leave. 204 C.S.M. WAGSTAFF G.H. to 48 Div. S of I. | K.G.D. |
| " | 24/2/16 | | A Coy relieved B and C relieved D. situation normal. Casualties nil. Capt R.J.C. LITTLE returned from leave. LIEUT + Q.M. C.F. FOOTE discharged from Hospital. Snow. | K.G.D. |
| " | 25/2/16 | | B Coy relieved A, and D relieved C. Situation normal. Casualties nil. Snow. Capt F.E. FRANCILLON admitted to Hospital. Strength Officers 31. O.R. 902. — | K.G.D. |
| " | 26/2/16 | | Dispositions altered as follows:— A Coy (Capt L.R.C SUMNER) 2 platoons Trenches XI to XIV inclusive in support 1 platoon BIRON &, into 1 platoon BUCQUOY RD B Coy (Capt R.J.C. LITTLE) In reserve - 4 Platoons RUE GRANDE. C Coy (Capt H.E.B. SESSIONS) 2 platoons Tr. XV to XVIII inclusive. In support 2 platoons. BIRON, REMAUD. BRICKFIELDS. D Coy (Capt F.W. COLE) 2 platoons Trs XIX to XXI and PAS DE TIR in support 2 platoons PUISIEUX RD. | K.G.D. |

# WAR DIARY
## or
## INTELLIGENCE SUMMARY.

*(Erase heading not required.)*

Army Form C. 2118.

| Place | Date | Hour | Summary of Events and Information | Remarks and references to Appendices |
|---|---|---|---|---|
| HEBUTERNE | 26/4/16 | | Situation normal. Snow. Casualties nil 2/Lts E. CARLISH and G.H. ALINGTON 5F ROYAL SUSSEX REGT attached for instruction | KGD |
| " | 27/4/16 | | B Coy relieved D Coy. 2/Lt N.H. GRAVES SMITH to 48E Div. S. of I. Situation normal casualties nil. | KGD |
| " | 28/4/16 | | D Coy relieved A Coy. Situation normal. Casualties nil. Thaw and Rain 2/LTS E. CARLISH and G.H. ALINGTON 5F ROYAL SUSSEX REGT rejoined unit | KGD |
| " | 29/4/16 | | A Coy relieved C Coy. Situation normal. Casualties nil. Weather unsettled. 2/Lt W.S.H. PARKER 1st KINGS DRAGOON GUARDS left to rejoin unit. Strength Officers 31 O.R. 890. | KGD |

145th Brigade.
48th Division.
----------

1/5th BATTALION

GLOUCESTERSHIRE REGIMENT

MARCH 1916

CONFIDENTIAL.

The A.G.

BASE.

Herewith diary for Month ending 31/3/16.

*[signature]*
Lt-Col

5/4/16.                    Commanding 1/5th Gloster Regiment.

# WAR DIARY 1/5th GLOSTER REGT

## INTELLIGENCE SUMMARY

Army Form C. 2118.

(Erase heading not required.)

| Place | Date | Hour | Summary of Events and Information | Remarks and references to Appendices |
|---|---|---|---|---|
| HEBUTERNE | 1/3/16 | | Division transferred to 10th Corps 4th Army. Situation normal. Coll. Casualties NIL | 3PW |
| " | 2/3/16 | | Battalion relieved by OXFORD and BUCKS L.I. BUCKS BATTN. and moved to SAILLY AU BOIS to form Divisional Reserve. Some Snow Casualties NIL Lt Col. J.H. COLLETT returned from leave and assumed command. | 3PW |
| SAILLY | 3/3/16 | | Battalion Transport moved from BUS to BAYENCOURT. C.O. infected recent large draft. Lt. Adj. J.P. WINTERBOTHAM and 2nd Lt L.T. CLAYTON returned from leave. Fine and cold. Casualties NIL | 3PW |
| " | 4/3/16 | | Heavy snow. normal. Casualties NIL | 3PW |
| " | 5/3/16 | | In billets. Normal. Fine London Gazette of 25th February 1916 Lt A.E.R. WELSH to be 2nd Lt in 1st Battn. SOUTH WALES BORDERERS | 3PW |

# WAR DIARY 1/5 GLOSTER REGT

## INTELLIGENCE SUMMARY

Army Form C. 2118.

(Erase heading not required.)

| Place | Date | Hour | Summary of Events and Information | Remarks and references to Appendices |
|---|---|---|---|---|
| SAILLY | 6/3/16 | | Battalion moved to HEBUTERNE and relieved 1/4th ROYAL BERKS in G Section. Right - K 23 b 2-2 to Left - K 16 b 8-4. Unit on our left OXFORD and BUCKS L.I. BUCKS BATTN on our Right. 144th I Brigade 4th and 6th GLOUCESTER REGT. Dispositions: - C Coy (capt. H.E.B SESSIONS) Tm 32 to 30 inclusive. A - (capt. G.F COLLETT) - 29 to 26 " B - (capt. R.J.C. LITTLE) - 25 to 22 " D - (capt. F.W. COLE) in reserve. Battalion Headquarters - Tn VERCINGETORIX K 22 c 2 - 9½. C & D Coy relieve each other every 24 hours. Normal. Fire Casualties NIL 2nd Lt L J CLAYTON to Hospital | SPO. |
| HEBUTERNE | 7/3/16 | | Coll. Snow. Quiet. Casualties NIL. Strength 30 Officers 885 O.R. | SPO. |
| " | 8/3/16 | | Snow. Cold. Normal. Casualties NL. Notified that Whole Division was transferred to 8th Corps. 4th Army. | SPO. |

# WAR DIARY

## INTELLIGENCE SUMMARY

1/5th GLOSTER REGT — Army Form C. 2118.

| Place | Date | Hour | Summary of Events and Information | Remarks and references to Appendices |
|---|---|---|---|---|
| HEBUTERNE | 9/3/16 | | Normal. Heavy snow at night. Casualties NIL. Capt FRANCILLON returned from Leafield 9/3/16. London Gazette of 23/2/16 Major J.F. TARRANT to be temporary Lt COLONEL | |
| " | 10/3/16 | | 4th R BERKS relieved OXFORD and BUCKS L.I. BUCKS BATTN on our left. Quiet. Casualties NIL. Cold. Some snow. | SPW |
| " | 11/3/16 | | Quiet. Casualties NIL Fine. Transport :- 2nd Lt G HAWKINS D Coy to B Coy 2nd Lt K.G. DURRANT C Coy to B Coy. Strength 2nd Lt W.J PEAREE joined Battalion posted to C Coy. Also 2nd Lt A.H SYMONDS posted to D Coy. Both from 3/5th GLOUCESTER REGT. | SPW |
| " | 12/3/16 | | Fine. Normal. Casualties NIL | SPW |
| " | 13/3/16 | | Fine. Strahan wounded. Casualties: 11.30 P.M. No 66 Sergt DURRETT T A Coy killed by rifle bullet Tr. 29 Sheet 57D Trench map 3 & 4 Parts of | SPW |

# WAR DIARY

## 1/5th GLOSTER REGT

### INTELLIGENCE SUMMARY

Army Form C. 2118.

Instructions regarding War Diaries and Intelligence Summaries are contained in F. S. Regs., Part II. and the Staff Manual respectively. Title pages will be prepared in manuscript.

(Erase heading not required.)

| Place | Date | Hour | Summary of Events and Information | Remarks and references to Appendices |
|---|---|---|---|---|
| HEBUTERNE | 13/3/16 | | K.19 & 51. | TRW |
| - | 14/3/16 | | Battalion relieved by BUCKS BATTN OXFORD and BUCKS L.I. and marched with billets at SAILLY AU BOIS. Headquarters and A & C Coys in common. B in afternoon and D after dark. Sergt DURRETT buried at Kilby Cemetery HEBUTERNE K.9.c.9.2 (Sheet 57D 1/40000). Five Casualties M.L. Capt R.M.F. COOKE rejoined from Army School of Instruction FLIXECOURT. 2nd Lt GRAVES-SMITH rejoined from 48th Div School of Instruction and 2nd Lt CRUICKSHANK went to 48th Div School for course of Instruction. Strength 32 Officers 844 O.R. | TRW |
| SAILLY | 15/3/16 | | In billets. Fine | TRW |
| " | 16/3/16 | | In billets. Fine | TRW |
| " | 17/3/16 | | Drill | TRW |

# WAR DIARY
## INTELLIGENCE SUMMARY.

*(Erase heading not required.)*

1/5th GLOSTER REGT    Army Form C. 2118.

Instructions regarding War Diaries and Intelligence Summaries are contained in F. S. Regs., Part II. and the Staff Manual respectively. Title pages will be prepared in manuscript.

| Place | Date | Hour | Summary of Events and Information | Remarks and references to Appendices |
|---|---|---|---|---|
| SAILLY | 18/3/16 | | Battalion moved to HEBUTERNE and relieved 4th ROYAL BERKS & Section dispositions:- <br> A Coy (Capt. G.F. COLLETT) Trs XI to XIV BIRON SAP <br> B Coy (Capt. R.I.C. LITTLE) Trs XV to XVIII <br> C Coy (Capt. R.H.F. ROOKE) Trs XIX to XXI PAS DE TIR and Saps of Tr XVIII <br> D " (Capt. F.W. COLE) in Reserve <br> Headquarters - The KEEP RUE GRANDE <br> Unit on our right 1/1 BUCKS BATTALION OXFORD and BUCKS L.I. on our Left 4th OXFORD and BUCKS L.I. <br> Fine. Fair amount of shelling by enemy. Casualties Nil. 2nd Lt. C.S. MILLARD gazetted 5/10/14 joined the Battalion from 3/5th Glos. Regt. and was posted to A Coy. Capt. R.I. SULLIVAN used to be Col. H.M. and Capt. R.H. BRODERICK 2nd Fd Ambulance took over his duties. Casualties 4369 Pte EDWARDS G. A Coy wounded very slight. | SPW |
| HEBUTERNE | 19/3/16 | | At 2 a.m. enemy guns opened heavy fire on front line trenches chiefly on the 146th Brigade line on our right, with a good many on our left company. | SPW |

1577  Wt. W10791/1773  500,000  1/15  D. D. & L.  A.D.S.S./Forms/C. 2118.

Army Form C. 2118.

# WAR DIARY  1/5 GLOSTER REGT
## INTELLIGENCE SUMMARY.

*(Erase heading not required.)*

Instructions regarding War Diaries and Intelligence Summaries are contained in F. S. Regs., Part II. and the Staff Manual respectively. Title pages will be prepared in manuscript.

| Place | Date | Hour | Summary of Events and Information | Remarks and references to Appendices |
|---|---|---|---|---|
| HEBUTERNE | 19/3/16 | | The Battalion stood to until about 3 AM when Artillery on both sides ceased fire. Casualties NIL. Rest of day quiet. Fine. Sufficient to London Gazette 18/3/16 Capt. G.F. COLLETT to be temporary Major 26th January 1916 | SPW SPW |
| - | 20/3/16 | | Fine. Situation quiet. Casualties 2614 Pte CLIFT G.A. slightly wounded | SPW |
| - | 21/3/16 | | Draft of 40 O.R. joined Battalion. Fine. Casualties NIL | SPW |
| - | 22/3/16 | | 4 Officers and 16 N.C.Os of the 18th R. WEST YORKSHIRE REGT attached for 6 days for instruction. Left N.C. 2 SESSIONS returned from leave and Casualties NIL. Enterprise. At 11.45 P.M. Capt. L.R.C SUMNER, 2nd Lt HAWKINS and 2 G.L.O.R left Tr 21 and proceeded towards enemy wire at K17 D 2.9 with the object of entering enemy trenches. Party was disposed as follows. Party No 1 wire cutting - 8 men - No 2 attacking No 3 attacking 8 men - 2nd Lt HAWKINS and 2 Orderlies - No 4 Souvenir Collectors & men - covering party 3 N.C.Os and 19 O.R under | SPW |

1577 Wt W10791/1773 500,000 1/15 D.D. & L. A.D.S.S./Forms/C. 2118.

# WAR DIARY
## INTELLIGENCE SUMMARY.
*(Erase heading not required.)*

Instructions regarding War Diaries and Intelligence Summaries are contained in F.S. Regs., Part II. and the Staff Manual respectively. Title pages will be prepared in manuscript.

Army Form C. 2118.

| Place | Date | Hour | Summary of Events and Information | Remarks and references to Appendices |
|---|---|---|---|---|
| MESNIL TERNE | 22/3/16 | | Capt. L.R.E. SUMNER will lie on ladders out 4 ladders leaves | SPW |
| " | 23/3/16 | | The party was in position at 12.30 A.M. ready for the artillery barrage to open. The Garden began in conjunction with a similar one further up. 143rd Brigade on our left. At 12.45 A.M. the 143 Brigade informed that they would be late. No message came from the left. By 1.5 A.M. Capt. SUMNER gave the order to fire and the barrage opened. The wire cutters advanced at once and commenced cutting wire. After 10 minutes about 7 or 8 wire cutters had been out leaving about double the amount to be done. Rifle grenades were fired & the wire cutters and 2nd hand HAWKINS hurled bombs & was unable to cut through. All over the front lines all returned safely to our trenches. Our artillery ceased fire at 1.35 T.M. Casualties No.16817 GODWIN A C. Coy machine gun killed, No. 1987 Pte JENNINGS W.F. A Coy very slightly R.O.S. Day very quiet. Fire | SPW |
| " | 24/3/16 | | Normal. Heavy snow at night. Casualties 2314 Pte CARTER E.T. A Coy slightly wounded. | SPW |

# WAR DIARY

## INTELLIGENCE SUMMARY

1/5 GLOSTER REGT

| Place | Date | Hour | Summary of Events and Information | Remarks and references to Appendices |
|---|---|---|---|---|
| HEBUTERNE | 25/3/16 | | Normal and Quiet. Casualties NIL. Fine | SRO |
| — | 26/3/16 | | Relieved by 1/1 Bucks BATTN. OXFORD and BUCKS L.I. and marched to SAILLY AU BOIS to form Divisional Reserve. Fine. Casualties NIL. Strength 33 Officers 922 O.R. Capt. R.T.E. LITTLE and Sergt. FAVILLE left for FLIXECOURT School of Instruction | SRO |
| SAILLY | 27/3/16 | | In Billets. Very quiet. 145th Brigade Headquarters moved to SAILLY. Capt. R.I. SULLIVAN returned from sick leave. Fine. | SRO |
| — | 28/3/16 | | 2nd Lieut. P. BADHAM gazetted 27th July 1915 joined Battalion from Base and was posted to A Coy | SRO |
| — | 29/3/16 | | In billets. Quiet. Fine | SRO |
| — | 30/3/16 | | Battalion moved to HEBUTERNE and relieved 4th ROYAL BERKS in G Sector. Trenches K.23.b to K.10-5 inclusive | SRO |

# WAR DIARY

1/5 GLOSTER REGT Army Form C. 2118.

## INTELLIGENCE SUMMARY

| Place | Date | Hour | Summary of Events and Information | Remarks and references to Appendices |
|---|---|---|---|---|
| HERU LERNE | 30/3/16 | | Dispositions:- | |
| | | | A Coy (Capt F.W COLE) Trenches K 23 - 6 - 7 and 8 | |
| | | | A Coy (Major G.F COLLETT) Trenches K 23-9 and 10 - K 19 — 1 and 2 | |
| | | | B " (Capt COOKE) Trenches K 19 3-4-9-5 and PAS DE TIR | |
| | | | C " (Capt H.E.R. SESSIONS) In Battalion reserve | |
| | | | Battalion Headquarters - In VEREINGETORIX K 22 & 23 - 9 | |
| | | | C and D Companies to relieve each other every 24 hours | |
| | | | Unit on our right 144th I Brigade 4th GLOUCESTER REGT Unit on our left | SRD |
| | | | 4th OXFORD and BUCKS L.I. | |
| | | | Fine Situation normal Casualties NIL | |
| | 31/3/16 | | Normal. Fine and left escualties NIL | |
| | | | Strength 34 Officers 912 O.R. London Gazette 30/3/16 47.C HAWKINS to | SRD |
| | | | be Temporary Lieutenant 25/2/16 Capt SUMNER and Capt W. FOOTE | SRD |
| | | | left the Battalion for leave | Two |

1577 Wt. W10791/1773 500,000 1/15 D.D. & L. A.D.S.S./Forms/C. 2118.

145th Brigade.

48th Division.

----------

1/5th BATTALION


GLOUCESTERSHIRE REGIMENT


APRIL 1916

To the Officer i/c

A.G. Office at the Base.

Herewith War Diary for month of April, please.

G. Hawkins
Lieut. & Actg. Adjt.
1/5th Gloucester Regiment.

4/5/16.

Army Form C. 2118.

# WAR DIARY
## of
## INTELLIGENCE SUMMARY. 1/5th GLOSTER REGT

*(Erase heading not required.)*

Instructions regarding War Diaries and Intelligence Summaries are contained in F. S. Regs., Part II. and the Staff Manual respectively. Title pages will be prepared in manuscript.

| Place | Date | Hour | Summary of Events and Information | Remarks and references to Appendices |
|---|---|---|---|---|
| HEBUTERNE | 1/4/16 | | Fine Col. Quiet. Casualties NIL. Patrol of Bucks Battn in our left encountered strong party of enemy near POPLARS on PUISIEUX ROAD and engaged the enemy. | |
| " | 2/4/16 | | Battalion was relieved in G. Section Northworks w/c and w/daly Tr. K17-2 by 1/7th WORCS REGT and will on relief of 48th Divn. (relief by Col. over trenches Northworks in being Battalion pml from F.T.K17-2 inclusive to F.T.K10-2 inclusive.<br><br>Dispositions:—<br>B Coy with 1 officer and 27 O.R. of 48th Divn Cyclist Coy (Capt. R.H.F. COOKE) Trenches K17-2 inclusive to K16-3 inclusive.<br>C Coy (Capt H.C.B. SESSIONS) F.T. K17-3 inclusive to F.T. K10-2 inclusive and REYNAUD.<br>D Coy (Capt F.W. COLE) in Battalion Reserve billets in RUE GRANDE.<br>A Coy (Major G.F. COLLETT) Brigade Reserve in the KEEP<br>Battalion Headquarters — RUE GRANDE. The MILL with Unit on our right 1/4 WORCS REGT. on L.(L—1/4—OXFORD & BUCKS L.I. — Two<br><br>G. ? [signature] Major<br>Commdg. 5th Bn GLOUCESTER REGT. | |

1577  Wt. W10791/1773  500,000  1/15  D. D. & L.  A.D.S.S./Forms/C. 2118.

Army Form C. 2118.

# WAR DIARY
# INTELLIGENCE SUMMARY.

(Erase heading not required.)

1/5th GLOSTER REGT

| Place | Date | Hour | Summary of Events and Information | Remarks and references to Appendices |
|---|---|---|---|---|
| HEBUTERNE | 2/4/16 | | Fine. Quiet. Casualties NIL | TRW |
| " | 3/4/16 | | Normal – Fine – Casualties Nil. Capt. F.E. FRANCILLON and Sergt HILL B Coy went to Base to train reinforcements | TRW |
| " | 4/4/16 | | Battalion relieved by 1/4 ROYAL BERKS REGT and moved to SAILLY to form Brigade Reserve. Casualties NIL Fine | TRW |
| SAILLY | 5/4/16 | | Battalion H.Q and A + B Companies moved to COUIN and were billetted in Huts and S 2 A 3-6. Major C.F. COLLETT in command of detachment at SAILLY | TRW |
| COUIN & SAILLY | 6/4/16 | | In billets fine normal. Major N.H. WALLER returned from leave and took over command of SAILLY detachment | TRW |
| " | 7/4/16 | | Normal fine | TRW |

C.T. Colish. Major
COMMDG. 5TH BN GLOUCESTER REGT.

Army Form C. 2118.

## INTELLIGENCE SUMMARY.
(Erase heading not required.)

1/5 GLOSTER REGT.

| Place | Date | Hour | Summary of Events and Information | Remarks and references to Appendices |
|---|---|---|---|---|
| COLIN SALLY | 8/4/16 | | In billets. Fine | TRO |
| " | 9/4/16 | | In billets. Fine. Capt F.W. COLE and Lt G. HAWKINS went on leave. 8.P.M. Parties of 8 officers 32 N.C.Os and 288 O.R. and 5 officers 27 N.C.Os and 277 O.R. under Major G.F. ROLLETT dug and wired respectively a new trench from reference North end of F.T. K17/15 400 yards to point K17 a 0 7½ thence 75 yards N.N.E. with similar trench from 4 OXFORD and BUCKS L.I. returned 125 yards N.N.E to point K11 e 22 thence 150 yards N.N.W. to K11 e 04 thence 200 yards W. to join up with dug out at Southern end of F.T. K10/2. Covering parties were supplied by 4th ROYAL BERKS on the right and 1/1 BUCKS BATT'N OXFORD and BUCKS L.I. on the left. The new trench is about an average distance of 200 yards in rear of our all present line trenches. Night was fine with double shadowing the moon. Work was carried on & began at 6.P.M. The morning forty completed line of knife rests with safe joined and dialed down by about 2.A.M. Diggy forty finished about 3.30 A.M. Enemy made no attack | TRO |

C. 7 Gaskell Major

COMDG. 5TH BN GLOUCESTER REGT.

1577 Wt.W10791/1773 500,000 1/15 D. D. & L. A.D.S.S./Forms/C. 2118.

# WAR DIARY

## INTELLIGENCE SUMMARY.

1/5 GLOSTER REGT.

(Erase heading not required.)

Army Form C. 2118.

| Place | Date | Hour | Summary of Events and Information | Remarks and references to Appendices |
|---|---|---|---|---|
| COUIN SAILLY | 10/4/16 | | Salvoes of 77 mm shrapnel and H.E. with some machine gun fire. Casualties :- 4346 Pte EAKETTS E.A. D Coy Shrapnel in head Slight. 1527 L/C SPROAT A.L. A Coy Shell Slight. 4 Dnr GURNEY B Coy Shell shock. Rest of day fine. | CWO |
| | 11/4/16 | | In billets. Normal. Heavy rain all day. Capt SUMNER and L/c Dr Mr FOOTE rejoined from leave. | CWO |
| | 14/4/16 | | Battalion moved to HEBUTERNE and relieved 4 ROYAL BERKS in J Section by 11 AM. Dispositions :— <br> A Coy (Major G.F. ROLLETT) Trenches K.17/2 exclusive to K.16/3 inclusive <br> C " (Capt H.E.S. SESSIONS) " K.17/3 " to K.10/2 and REMAUD inclusive <br> D " (Lieut P. SNOWDEN) Cellars in RUE GRANDE — Battalion Reserve <br> B " (2/Lt R.M.F COOKE) The KEEP — Brigade Reserve <br> Battalion Headquarters — The MILL RUE GRANDE | TRW |

G.F. Colech

Major
COMDG. 5TH BN GLOUCESTER REGT.

# WAR DIARY
## INTELLIGENCE SUMMARY

**Army Form C. 2118.**

5 GLOSTER REGT

| Place | Date | Hour | Summary of Events and Information | Remarks and references to Appendices |
|---|---|---|---|---|
| HEBUTERNE | 12/4/16 | | Unit on our Right – 1/4th I.R. Brigade. on our Left 1/1 BUCKS BATTN OXFORD and BUCKS L.I. Casualties 2 O.R. wounded. Heavy rain. | SPW |
| " | 13/4/16 | | Owing to 5th ROYAL SUSSEX being withdrawn from line on left Battalion was ordered to take over 3 more infantry posts on left, extreme left of Left Company retained by F.T. K10/3 BIRON avenue, Capt. E.G. KILLICK 2nd Lt. S.I. WELFORD and J.B. BRADFORD |  |
|  |  | 9 p.m. | Party of 2 = 4 officers and 200 O.R. from 1st Bucks L.I. continued digging a communication trench from our ref from F.T. K16/5 along North side of PUISIEUX ROAD. 2 Company provided two posts in front of new fire trench Capt COOKE in command. At 11.30 P.M. enemy opened heavy howitzer and walt trenchmortar 77 mm 15 c.m. and 10.5 c.m. along front of new trench for 15 minutes and this was repeated at 12 midnight. At 12.15 A.M. an enemy patrol of about 15 men approach post under Corporal E. BRIEN No.2748 & Lay rapid fire was opened and one man shot shortly after none of the party returned Unter Offizier TANIEYE 5 KOMP I.R 66 was subsequently brought in dead The work was finished about 1.30 A.M. Casualties 1 S.O.R. wounded including G.7 Cobb — | SPW |

COMMDG. 5TH BN GLOUCESTER REGT.

# WAR DIARY
## or
## INTELLIGENCE SUMMARY.

*(Erase heading not required.)*

5 GLOSTER REGT

| Place | Date | Hour | Summary of Events and Information | Remarks and references to Appendices |
|---|---|---|---|---|
| HEBUTERNE | 14/4/16 | | 7 shell shock. Rest of day fine and quiet except for occasional shells and some minenwerfers. Some artillery fire at night. Unteroffizier JÄNIKE buried in military cemetery HEBUTERNE | SWO |
| " | 15/4/16 | | Fine. Fairly quiet in day. 11.30 PM Enemy again on our lines, trench with minenwerfer and guns of various calibre and at 12.5 PM. Casualties fire O.R. and one shell shock wounded. Draft 2 N.C.Os and 11 O.R. arrived. Strength 34 Officers 888 O.R. | SWO |
| " | 16/4/16 | | Fine sunny day. Casualties 4 O.R. wounded by shell fire. Enemy shelled at intervals during the night on rear and old trenches. D Company relief B Coy relieved A Coy and D by relieved C by. Enemy shelled all fine and communication trenches throughout the day with occasional intense outbursts at night. | SWO SWO |
| " | 17/4/16 | | by shell fire :— No 2811 Pte DANCEY S.V. D Coy. No 4358 Pte SMITH A B Coy. No 3008 Pte BROWN N.S. B Coy. No 4427 Pte BERRY W B Coy (died of wounds 3 hours later.) Wounded 5 O.R. Walter Fine | SWO |

G.F. A---- Major
COMMDG. 5TH BN GLOUCESTER REGT.

# WAR DIARY
## INTELLIGENCE SUMMARY.

*(Erase heading not required.)*

Army Form C. 2118.

5th GLOSTER REGT

| Place | Date | Hour | Summary of Events and Information | Remarks and references to Appendices |
|---|---|---|---|---|
| HEBUTERNE | 17/4/16 | | All the above killed were buried in military cemetery HEBUTERNE | BOW |
| " | 18/4/16 | | Some shelling during the day. Enemy artillery very active in shelling the village with effective reply by our guns. Casualties 4 & 2 wounded. Weather very wet | JRW |
| " | 19/4/16 | | Very wet. Situation quiet. Casualties 2 O.R. wounded left coy, a/c Lt E. HAWKINS returned from leave. Former took over command of B Coy | JRW / BW |
| " | 20/4/16 | | Battalion were relieved by 4 ROYAL BERKS and moved to Brigade Reserve H.Q. and C & D Coys in huts at COUIN A & B Coys under MAJOR G.F. COLLETT in billets at SAILLY. Weather very wet. No 4381 Pte STEELE H.G. D coy died in Field Ambulance | JRW |
| COUIN & SAILLY | 21/4/16 | | Battalion H.Q. & C & D Coys moved to billets in SAILLY. No 4381 Pte STEELE H.G. buried in military cemetery HEBUTERNE. Weather very wet | BW |

G.F. Collett
Major
Commdg. 5th Bn GLOUCESTER REGT.

Army Form. C. 2118.

# WAR DIARY
# or
# INTELLIGENCE SUMMARY.

(Erase heading not required.)

5 Gloucestershire Regt.

| Place | Date | Hour | Summary of Events and Information | Remarks and references to Appendices |
|---|---|---|---|---|
| SAILLY | 22.4.16 | | In Billets. Fine | G.H. |
| " | 23.4.16 | | " " Lieut & Adjt J.P. WINTERBOTHAM left for the 4th ARMY School of Instruction FLIXECOURT, Lieut G. HAWKINS took over the duties of Adjutant. "B" Shooting range commenced. Capt R.J.C. LITTLE & 1 O.R. returned from 5th Army School of Instruction FLIXECOURT. | G.H. |
| " | 24.4.16 | | In Billets. Fine. General FANSHAWE held a Staff Conference at the DELL SAILLY - COIGNEUX Road attended by Lt Col COLLETT & Lt G HAWKINS. The CORPS COMMANDER General Sir AYLMER HUNTER-WESTON visited the Bn. No 26449 Pte ROE. W. died of wounds & was buried at No 4 C.C.S. BEAUVAL | G.H. |
| " | 25.4.16 | | In Billets. Fine. General FANSHAWE held a Staff Conference at COIGNEUX | G.H. |
| " | 26.4.16 | | In Billets. BRIG GEN H.P. DONE Conducted a Regtl Tour. Twelve Officers attended. One Officer & 50 O.R's A Coy inoculated | G.H. |
| " | 27.4.16 | | In Billets. Fine. Routine work of Company training, shooting practice, inoculation | G.H. |

G.T. Collett, Major
COMDG. 5th Bn GLOUCESTER REGT.

Army Form C. 2118.

# WAR DIARY
## or
## INTELLIGENCE SUMMARY.

(Erase heading not required.)

5 Gloucestershire Regt

| Place | Date | Hour | Summary of Events and Information | Remarks and references to Appendices |
|---|---|---|---|---|
| | | | Carried on | |
| SAILLY | 28.4.16 | | In Billets. Fine. Routine work carried on. | G.N. |
| " | 29.4.16 | | In Billets. Fine. Brigade exercise consisting of an advance from T16d through COIGNEUX practised by the B'n with the 1/4 O.B.L.I. on the right flank. | G.N. |
| | 30.4.16 | | In Billets. Fine. Lt Col J.H. COLLETT unfortunately assumed Command of the 145 Infantry Brigade vice Brig. Gen. N.P. DONE on leave. Major G.F. COLLETT assumed Command of the B'n. Strength Thirty three (33) Officers Eight hundred & Eighty two (881) other Ranks. Lt C.W. WINTERBOTHAM & 1 O.R. (returned from) to School of Instruction A.8. Div at COUIN. Lt L.W. MOORE & 1 O.R. went to A.8.Div School of Instruction at COUIN. | G.N. |

G.F. Collett Major

COMDG. 5TH Bn Gloucestershire Regt.

1577 Wt. W10791/1773 500,000 1/15 D.D.&L. A.D.S.S./Forms/C.211B.

145th Brigade.

48th Division.

-----

1/5th BATTALION

GLOUCESTERSHIRE REGIMENT

M A Y   1 9 1 6

D.A.G.
3rd Echelon.
G.H.Q.

Herewith War Diary for month ending 31st May 1916.

J.P.W. Carlott
Lieut for Major
COMDG. 5TH BN. GLOUCESTER REGT.

2/6/16.

Army Form C. 2118.

1/5 Gloucestershire Regt

# WAR DIARY
## INTELLIGENCE SUMMARY.
(Erase heading not required.)

| Place | Date | Hour | Summary of Events and Information | Remarks and references to Appendices |
|---|---|---|---|---|
| SAILLY | 1.5.16 | | In Billets. Fine. Routine work of Company Training, shooting practice, inoculation carried on. SAILLY shelled with 15 c.m shells between 9am-11am. Capt. R.I. SULLIVAN (RAMC) & Capt R.M.F. COOKE went on leave. Strength 33 Officers 681 other ranks | G.A. |
| NEUVETERNE | 2.5.16 | 11 A.M | B" marched to NEUVETERNE & relieved 4 GLOUCESTERSHIRE REGT in J.Section by 11.a.m<br>Dispositions<br>A Coy (Capt L.R.C. SUMNER). Trenches K17.2 (Inclusive) to K18.3 (inclusive).<br>B. Coy (Lt C.S. NASON) cellars in RUE GRANDE. B" Reserve<br>C Coy (Capt N.C.B. SESSIONS) Trenches K17.3 to K18.2 & REMAUD (inclusive)<br>D Coy (Capt F.W. COLE) THE KEEP Bde Reserve<br>B" H.Q. THE MILL RUE GRANDE<br>Unit on our right 1/4 O.B.L.I. Unit on our left Bucks Bn O.B.L.I.<br>Wet & quiet. Casualties Nil. Four Officers of the 8th MIDDLESEX Regt came up to examine our line with a view to taking over details part of it | |

Army Form C. 2118.

# WAR DIARY

## INTELLIGENCE SUMMARY.

(Erase heading not required.)

1/5 GLOSTER REGT

Instructions regarding War Diaries and Intelligence Summaries are contained in F.S. Regs., Part II. and the Staff Manual respectively. Title pages will be prepared in manuscript.

| Place | Date | Hour | Summary of Events and Information | Remarks and references to Appendices |
|---|---|---|---|---|
| HEBUTERNE | 2/5/16 | | north of PUISIEUX ROAD (inclusive) | G.N. |
| HEBUTERNE | 3/5/16 | | Fine. Quiet. Casualties nil. Enemy appeared to be very nervous. Numerous flares were sent up & machine guns were unusually active. Probably a relief is taking place. Bombs were thrown from the CHRISTMAS TREE; they all fell short & on rapid fire being opened a small party of the enemy were seen to be running back. A man of the 2nd GUARDS DIVISION gave himself up to the BUCKS B'n O.B.L.I. on our left. | G.N. |
| HEBUTERNE | 4/5/16 | | Fine, very hot. Quiet. Casualties No. 1171 Pte GOULD.C. wounded by shrapnel. The 145 Brigade was relieved of that part of its line north of the PUISIEUX ROAD (inclusive) by the 164 Infantry Brigade 56th Division. The Battalion handed over to the 8th MIDDLESEX REGT. that part of its line North of the PUISIEUX ROAD Dispositions. A. Coy (Capt L.R.C SUMNER) held the Right Sub-sector, from 2nd BARRICADE | G.N. |

1577 Wt W10791/1773 500,000 1/15 D.D. & L. A.D.S.S./Forms/C. 2118.

**WAR DIARY**
or
INTELLIGENCE SUMMARY.     1/5 GLOSTER REGT

Army Form C. 2118.

| Place | Date | Hour | Summary of Events and Information | Remarks and references to Appendices |
|---|---|---|---|---|
| | | | to Head of Trench BUGEAUD inclusive. C Coy (Capt A.C.B. SESSIONS) from this point to the PUISIEUX ROAD (exclusive) D Coy (Capt F.W. COLE) in Bn Reserve. B Coy (Lt C.S. NASON) in Bde Reserve at SAILLY Headquarters at the Cross Roads in K 16 a 2 7. The relief was completed by 6 p.m. The Boundary between the 56 Division (3rd ARMY) & the 48 Division (4th ARMY) is PUISIEUX ROAD & a line running parallel & 50 yds N.E. of BRIGADE ROAD. Unit on our Right 1/4 O.B.L.I's  unit on our left 8 MIDDLESEX REGT | G.H. |
| HEBUTERNE 5.5.16 | | | Quiet. Fine. Casualties Nil. | G.H. |
| HEBUTERNE 6.5.16 | | | Quiet. Fine. Casualties Nil. Into Coy. Relief. A Coy relieved by B Coy, & went into Bn Reserve C Coy relieved by D Coy & went into Brigade Reserve SAILLY. | G.H. |

Army Form C. 2118.

# WAR DIARY
## INTELLIGENCE SUMMARY.
(Erase heading not required.)

1/5 GLOSTER REGT

| Place | Date | Hour | Summary of Events and Information | Remarks and references to Appendices |
|---|---|---|---|---|
| HEBUTERNE | 7.5.16 | | Quiet. Showery. Casualties Nil. B.Coy sent out 2 N.C.O.s & 10 men on a standing Patrol but nothing unusual was noticed. | G.N. |
| HEBUTERNE | 8.5.16 | | Quiet. Showery. Casualties Nil. Lt. W. FREAM & Lt. G. LISTER went on leave | G.N. |
| HEBUTERNE | 9.5.16 | | Showery. Casualties one man wounded by BOMB. At 1.40.a.m a party of Germans was heard to enter our trench. Cpl. ABEL (D Coy) in charge of our left post, immediately followed his group out of the Advanced Trench into a pit behind. Bombs were at once thrown by the enemy into the bay he vacated. One of our men was wounded in the cheek. Our men threw bombs, drove the Germans out of the trench, opened rapid fire & then cleared the trench by the orthodox bombing tactics. The enemy got in by the PUISIEUX ROAD barricade. A search was at once made for souvenirs but without any success otherwise quiet. | |
| HEBUTERNE | 10.5.16 | | Wet. Casualties Nil. B" relieved by BUCKS B" O.B.L.I. Owing to advance | |

Army Form C. 2118.

# WAR DIARY
# INTELLIGENCE SUMMARY.
(Erase heading not required.)

1/5 GLOSTER REGT

| Place | Date | Hour | Summary of Events and Information | Remarks and references to Appendices |
|---|---|---|---|---|
| | | | that the SAILLY-HEBUTERNE Road was not to be used by daylight, the relief was late; the last company arrived at COIGNEUX at 12.30 a.m. | G.N. |
| COIGNEUX | 11.5.16 | | In Huts. In Brigade Reserve. Fine. "B" supplied a working party of 4 Officers & 81 O.R. for digging a cable trench between VERCINGETORIX and the front line. | G.N. |
| COIGNEUX | 12.5.16 | | In Huts. Showery. Capt R.M.F. COOKE & Capt R.L. SULLIVAN (R A M C) returned from leave. Capt COOKE took over Command of B. Coy. | G.N. |
| COIGNEUX | 13.5.16 | | In Huts. Wet. "B" supplied a working party of 5 Officers & 45 O R. | G.N. |
| COIGNEUX | 14.5.16 | | In Huts. Showery. "B" supplied a working party of 13 Officers 604 O.R's for night work at COLINCAMPS | G.N. |
| AUTHIE | 15.5.16 | | "B" moved to billets in AUTHIE, the 144th Bde relieving the 145 Bde, but 1/4 W R SNOWDEN & Lt E CONDER went on leave. Very heavy shelling; the Germans raided the 1/4 R BERKS in G Sectn. | G.N. |

Army Form C. 2118.

# WAR DIARY
## INTELLIGENCE SUMMARY
(Erase heading not required.)

1/5 GLOSTER REGT

| Place | Date | Hour | Summary of Events and Information | Remarks and references to Appendices |
|---|---|---|---|---|
| AUTHIE | 16.5.16 | | In Billets. Fine. Routine | G.H. |
| AUTHIE | 17.5.16 | | In Billets. Fine. Routine. 2Lt C.S. MILLARD left for England with instructions to report in writing to the War Office. | G.H. |
| BEAUVAL | 18.5.16 | | The Battalion marched with the 145 Infantry Bde to BEAUVAL, marching past the Corps Commander Sir AYLMER HUNTER-WESTON at MARIEUX. Owing to the strenuous heat 80 O.R's fell out. Billets at BEAUVAL the first. | G.H. |
| BEAUVAL | 19.5.16 | | In Billets. Coy paraded for inspections etc. Lt G. LISTER & Lt W FREMM returned from leave | G.H. |
| BEAUVAL | 20.5.16 | | In Billets. Fine. Coys paraded for training from 7am - 11am. 92 Officers & 92 O.R's were away on working parties. | |

1577 Wt. W10791/1773 500,000 -1/15 D. D. & L. A.D.S.S./Forms/C. 2118.

Army Form C. 2118.

# WAR DIARY
## INTELLIGENCE SUMMARY.   1/5 GLOSTER REGT.

(Erase heading not required.)

Instructions regarding War Diaries and Intelligence Summaries are contained in F. S. Regs., Part II. and the Staff Manual respectively. Title pages will be prepared in manuscript.

| Place | Date | Hour | Summary of Events and Information | Remarks and references to Appendices |
|---|---|---|---|---|
| BEAUVAL | 21/5/16 | | In Billets. Fine. Bn paraded for Brigade Church Parade at 10 a.m. 3 Officers 246 O.R's were away on working parties. Inoculation started. Lt & Adjt. T.P. WINTERBOTHAM returned from III Army School and assumed duties of Adjutant. | G/1 SPW SPW |
| " | 22/5/16 | 7 A.M. | Battalion Route march via BEAUQUESNE. Fine and hot. | SPW |
| " | 23/5/16 | 7 A.M. | Battalion Training. Lieut. General Sir AYLMER HUNTER-WESTON K.C.B. Commanding VIII Corps visited Battalion and watched Training. Lieut H.S. KING and C.S. NASON left for leave | SPW SPW |
| " | 24/5/16 | | In billets. Fine. Training | SPW |
| " | 25/5/16 | | In billets. Fine Training | SPW |
| " | 26/5/16 | | In billets. Fine | SPW |

Army Form C. 2118.

# WAR DIARY
## INTELLIGENCE SUMMARY.
*(Erase heading not required.)*

1/5 GLOSTER REGT.

| Place | Date | Hour | Summary of Events and Information | Remarks and references to Appendices |
|---|---|---|---|---|
| BEAUVAL | 27/5/16 | 7 A.M. | Brigade Route moved via CANDAS - MONTRELET - BONNEVILLE - VALHEUREUX. Led. Gen. Sir A. HUNTER WESTON addressed officers. Fine and hot. | SPW |
| — | 28/5/16 | 10 A.M. | Brigade Church Parade. G.O.C. 48th Division present. Fine | SPW |
| | | 2:30 P.M. | Field General Court martial assembled at Brigade H.Q. on no 602 C.S.M. L.H. HORNE for offence in respect of a green envelope. President Major L.L.C. REYNOLDS 1/1 BUCKS BATTN. Court adjourned for further evidence | SPW |
| — | 29/5/16 | | Fine. Training | SPW |
| — | 30/5/16 | | Fine. Training | SPW |
| — | 31/5/16 | 4 A.M. | Brigade moved to COULONVILLERS via CANDAS - FIENVILLERS - BERNAVILLE - BEAUMETZ - LES MASURES. Arrived in billets about 11.30 AM | SPW |

Army Form C. 2118.

# WAR DIARY
## or
## INTELLIGENCE SUMMARY.

1/5 GLOSTER REGT

*(Erase heading not required.)*

| Place | Date | Hour | Summary of Events and Information | Remarks and references to Appendices |
|---|---|---|---|---|
| COULONVILLERS | 31/5/16 | | Fine and hot. Six men fell out on march. Lt. C.O. Winterbotham and L.W. Moore went on leave. | PW |

Commdg 5th Bn Gloucester Regt.

145th Brigade.
48th Division.
----------

1/5th BATTALION

GLOUCESTERSHIRE REGIMENT

JUNE 1916

# WAR DIARY
## INTELLIGENCE SUMMARY.

1/5 GLOSTER REGT    Vol 16

| Place | Date | Hour | Summary of Events and Information | Remarks and references to Appendices |
|---|---|---|---|---|
| COULONVILLERS | 1/6/16 | 6 A.M. | In billets. Training on new training area. Fine and cool | SFW |
| " | 2/6/16 | 12.15 AM | In billets. Training in open under brigade scheme. Fine | SFW |
| " | 3/6/16 | | Training. Fine. | SFW |
| " | 4/6/16 | 9 A.M. | Battalion marched independently and billeted in CAPENNES. Brigade H Q at ARGENVILLERS | SFW |
| CAPENNES | 5/6/16 | 6 A.M. | Training. Honours list 3rd June 1916. C.M.G. - Lt Col J H COLLETT - Military cross - Capt H. E B SESSIONS | SFW |
| " | 6/6/16 | 4 P.M. | Training including night work and brigade march in due order reached billets 3.30 AM. Some rain | SFW |
| " | 7/6/16 | 2 P.M. | Brigade horse show at ARGENVILLERS. Battalion secured 1st prize. Some rain during day | SFW |

# WAR DIARY

## INTELLIGENCE SUMMARY.    1 1/5 GLOSTER REGT.

Army Form C. 2118.

Instructions regarding War Diaries and Intelligence Summaries are contained in F.S. Regs., Part II and the Staff Manual respectively. Title pages will be prepared in manuscript.

| Place | Date | Hour | Summary of Events and Information | Remarks and references to Appendices |
|---|---|---|---|---|
| CAPENNES | 8/6/16 | | F.G. Coot tried on 602 C.S.M. HORNE L.H. matter old. Finding guilty. Sentence — To be reduced to rank of Sergeant. Battalion paraded at 2.30 P.M. for Divisional Training with 144th I. Bde. | SPW |
| — | 9/6/16 | | Divisional Training with 144th I. Bde at 6. Atr. Fire. | STW |
| OUTREBOIS | 10/6/16 | | 145th I Bde marched to OUTREBOIS via YVRENCHEUX — MAISON PONTHIEU — AUXI-LE-CHÂTEAU — WAVANS — MÉZEROLLES arriving in billets about 5 P.M. Fire with some showers | PW |
| COIGNEUX | 11/6/16 | 6 A.M. | 145th Bde marched to COIGNEUX via HEM — FRESCHVILLERS — SARTON — THIEVRES — AUTHIE arriving in billets about 5 P.M. Three hour halt at SARTON. Major G.F. COLLETT went to FIXÉCOURT for C.O.s course and Capt. R.S.C. LITTLE assumed command of the Battalion. Capt. COLE 2nd in command. Lt FREAM O.C. D Coy. Some showers | BPW |
| — | 12/6/16 | | The Battalion relieved 9th ROYAL WARWICKS in Sector | CWZ |

1577   Wt. W10791/1773  500,000  1/15  D.D. & L.   A.D.S.S./Forms/C. 2118.

Army Form C. 2118.

# WAR DIARY
# or
# INTELLIGENCE SUMMARY.
(Erase heading not required.)

1/5 GLOSTER REGT

| Place | Date | Hour | Summary of Events and Information | Remarks and references to Appendices |
|---|---|---|---|---|
| HEBUTERNE | 12/6/16 | | Dispositions :- <br> A Coy (Capt. L.R.E. Sumner) 2nd Reservists on SERRE ROAD to junction of BUGEAUD and F.T.K. 4-5 <br> C Coy (Lieut. H.P. SNOWDEN) from junction of BUGEAUD with F.T K17 4-5-6 PUSIEUX - HEBUTERNE Road <br> B - (Capt. R.H. COOKE) - In support - cellars near Billet No. 4 and Dug-outs in RAGLAN. <br> D - (Lt. F. FREAH) - In Reserve. Billets at SAILLY - AU - BOIS <br> Battalion H.Q. Billet 162 at junction of PUISIEUX and SERRE - HEBUTERNE ROADS. <br> Unit on our right 1/4th OXFORD and BUCKS L.I. <br> " " " left " <br> Situation normal - At night some maneuvering in PUISIEUX ROAD and windmill amount of tracline gun fire. Casualties NIL | TPW |
| " | 13/6/16 | | Normal. Rain. Casualties NIL | TPW |

# WAR DIARY

## INTELLIGENCE SUMMARY

1/5 GLOSTER REGT

(Erase heading not required.)

Army Form C. 2118.

Instructions regarding War Diaries and Intelligence Summaries are contained in F. S. Regs., Part II. and the Staff Manual respectively. Title pages will be prepared in manuscript.

| Place | Date | Hour | Summary of Events and Information | Remarks and references to Appendices |
|---|---|---|---|---|
| HEBUTERNE | 14/6/16 | | Lt Col. J.H. COLLETT rejoined and resumed command of the Battalion. Capt P.E. FRANCILLON also rejoined. 2nd Lts K.G and J.G DURRANT went on leave. Considerable rain. Situation quiet. Casualties NIL. At 11 PM line full manned to midnight. | 3RD |
| " | 15/6/16 | | Situation normal. Enemy quiet except for M.Gun fire. Casualties NIL | 3RD |
| " | 16/6/16 | | Battalion relieved by 4th R BERKS and marched back to billets near the DELL S/W of SAILLY-AU-BOIS. (J16 D 68) Casualties on relief NIL | 3RD |
| SAILLY (DELL) | 17/6/16 | | Fine. Brig washing parties. Majors G.F COLLETT returned from FLIXECOURT | 2ND |
| " | 18/6/16 | | Normal fine | 2ND |

1577  Wt. W10791/1773  500,000  1/15  D. D. & L.   A.D.S.S./Forms/C. 2118.

# WAR DIARY
## INTELLIGENCE SUMMARY.
*(Erase heading not required.)*

1/5 GLOSTER REGT

| Place | Date | Hour | Summary of Events and Information | Remarks and references to Appendices |
|---|---|---|---|---|
| SAILLY (THE DELL) | 19/6/16 | | Normal. Mentioned in despatches Lt Col. J.H. COLLETT. C.M.G. No 2717 Serj. R.D. THOMPSON No 1132 Serj. C.F. HARRIS | Fine |
| " | 20/6/16 | | 2nd Lt C. BRIEN joined from St OMER and was posted to D Coy | Fine |
| " | 21/6/16 | | Lt NASON and 2nd Lt BELL with 100 O.R. left for LOUVENCOURT. Fine and dull | Fine |
| " | 22/6/16 | | Battalion moved to bivouac near COUIN (T8a). Fine | B.M.W. |
| COUIN | 23/6/16 | | Company training. Some rain | B.M.W. |
| " | 24/6/16 | | 2nd Lt KNIGHT joined the Battalion posted to B Coy. Draft of 25 O.R. arrived. Rain | B.M.W. |
| " | 25/6/16 | | Church parade interrupted by enemy aeroplanes. Fine | B.M.W. |

# WAR DIARY
## of
## INTELLIGENCE SUMMARY.

(Erase heading not required.)

1/5 GLOSTER REGT.

Instructions regarding War Diaries and Intelligence Summaries are contained in F. S. Regs., Part II. and the Staff Manual respectively. Title pages will be prepared in manuscript.

| Place | Date | Hour | Summary of Events and Information | Remarks and references to Appendices |
|---|---|---|---|---|
| COUIN | 26/6/16 | | Training. Rain | SPO |
| — | 27/6/16 | | Six shells fell near bivouac during g.m. DONE's section of A Coy. in assault order. Casualties NIL. | PM |
| — | 28/6/16 | | L⁴ NASON 2/Lt BELL and 102 O.R. rejoined from LOUVENCOURT. Rain. | 3W |
| — | 29/6/16 | | Bivouac moved further West to SP a 6-1. (Sheet 57 D 1:40,000) | SPO |
| | 30/6/16 −1/7/16 | | Strength Officers 35 O.R. 913. Lt SNOWDEN rejoined from 4th Div. School. | SPO |

S.D. Gale
Lieut. for LT. COLONEL
COMDG. 5TH BN GLOUCESTER REGT.

145th Inf.Bde.
48th Div.

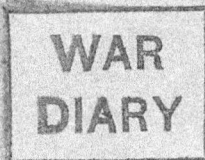

1/5th BATTN. THE GLOUCESTERSHIRE REGIMENT.

J U L Y

1 9 1 6

# WAR DIARY

## INTELLIGENCE SUMMARY.

*(Erase heading not required.)*

Army Form C. 2118.

1/5 GLOUCESTERSHIRE REGT

| Place | Date | Hour | Summary of Events and Information | Remarks and references to Appendices |
|---|---|---|---|---|
| COUIN 57/a 6.1 | 1/7/16 | 9 AM | Brigade marched to MAILLY-MAILLET and bivouaced at P18 & 44 (Map reference Sheet 57 D S.E 1:20000). Artillery continuous on front. Fine. Lt R.H.G. BATTEN, 1/5 R.H.A. | SPW |
| MAILLY-MAILLET | 2/7/16 | | HARRISON, 2Lt LYETT W.B., 2/Lt LE FARRIMOND J, 2nd Lt S. THOMPSON and 2Lt E.T.H.A. WOOD and NORTHANTS Regt joined. Orders received to attack 3 lines of German trenches North of HAMEL (Q.18 a and c Map reference as above) at 3.30 AM. of 3/7/16. 4th R BERKS on right of Battalion. 144 I Bde on left. 1/OXFORDS Brigade Reserve. 1/1 BUCKS Divisional Reserve. Brigade less BUCKS Battn. relieved Le MESNIL and front line trenches were reinforced. W8 by SOUTH WALES BORDERERS Co. About Midnight the whole operation was cancelled and Battalion returned to Bivouac at MAILLY-MAILLET at about 3 AM. Casualties NIL. | SPW |
| MAILLY-MAILLET | 3/7/16 | 5 PM | Brigade marched to COUIN Bivouac 57 Y a 6-1 with some Infantries as on morning 1/7/16 | mel |
| COUIN | 4/7/16 | 6 PM | Battalion relieved 5th R WARWICKS in H section Unit on left 1/6 R WARWICKS on Right 1/4 OXFORD and BUCKS L.I. S/60 Division - on Right 1/4 OXFORD and BUCKS L.I. | SPW |

Army Form C. 2118.

# WAR DIARY
## INTELLIGENCE SUMMARY.
1/5 GLOUCESTERSHIRE REGT.

*(Erase heading not required.)*

| Place | Date | Hour | Summary of Events and Information | Remarks and references to Appendices |
|---|---|---|---|---|
| HEBUTERNE | 4/7/16 | | Dispositions:- | |
| | | | A Coy (Capt L.R.C. SUMNER) Trenches. 3rd Barricade SERHED ROAD to F.T.K17'S | |
| | | | C " (Capt R.H.F. COOKE) " F.T.K17.5 exclusive to PUISIEUX ROAD | |
| | | | B " (Capt LITTLE) Fort GROSVENOR | |
| | | | D " (Capt F.W. COLE) SAILLY Bivouac THE DELL | |
| | | | Bn. H.Q. Billet 81. | |
| | | | Fine. Casualties NIL | |
| | 5/7/16 | | Heavy rain. Considerable artillery activity especially in villages. Casualties NIL. | |
| - | 6/7/16 | | 5 P.M. Inter-company relief. B relieved A and D - C. Coy. SESSIONS rejoined from FLIXECOURT. Casualties No 2563 Pte. ROBERTS A B Coy killed by shell in trenches and buried in village cemetery HEBUTERNE. No. 4818 Pte ROBERTS B A Coy wounded by his own rifle in trenches. Heavy rain | |

Army Form C. 2118.

# WAR DIARY
## INTELLIGENCE SUMMARY.
(Erase heading not required.)

1/5 GLOUCESTERSHIRE REGT

| Place | Date | Hour | Summary of Events and Information | Remarks and references to Appendices |
|---|---|---|---|---|
| HEBUTERNE | 7/7/16 | | Rain. Casualties. No 2862 Pte PACKER W.H. D Coy grenade shell. No 11189 L/C GIBBONS A/B Coy wounded shell. Lt MOORE and Sergt HUXFORD to FLIXECOURT. Trenches very wet. 8 AM smoke cloud discharged from front line. | TRW |
| " | 8/7/16 | | Relieved by 1/4th R. BERKS. Casualties in working party at night. No 1552 Pte BISHOP S.E. C Coy and No 2276 Pte LATWORTH T C Coy wounded shrapnel. Fine. Long carrying party to remove cylinders from trenches | TRW |
| " | 9/7/16 | | In bivouac. Fine. Working parties at night. Lt C.W. WINTERBOTHAM att. 6 Co attached to staff eff. 1st & 3rd I.B.de | TRW |
| " | 10/7/16 | | In bivouac. Fine. Lt BATTEN L.E HARRISON L.E HEWETT. 2nd Lt THOMPSON eff to join 6th & 8th WARWICKS. New Trench and three communicators dug from 2nd Reserve on SERRE - HEBUTERNE ROAD to junction of WATSON and 1st DONE. eff H.E.R. SESSIONS in charge. Casualties No 2795 Pte SCRUBY A C Company wounded. Fine | TRW |

1577 Wt.W10791/1773 500,000 1/15 D.D.&L. A.D.S.S./Forms/C. 2118.

**Army Form C. 2118.**

# WAR DIARY
# INTELLIGENCE SUMMARY

(Erase heading not required.) 1/5 GLOUCESTERSHIRE REGT.

| Place | Date | Hour | Summary of Events and Information | Remarks and references to Appendices |
|---|---|---|---|---|
| SAILLY AU BOIS [DELL] | 11/7/16 | | Draft of 54 O.R. from Regular and Service Rolls. Large party of enemy aero and much interfered with by our and artillery fire. | STW |
| | 12/7/16 | 7 A.M. | Battalion relieved 1/4 R. BERKS in H. Section. Dispositions:- A Coy (Capt SUMNER) 2nd Bouereale SERTER ROAD to junction of RUSSAUD and front trench.  C Coy (Capt SESSIONS) From left of A Coy to PUISIEUX ROAD.  B - (Capt LITTLE) SAILLY (DELL) Buonee  D - (Capt F.W COLE) Fort GROSVENOR  H.Q. R.COLL 81  Units on our right 1/4 OXFORD and BUCKS L.I. On left 56th Division under SCOTTISH. Fine. Casualties 2 O.R. D Coy wounded slightly | STW |
| HEBUTERNE | 13/7/16 | 11P.M. | The Battalion were ordered to attempt a raid an enemy line about K.14. b.-1.-1. Lieut KING in charge with 2/Lt BADHAM and HOUGHTON with 60 O.R proceeded to enemy wire. After attempts were made from | |

# WAR DIARY
## INTELLIGENCE SUMMARY

(Erase heading not required.)  1/5 GLOUCESTERSHIRE REGT

Army Form C. 2118.

| Place | Date | Hour | Summary of Events and Information | Remarks and references to Appendices |
|---|---|---|---|---|
| HEBUTERNE | 13/7/16 | | Enemy were well driven back by rifle fire and bombers. Party returned about 12.30 A.M. Casualties, 2nd Lt. HOUGHTON wounded and 5 O.R. wounded | Nil |
| | 14/7/16 | 3.0 AM | Smoke candles and P. Bombs fired from our front trenches. Enemy put down a heavy barrage on trenches. Fire. Casualties. NIL. Lt. Col. COLLETT went to command the section of 145th Bde at SAILLY. Major G.F. COLLETT took over command of Battalion. Normal. Fire Casualties NIL. | Nil |
| " | 15/7/16 | | | |
| " | 16/7/16 | 4 P.M. | Relieved by 15th Bn. WELSH REGT, and moved to bivouac COUIN (J7a 6.1) less 6 Officers and 3 platoons left to guide WELSH. Fire. Casualties NIL. | 3Gd |
| COUIN | 17/7/16 | | Battalion moved by motor lorries to BOUZINCOURT arriving in billets in village about 5. P.M. Lt. Col. COLLETT resumed and took over command of Battalion. Strength 35 Officers 937 O.R. | 3Ad |
| BOUZINCOURT | 18/7/16 | 9 P.M. | In billets. 9 P.M. Working party under Captain SESSIONS of 200 moved up and dug trench East of OVILLERS-LA-BOISSELLE about X 9 b (map reference trench map OVILLERS 57 D S.E 4 Edition 2 B 1:10,000 Casualties 1 O.R. wounded | 3rd |

Army Form C. 2118.

# WAR DIARY
# or
# INTELLIGENCE SUMMARY

(Erase heading not required.)

1/5 GLOUCESTERSHIRE REGT

Instructions regarding War Diaries and Intelligence Summaries are contained in F. S. Regs., Part II. and the Staff Manual respectively. Title Pages will be prepared in manuscript.

| Place | Date | Hour | Summary of Events and Information | Remarks and references to Appendices |
|---|---|---|---|---|
| BOUZINCOURT | 19/7/16 | | 6 P.M. Battalion took over from 1/6 ROYAL WARWICKS captured German Trenches N. & E. of OVILLERS - LA - BOISSELLE about x 2 b - x 3 c - X 8 b. (Map Ref. as above) Dispositions :- Battalion H.Q. - x 8 b - 7½ - 8½ A Coy (Capt. L.R.E. SUMNER) In Reserve Trench X 14 a 5½ - 60 to X 14 a 50-8½ B Coy (Capt. R.S.C. LITTLE) Trench x 3 c 8-3 to x 3 c 0 2 (Point 02) and thence to x 8 b 65-35 C Coy (Capt. H.E.B SESSIONS) In Support. Trench x 8 D 2-4 to x 8 D 15-60 D Coy (Capt. F.W. COLE) Trench x 2 D 2-2 to x 8 b 65-35 and thence to x 2 D 4-3 Unit on left 144 I Bde. on right 1/4 R. BERKS. Officers taken up to trenches. C.O. Adj. M.O. Le CONDER & Lt CRUICKSHANK and 4 officers including O.C. Coys. remainder of officers and 5% O.R. left at BOUZINCOURT 11. P.M. B Company ordered to bomb up trench to capture Point 79 = Trench junction X 3 c 66-89. Point 79 found to be strongly held and | 3 PRO |

Army Form C. 2118.

# WAR DIARY / INTELLIGENCE SUMMARY

(Erase heading not required.) 1/5 GLOUCESTERSHIRE REGT.

| Place | Date | Hour | Summary of Events and Information | Remarks and references to Appendices |
|---|---|---|---|---|
| | 19/7/16 | | Trench work in front of enemy conceals which was not enfiladed. Our bombers was advanced and a new post established at X3c.55-70. Draft of 32 O.R. arrived at BOUZINCOURT. Fine | RFW |
| OVILLERS LA BOISSELLE | 20/7/16 | | Fine. Continued shelling throughout day. Battalion H.Q. moved to X14a.55-60 under Bde Orders, old Battalion H.Q. occupied by night trench company H.Q. Inter-company relief. A boy relieved B and C coy D at 6 P.M. Casualties Lt. C.B. NASON accidentally wounded. O.R. 3 killed 9 wounded. |  |
| | | 11.30 TH | Battalion was ordered to attack Points 79 and 40. = X3c.4.0. 1/4 OXFORD and BUCKS L.I. attacking immediately on my right. The attack A and C companies to advance to my left. The attack was met with heavy shell and machine gun fire and failed to take objective. Casualties missing believed killed Lt. W. FREAM 2d Lt. C.V.N PUCKRIDGE and 2nd Lt. I.J. FARRIMOND Wounded Capt. H.E.B SESSIONS 2/Lt. F.P. BADHAM. O.R. missing 45 killed 5 Wounded 59. |  |
| | 21/7/16 | | Heavy shelling during the day. Draft of 68 O.R. arrived BOUZINCOURT. Capt. R.F.H. COOKE took command of C company | RFW |

# WAR DIARY

## INTELLIGENCE SUMMARY

1/5 GLOUCESTERSHIRE REGT

| Place | Date | Hour | Summary of Events and Information | Remarks and references to Appendices |
|---|---|---|---|---|
| OVILLERS LA BOISSELLE | 21/7/16 | | Battalion drilling during the night and day. Draft 75 O.R arrived BOUZINCOURT. Gas company relief B to A and D to C. 11.P.M. B Company and bombing party of trench to attack point 79 and D Company attempted to capture point 40. B Company needed but finding no cover there were compelled to fall back in the main and found machine wounded at Bouzinecourt at first directly down on our length of trench. Weather Fine. Casualties 2nd Lt R.E. KNIGHT wounded and died of wounds 2nd Lt R.E. DURRANT and 2nd Lt F.R. BELL wounded. O.R. 1 killed and 3 wounded. | RW |
| " | 22/7/16 | | Heavy Shelling during day. Inter-company relief A to B and C to D. Weather Fine | |
| " | 23/7/16 | 12.35 A.M. | 145 I.Bde ordered to attack in conjunction with 144 I Bde on left Dividing line Railway in X 3 e inclusive to 145 I.Bde. Battalion attacked Point 02 to 79 on right and Railway on left to capture Pt. 79 from Wall and 40 from East. 1/4 OXFORD and | RW |

# Army Form C. 2118.

## WAR DIARY
## INTELLIGENCE SUMMARY

(Erase heading not required.)

1/5 GLOUCESTERSHIRE REGT

| Place | Date | Hour | Summary of Events and Information | Remarks and references to Appendices |
|---|---|---|---|---|
| OVILLERS LA BOISSELLE | 23/7/16 | | BUCKS L.I. to attack Pt 81 = X3 B 81 with left of attack just East of Point 28 = X 3 D 2-8. 144 I. Bde to attack Pt. 40 = X 3 d 4-0 from North Battalions of 145 I. Bde to join hands North of and in Trench 79 – 11 = X 3 B 1-1. A Company on Right – C on left – B in support – D in reserve. The attack was quickly discovered by enemy who were holding all Trenches strongly. Heavy barrage of arte. [artillery] and machine gun fire were opened and in spite of being reinforced by B coy. [company] and heavily shelled objectives were not reached. A fresh attack after was planned by our 7 min. offside A Coy. objective also failed Stokes guns and old trench mortars used during February bombardment. Casualties. Wounded and died of wounds 2nd LT W.B. LYETT NORTHANTS REGT attached. Wounded Capt R.J.C. LITTLE Capt. F.W. COLE Capt L.R.E. SUMNER Capt. R.N.F. COOKE LT. H.S. KING 2nd LT L.J. CLAYTON 2nd LT W.J. PEARCE. O.R. Killed 12. Missing 23. Wounded 113. At about 3.30 A.M. The Battalion were withdrawn to reserve line being | 340 |

Army Form C. 2118.

# WAR DIARY
## or
## INTELLIGENCE SUMMARY
*(Erase heading not required.)*

Instructions regarding War Diaries and Intelligence Summaries are contained in F. S. Regs., Part II. and the Staff Manual respectively. Title Pages will be prepared in manuscript.

| Place | Date | Hour | Summary of Events and Information | Remarks and references to Appendices |
|---|---|---|---|---|
| OVILLERS LA-BOISSELLE | 23/7/16 | | relieved by 1/1 BUCKS BATTN OXFORD and BUCKS L.I. who after a few hours bombardment captured trench 28 - 11 - 79 about 120 of whom surrendered including 2 machine guns. 11 P.M. Battalion relieved by 1/4 R BERKS and moved to Bouzincourt East of ALBERT at W 29 B 9-4 | BW |
| Bouzincourt East of ALBERT W29 B9-4 | 24/7/16 | 9 PM | A & B companies moved up to support 1/4 R BERKS whilst Major G.F. COLLETT Remainder of Battalion in Bivouac. Casualties 10 R. wounded. | BW |
| " | 25/7/16 | 9 AM | Battalion relieved 1/4 R BERKS in trenches as on 19/7/16. C in right. B in support. A in reserve. Major G.F. COLLETT in command. 4 P.M. Battalion relieved by 1/4 GLOSTER REGT and marched to Bouzincourt left in morning. Casualties O.R. wounded 3. Draft 30 O.R. arrived Bouzincourt. Weather fine. | BW |
| " | 26/7/16 | 9 AM | Battalion moved to LEALVILLERS halting for dinner near BOUZINCOURT where Lt. Col. COLLETT assumed command. | BW |

Army Form C. 2118.

# WAR DIARY
## or
## INTELLIGENCE SUMMARY

(Erase heading not required.)

Instructions regarding War Diaries and Intelligence Summaries are contained in F. S. Regs., Part II. and the Staff Manual respectively. Title Pages will be prepared in manuscript.

| Place | Date | Hour | Summary of Events and Information | Remarks and references to Appendices |
|---|---|---|---|---|
| LEAVILLERS | 27/7/16 | | In billets. Weather fine. Draft 49 O.R. arrived | Two |
| " | 28/7/16 | | 85 O.R. of 1/4 and 1/6 GLOSTERS sent to 144 I.Bde. Battalion moved with Brigade to BEAUVAL via ARQUEVES-RAINCHEVAL-BEAUQUESNE. Very hot. | |
| BEAUVAL | 29/7/16 | | 8 AN Brigade moved to CRAMONT via CANDAS-FIENVILLERS-BERNAVILLE BEAUMETZ-LONGVILLERS. Very hot. moved. Draft 6 O.R. | Two |
| CRAMONT | 30/7/16 | | In billets. Very fine and hot | Two |
| " | 31/7/16 | | Fine hot. Draft 26 O.R. Strength. Officers 20 (6 clerks employed) 843 O.R. | Two |

J Molcott
2/6
Lt Col Commanding
1/5 GLOSTER REGT.

145th Brigade.
48th Division.
------

1/5th BATTALION

GLOUCESTERSHIRE REGIMENT

AUGUST 1 9 1 6

Headquarters
145th Inf. Bde.

Herewith War Diary for Month of August, please.

E.J. Collett

Major,
Cmdg. 1/5th Bn. Gloster Regt.

1/9/16

# WAR DIARY
## or
## INTELLIGENCE SUMMARY

(Erase heading not required.)  1/5 GLOUCESTERSHIRE REGT.

Army Form C. 2118.

| Place | Date | Hour | Summary of Events and Information | Remarks and references to Appendices |
|---|---|---|---|---|
| CRAMONT | 1/8/16 | | Fine. Following officers joined and were posted. 2nd Lt. R.L. HARKSWORTH - D Coy<br>" W.F. BIGGER - B<br>" V.R. BINGHAM-HALL B - 15th GLOSTER REGT<br>" F. CHAPMAN A Coy<br>" K.E. CHURCH C Coy | |
| " | 2/8/16 | | In billets. Fine. Lt. L.W. MOORE rejoined from FLIXE COURT and took over command of B Coy. | |
| " | 3/4/16 | | Very hot. Lt. HAWKINS took over command of C company. | |
| " | 4/8/16 | | In billets. Fine. Company training & Bombing | |
| " | 5/8/16 | | " Draft 10 OR arrived. Company training | |
| " | 6/8/16 | | " Sunday. Very hot. | |
| " | 7/8/16 | | Fine. 2nd Lt. E.H. HARVEY } joined from 3/5 Battalion and were posted to C B Coy<br>" N. YEARS } A | |

Army Form C. 2118.

## INTELLIGENCE SUMMARY

(Erase heading not required.) 1/5 GLOSTER REG-T

| Place | Date | Hour | Summary of Events and Information | Remarks and references to Appendices |
|---|---|---|---|---|
| CRAMONT | 8/8/16 | | In billets. Fine. Strength 27 Officers 886 O.R. Harvesting party supplied to farmers | RW |
| " | 9/8/16 | 7.30AM | Battalion moved with the Brigade to BEAUVAL via BEAUMETZ-BERNAVILLE CANDAS. Very hot march | RW |
| BEAUVAL | 10/8/16 | 4 AM | Battalion moved with the Brigade to VARENNES. Fine | RW |
| VARENNES | 11/8/16 | 7 AM 3 P.M. | Battalion moved with Brigade and billeted in BOUZINCOURT. Moved out of BOUZINCOURT to bivouac west of BOUZINCOURT. Wind distant. | RW |
| BOUZINCOURT (Bivouac) | 12/8/16 | | In bivouac. fine | RW |
| " | 13/8/16 | 9.30 AM | Relieved 7th SUFFOLK REGT in Reserve Trenches W.21 a central. | |
| Reserve trenches W.21 a (central) | 14/8/16 | | Relieved 1st ROYAL BERKS in support trenches south of OVILLERS-LA-BOISSELLE. Infantry :- 1 O. Trench X.14. a. 5.8. B. Coy (Lt MOORE) in M. Street - e Coy (Lt HAWKINS) in M. Street. D. Coy. (Lt SNOWDEN) in St Street | BW |

# WAR DIARY
## INTELLIGENCE SUMMARY

(Erase heading not required.) 1/5 GLOSTER REGT

| Place | Date | Hour | Summary of Events and Information | Remarks and references to Appendices |
|---|---|---|---|---|
| OVILLERS- LA BOISSELLE | 14/8/16 | | A Coy (2nd Lt D.G. DURRANT) in 2nd Street. C Coy also relieved 2nd Street half of 1/4 OXFORD + BUCKS L.I. in SKYLINE Trench and 74 - Bond with ANZACS on right. heavy shells in the way up. Casualties OR 5 killed wounded 16. Lt. E.W. WINTERBOTHAM rejoined from 143 I. Bde. | |
| " | 15/8/16 | | C company party on way to relieve field next ANZACS heavily shelled. Lt. HAWKINS buried by shell and injured. OR 1 killed and 1 missing. A and D companies attacked trench X 2 A 76 & 74. Attacked did not succeed. Casualties. Officers killed 2nd Lt D.G. DURRANT wounded 2nd Lt S.M.A. WOOD, 2nd Lt R.L. HARTSWORTH, 2nd Lt E.N. YEARS, 2nd Lt F. CHAPMAN O.R. 3 killed - 99 wounded 21 missing. | |
| " | 16/8/16 | | Relieved by R. BERKS and moved to gun pits W 24 A 34. Lt. E.W. WINTERBOTHAM assumed command of C Coy and 2nd Lt RATCLIFF of A Coy | |
| GUN PITS W24 A34 | 17/8/16 | | In bivouac | |

# WAR DIARY
## or
## INTELLIGENCE SUMMARY

(Erase heading not required.)

**1/5 GLOSTER REGT**

| Place | Date | Hour | Summary of Events and Information | Remarks and references to Appendices |
|---|---|---|---|---|
| GUN PITS W.24.A.3.4. | 18/8/16 | | Battalion moved up & suffered casualties in an 14/8/16. Bomb & carrying parties moved up to support 4th R.BERKS during attack following successful attack by 143 & R.Bde. in which about 400 prisoners were taken. Casualties 3 O.R. wounded. | 3M.O |
| Suffolk Trenches | 19/8/16 | 9 AM. | Relieved 4th & 2 BERKS in front line. Defenders R.Bde H.Q. x 3 & 57 Skyline Trench. Ration Trench and front line in x.2.6 | 3M.O |
| | | 7 PM | Relieved by 1st WORCESTER REGT 144 I. Bde and marched to Louvencourt W.12. D.15. Casualties O.R 11 wounded | 3M.O |
| BOUZINCOURT (Louvencourt) V.12. C.67 | 20/8/16 | | On Divisional Reserve. Lt F. BALFOUR rejoined from M.Gun company. 2nd Lt. M.H. GRAVES-SMITH rejoined from M.Gun course. 2nd Lt A L APPERLY joined for duty and was posted to C Company. Lt BALFOUR to B Coy Map Ref: Trench Map Sheet 57 D.S.E. 1:20,000. | 3M.O |
| | 21/8/16 | | In Divisional Reserve. 24 O.R. arrived on duty. | 3M.O |
| | | | | 3M.O |

Army Form C. 2118.

# WAR DIARY
## or
## INTELLIGENCE SUMMARY
*(Erase heading not required.)*

1/5 GLOUCESTERSHIRE REGT

Instructions regarding War Diaries and Intelligence Summaries are contained in F.S. Regs., Part II. and the Staff Manual respectively. Title Pages will be prepared in manuscript.

| Place | Date | Hour | Summary of Events and Information | Remarks and references to Appendices |
|---|---|---|---|---|
| BOUZIN- COURT VIVE 67 | 22/8/16 | | In Bivouac. Weather Fine | SPO |
| " | 23/8/16 | 6AM | Battalion moved to subflat trenches in rear of DONNETS POST vise X13 A17. A Company 2nd Lt RATCLIFF in command moved to suffolk 1/1 BUCKS BATTN. then holding front line. Strength of Officers 743 O.R. | SPO |
| DONNETS POST | 24/8/16 | | Lieut J.H. COLLETT went to Hosptl. Major G.F. COLLETT took over command of the Battalion. 25th Division on left of Brigade line attached and took German trig line trench No. 2 of THIEPVAL Regt commander as added Military medal to the following for gallantry No. 2425 Pte TRINDER A.J. and No. 2169 Stretcher Bearer NESBITT B. | SPO |
| " | 25/8/16 | 6AM | Battalion relieved 1/1 BUCKS Battn. OXFORD and BUCKS L.I. in the front line. Disposition:— B.H.Q. Trench X8 A 05 A Coy (2nd Lt RATCLIFF) Front line X31 D 81 - X2 a 19 - X2a 28 — X2 A 59 Bomb stop. | SPO |

# WAR DIARY or INTELLIGENCE SUMMARY

1/5 GLOUCESTERSHIRE REGT

| Place | Date | Hour | Summary of Events and Information | Remarks and references to Appendices |
|---|---|---|---|---|
| Trenches R31D91 & X8A05 | 25/8/16 | | D Coy. (Lt H.P. SNOWDEN) In support near X2a16. C " (Lt E.W. WINTERBOTHAM) near X2 & 38. B " (Lt L.W. MOORE) near Batt. H.Q. Held in left 25th Division, 3rd WORCESTERSHIRE REGT. Right 114 OXFORD and BUCKS L.I. Consolidation carried on. Enemy artillery very active and continuous fire by our guns. Casualties to OR wounded. Fine. | 2 W.O. |
| " | 26/8/16 | | In trenches. Casualties 3 O.R. wounded. Weather fine. Coys. Commander inspected the Military Medal to the following:— No. 3034 Sgt PALMER F. and No. 2532 Pte FRY F.W. 2nd Lt C. BRIEN rejoined the Battalion and was posted to C company. 2nd Lt F.S. WOLLARD 1/5 Royal WARWICKSHIRE REGT joined and was posted to B company. | 2 W.O. |

# WAR DIARY
## INTELLIGENCE SUMMARY

1/5 GLOUCESTERSHIRE REGT

| Place | Date | Hour | Summary of Events and Information | Remarks and references to Appendices |
|---|---|---|---|---|
| Trenches | 27/12/16 | 7pm | The Battalion was ordered to attack trench from R32 c 50 – 33 c company and R company on right and B company in support in two lines across the open. A company 2 platoons advanced up communication trench X 2 a 19 – R 31 c 31. Platoons halted for 3 minutes. Right company entered trench in their own barrage and left company at the moment of lift but will have casualties. The company platoons will consolidate position in the communication and a long part of German held out between points 31 and 31 but were ultimately forced to retire across the open between our lines. Just a counter attack for all but 3. Several lay-outs were rounded and the trench was consolidated and 200 about 50 prisoners were taken and the enemy's dead count were collected about 200 killed and wounded. One machine gun was captured. | Two |

# WAR DIARY
## or
## INTELLIGENCE SUMMARY

*(Erase heading not required.)*

1/5 GLOUCESTERSHIRE REGT

| Place | Date | Hour | Summary of Events and Information | Remarks and references to Appendices |
|---|---|---|---|---|
| Trenches | 27/9/16 | | Our casualties :— Killed :- Lt. L.W.MOORE, Lt. G.W.WINTERBOTHAM, 2nd Lt A.APPERLY Missing :- 2nd Lt E. BRIEN Wounded :- 2nd Lt. N.H.GRAVES-SMITH, 2nd Lt. W.F.BIGGER O.R. Killed 14, Wounded 84, missing 10. The Colonel and Commander who reconnoitred the myself. The 1/4th Ox.& Bucks L.I. Royal Berks and 143 I Bde attached Batalion on our right. Prisoners belonged to 5th Grenadier Guards Regt = BND Batalion was relieved by a company of 4- LANCASHIRE FUSILIERS and move to bivouac N.W. of BOUZINCOURT. Capt. F.E.FRANCILLON and 2nd Lt. K.H. ROBERTSON joined for duty. | |
| | 28/9/16 | | The c.in.c. under authority awarded the D.C.M. to the following:- No 2571 Corporal TAYLOR M. | END |

# WAR DIARY
## or
## INTELLIGENCE SUMMARY

(Erase heading not required.) 1/5 GLOUCESTERSHIRE REGT

| Place | Date | Hour | Summary of Events and Information | Remarks and references to Appendices |
|---|---|---|---|---|
| BOUZINCOURT Bivouac | 29/8/16 | | Battalion marched to Bus-les-Artois Strength 13 Officers 592 O.R. | |
| BUS-LES-ARTOIS | 30/8/16 | | In billets. Heavy rain | |
| " | 31/8/16 | | Baths - Fine | |

S.J. Colchester
Major
COMDG. 1/5th BN. GLOUCESTER REGT.

145th Brigade.

48th Division.

---

1/5th BATTALION

GLOUCESTERSHIRE REGIMENT

SEPTEMBER 1 9 1 6

# INTELLIGENCE SUMMARY

(Erase heading not required.) 1/5 GLOUCESTERSHIRE REGT.

| Place | Date | Hour | Summary of Events and Information | Remarks and references to Appendices |
|---|---|---|---|---|
| BUS-LES-ARTOIS | 1/9/16 | | In billets. Company training. Some rain. | |
| " | 2/9/16 | | Maj. Willets C.O.C. 48th (S.M.) Division inspected the Battalion and presented medals. Fine. F.G.C.M. held on 3338 Pte PHILLIPS E. charge "Neglecting to obey an Order". Accused dealt with. F.G.C.M. sentence promulgated. No. 3946 Pte MANN R.E. Charge :- Showing cowardice in the presence of the enemy. Sentence - Death Commuted by General Commanding Reserve Army to 5 years penal servitude on account of youth. | |
| " | 3/9/16 | | Battalion Church Parade. C.O. presented medals as follows:-<br>No. 133 C.S.M. FAVILLE A. (awarded Long Service (previously) D.C.M.<br>- 1891 Pte MILLICHAP P.S. - M.M.<br>- 2433 - WHITE J.H.C. M.M.<br>- 2168 - HACKFORD W.A. M.M<br>- 2571 Qr. TAYLOR H. D.C.M | |

E.J. Collett LT. COLONEL,
COMDG. 1/5th BN. GLOUCESTER REGT.

# INTELLIGENCE SUMMARY

(Erase heading not required.) 1/5 GLOUCESTERSHIRE REGT

| Place | Date | Hour | Summary of Events and Information | Remarks and references to Appendices |
|---|---|---|---|---|
| BUS-LES-ARTOIS | 3/1/16 | | F.G.C.M. Sentence promulgated. No 3338 Pte PHILLIPS C. Coy. Neglecting to obey an order. Awarded detention. Sentence 28 days F.P. No. 1 | SPO |
| " | 4/1/16 | | In billets. Rain. | |
| " | 5/1/16 | | In billets. Rain all day. 1 Bucks Battn. and 1/4 Oxfords + Bucks took over line from 1/5 & Worcesters & next MAILLY MAILLET. Following officers joined and were posted to Coys:— 2nd Lts (Temp Capts) A.T.L. GREAR & Conf. & command W.S. CONGDON — A Coy H.G. WELCH B " N.G. LAKE A " R.F. RUBINSTEIN B — | SPO |

C.J. Gilbert
Lt. Colonel
Commdg. 1/5th Bn. Gloucester Regt.

## INTELLIGENCE SUMMARY

(Erase heading not required.) 1/5 GLOUCESTERSHIRE REGT

| Place | Date | Hour | Summary of Events and Information | Remarks and references to Appendices |
|---|---|---|---|---|
| BUS-LES-ARTOIS | 6/9/16 | | In billets. Fine | RWO |
| " | 7/9/16 | | — companies route marched. Capt (Temp. Major) G.F. COLLETT appointed to command the Battalion vice death of Lt. Col. ⟨A⟩ | RWO |
| " | 8/9/16 | 9 AM | Battalion relieved 1st Bucks Battn Oxford and Bucks L.I. in trenches opposite BEAUMONT HAMEL — WATLING STREET (Q4 b 5.6) to New BEAUMONT ROAD (Q4 d 4.4) Inf Ref Sheet 57 D S.E. 1:20,000 Edition 2D Dispositions:— A Company (Lt. SNOWDEN) Right front line (2d Lt. RATCLIFF) Left " C " (Capt. A.T.L. GREAR) Support at WHITE CITY (Q4 A 4.3) B " (Capt. F.F. FRANCILLON) Reserve — The Bowery Q 3 D 57 Battalion H.Q. & Dressing Station — WHITE CITY | RWO |

C.F. Collett Lt-Colonel,
Comdg. 1/5th Bn. GLOUCESTER REGT.

WAR DIARY

# INTELLIGENCE SUMMARY

(Erase heading not required.)

1/5 GLOUCESTERSHIRE REGT

Instructions regarding War Diaries and Intelligence Summaries are contained in F.S. Regs., Part II. and the Staff Manual respectively. Title Pages will be prepared in manuscript.

| Place | Date | Hour | Summary of Events and Information | Remarks and references to Appendices |
|---|---|---|---|---|
| Trenches nr BEAUMONT HAMEL | 8/9/16 | | Unit in Right sub section. Relieved 1/4 R BERKS on left - ROYAL FUSILIERS on right. Situation quiet. Casualties NIL | Nil |
| " | 9/9/16 | | Inter company relief. C relieved A and B - D. Fine. Casualties NIL | Nil |
| " | 10/9/16 | | Relieved by 13th ROYAL SUSSEX and marched to huts in BOIS-DE-WARNIMONT. Left P.E. FRANCILLON took over duties of 2nd in command. Lt E CONDER to command C Coy - Lt E.G. HAWKINS to command B Coy. Military Crosses awarded Capt L H P SNOWDEN - 2 Lt H P HARVEY - C.S.M. TIBBLES W.S. A.C.M. Draft 13 O.R. — No 3028 Pte LANE J.D. Fine casualties NIL | Nil |
| BOIS DE WARNIMONT | 11/9/16 | 2 PM | Brigade moved to BEAUVAL via MARIEUX and BEAUQUESNE | Nil |
| BEAUVAL | 12/9/16 | | In billets. Fine. Lt P.T. BRETHERTON arrived Lt Colm Stanfell arrived and was posted to A Coy. Draft of 29 O.R. 20 Officers and 607 O.R. | Nil |
| " | 13/9/16 | | In billets. Rain | |

C P Christie Lt Colonel

# INTELLIGENCE SUMMARY

*(Erase heading not required.)*

| Place | Date | Hour | Summary of Events and Information | Remarks and references to Appendices |
|---|---|---|---|---|
| BEAUVAL | 14 Sept 16 | | In Billets. Fine. A draft of 14 O.R. arrived with 7 Officers of the Highland Light Infantry were posted to Coys as follows:- <br> 2.Lt A.M. BRIGGS to A Coy <br> 2Lt W.H. IRWIN to A Coy <br> 2Lt W. WALKER to B. Coy <br> 2Lt H.W. STEELE to C Coy <br> 2Lt W.S. WILSON to D. Coy <br> 2Lt C. LOGAN to D. Coy <br> 2Lt I.M. HENRY to D Coy | 9.11 |
| BEAUVAL | 15 Sept | | In Billets. Fine. "B" practised a field exercise. 2Lt G.E. RATCLIFFE, 2Lt H.W. CRUICKSHANK went on special leave. | G.H. G.N. |
| BEAUVAL | 16 Sept | | "B" paraded for Bn Training. Fine. | |
| BEAUVAL | 17 Sept | | In Billets. Fine. "B" practised a field exercise. Church Parade. | |
| BEAUVAL to VACQUERIE & GORGES | 18 Sept | | "B" moved with the 115 Infy. Bde to VACQUERIE via CANDAS, FIENVILLERS. <br> BERNAVILLE. "A" & C Coys & Hdqrs billetted in VACQUERIE, Two Coys billetted in GORGES. Very hot march. | G.H. |

C.D. Callender

## INTELLIGENCE SUMMARY

*(Erase heading not required.)*

Instructions regarding War Diaries and Intelligence Summaries are contained in F. S. Regs., Part II. and the Staff Manual respectively. Title Pages will be prepared in manuscript.

| Place | Date | Hour | Summary of Events and Information | Remarks and references to Appendices |
|---|---|---|---|---|
| VACQUERIE | 19 Sept | | Coys paraded from 9am – 11am, 2.30 – 4.30pm for training | G.H. |
| GORGES | | | Lt FOOTE & 20 O.R.s went on leave. 2 Lt H. McL. MILLER 7 Highland Light Infantry reported for duty & was posted to A Coy | |
| VACQUERIE GORGES | 20 Sept | | In Billets Wet. | |
| VACQUERIE GORGES | 21 Sept | | In billets. Showery. Bn practised Field Training. Capt S.H. NADEN (13th Gloucestershire Regt) arrived for duty & took over command of A Coy | G.H. |
| VACQUERIE GORGES | 22 Sept | | In billets Fine. All men not inoculated within the last six months ordered to be inoculated. Coy Training | G.H. |
| VACQUERIE GORGES | 23 Sept | | In billets. Fine. Routine work. Training of Junior N.C.O's practised | G.H. |
| VACQUERIE GORGES | 24 Sept | | In billets. Fine. Church Parade. 42 O.R's arrived as reinforcements. | G.H. |

C.J. Collett
LT. COLONEL
COMDG. 1/5th BN. GLOUCESTER REGT.

Instructions regarding War Diaries and Intelligence Summaries are contained in F.S. Regs., Part II. and the Staff Manual respectively. Title Pages will be prepared in manuscript.

# INTELLIGENCE SUMMARY

*(Erase heading not required.)*

| Place | Date | Hour | Summary of Events and Information | Remarks and references to Appendices |
|---|---|---|---|---|
| VACQUERIE GORGES | 25 Sept. | | In billets. Fine. Coy Training. Lt. H.P. SNOWDEN gazetted temp. Capt. whilst commanding a Coy. 23.8.16. | G.H. |
| VACQUERIE GORGES | 26 Sept. | | In Billets. Wet. 74 O.R.s arrived from the 3rd GLOUCESTER REGT. as reinforcement. | G.H. |
| VACQUERIE GORGES | 27 Sept. | | In Billets. Showery. Coy Training. | G.H. |
| VACQUERIE GORGES | 28 Sept. | | In Billets. Showery. In the afternoon the G.O.C. 145. 7 Bde conducted a repeated staff ride. | G.H. |
| VACQUERIE GORGES | 29 Sept. | | Bn moved to HUMBERCOURT via DOULLENS - GROUCHES - LUCHEUX. a wet march. | G.H. |
| HUMBERCOURT | 30 Sept. | | In Billets. Fine. Bn Strength; Effective Strength 32 Offs 885 O.Rs. Ration Strength 26 Offs 806 O.Rs. | G.H. |

C. F. Colsey
LT.-COLONEL,
COMDG. 1/5th BN. GLOUCESTER REGT.

145th Brigade.
48th Division.
----------

1/5th BATTALION

GLOUCESTERSHIRE REGIMENT

OCTOBER 1916

# INTELLIGENCE SUMMARY

*(Erase heading not required.)*

1/5 Gloucestershire Regt

Vol 20

| Place | Date | Hour | Summary of Events and Information | Remarks and references to Appendices |
|---|---|---|---|---|
| HUMBERCOURT | 1.X.16 | | Billets. Fine. Battalion paraded for divine Service. | |
| WARLINCOURT | | at 11.30.a.m. the B^n moved to WARLINCOURT. Billets were very crowded + consisted of summer huts. | G.N. |
| WARLINCOURT | 2.X.16 | | In billets. Wet. Routine. | G.N. |
| WARLINCOURT | 3.X.16 | | In billets. Wet. Routine + letters in huts. Draft of 12 O.R. arrived | G.N. |
| WARLINCOURT | 4.X.16. | | In billets. Wet. Routine + letters in huts. A draft of 4 O.R. arrived | G.N. |
| WARLINCOURT | 5.X.16. | | In billets. Fine. The 145 T Bde relieved the 143 T Bde in trenches K.10.B.07 | G.N. |
| | 6. | | K 3 d 90.05. Dispositions 1/1 Bucks B^n in trenches. Bde H.Q. of 1/4 R.Berks Shire Regt in SOUASTRE. 1/4 O.B.L.I + 1/5 Gloucestershire Regt remained in WARLINCOURT. | G.N. |
| WARLINCOURT | 6.10.16 | | In billets. Wet. Routine. 2 Lt A.T. DEATON arrived + was posted to C Co. | G.N. |
| NENU | 7.10.16 | | B^n moved to Huts in NENU via PAS. Lut 2Lt HOWARD G.G.L. + WHITE reported for duty. | G.N. |
| WARLINCOURT | 8.10.15 | | B^n returned to huts in WARLINCOURT via PAS. Showing. 2Lt F.S. GARLAND (A.Co) + 2 Lt A.R. STANLEY (C. Co.) All the above officers arrived from the 4th R.B. Glouc Regt. | G.N. |
| WARLINCOURT | 9.10.16 | | B^n returned to NENU, taking over billets from the BUCKS B^n. The Commander 7 Officers + Company Commanders went up to reconnoitre trenches at KABROTEUX | G.N. |

G.J.C___
LT-COLONEL
1/5th BN. GLOUCESTER REGT.

# INTELLIGENCE SUMMARY

1/5 Gloucestershire Regt

| Place | Date | Hour | Summary of Events and Information | Remarks and references to Appendices |
|---|---|---|---|---|
| HENU | 10.4.16 | | In billets. Fine. Company training | G.H. |
| HENU | 11.4.16 | | In billets. hot. 2 O.R. reinforcements arrived | G.H. |
| HENU | 12.4.16 | | In billets. hot. Capt A.S. HADEN left to join 2/2 Aux Bn West YORKS Regt | G.H. |
| HENU | 13.4.16 | | In billets. Fine. Coy training. | G.H. |
| HENU / HEBUTERNE | 14.4.16 | | Bn took over trenches in HEBUTERNE relieving the 1/4 R.BERKS. from K4.C.11. to K10.6.6.4. Map Ref 57 D N.E. | G.H. |
| | | | Dispositions. C Coy on the left. Lt CONDER B.Hq. K9.6.1.<br>D Coy on the right Capt SNOWDEN<br>B Coy in support in the Orchard - Cross St.<br>A Coy in Reserve in the Keep - B. FARM | |
| | | | 2 Lt N.G. KARR & 2nd Lt. D. WHITE reconnoitred the enemy's wire<br>Fairly quiet. Casualties. 2 O.R. C Coy wounded (one of which slightly) | |
| HEBUTERNE | 15.4.16 | | Into Coy Relief. B Coy relieved C Coy. A Coy relieved D Coy.<br>2 Lt R.F. ROBINSTEIN & Lt W.N. IRWIN reconnoitred the enemy's wire<br>Very quiet. A little shelling by the 2 Hedge Casualties 2 O.R. A Coy wounded<br>Capt SNOWDEN left for 3rd Army School of Instruction AUXI-LA-CHATEAU<br>2nd Lt F. HARVEY reported from L.G. Course at ETAPLES. Major H. WATHEN Capt F.R. ANGLILON to COURT joined the Bn & became second in Command | G.H. |

E.J. Collett Lt. Colonel
1/5th Bn. GLOUCESTER REGT.

# INTELLIGENCE SUMMARY
## 1/5 Gloucester Regt
*(Erase heading not required.)*

| Place | Date | Hour | Summary of Events and Information | Remarks and references to Appendices |
|---|---|---|---|---|
| HERBUTERNE / HENU | 16.x.16 | | Commenced D. Coy. E.O.R. arrival | G.A |
| HENU | 17.x.16 | | Bn relieved by 1/6 WORCESTER Regt marched to huts in HENU | G.A |
| HENU | 18.x.16 | | In huts. Showery. Coy Routine Baths etc | G.A |
| HENU | 19.x.16 | | In huts. Showery. Coy Training. Baths. Working Parties | JWC |
| WARLINCOURT | | | Bn moved to huts in WARLINCOURT via PAS. Wet | JWC |
| WARLINCOURT | 20.x.16 | | Bn moved via COUTERELLE and COULLEMONT to HUMBERCOURT. FINE | JWC |
| HUMBERCOURT | 21.x.16 | | In huts. Fine. A & B coys went for tactical exercise under Comdg. Offr to LA FOLIE FARM. 2nd LT WILSON rejoined | |
| HUMBERCOURT | | | B & D similar exercise under MAJOR COURT at LA BELLEVUE | Jhre |
| | | | Cattelin from hospital | JWC |
| HUMBERCOURT / BEAUVAL | 22.x.16 | | Batn marched via LUCHEUX — DOULLENS to BEAUVAL arriving 2.30 p.m. Fine | |
| BEAUVAL / TALMAS | 23/10/16 | 2 P.M | Batn marched to BEHENCOURT. Fine | 3 PLD |
| TALMAS / BEHENCOURT | 24/10/16 | 8.30 AM | Batn marched to BEHENCOURT via RUBEMPRE — MOLLIENS and BEAUCOURT | 3 PLD |

G J Colt
LT COLONEL
1/5 REGT

**INTELLIGENCE SUMMARY**

*(Erase heading not required.)* 1/5 GLOSTER REGT

Instructions regarding War Diaries and Intelligence Summaries are contained in F. S. Regs., Part II. and the Staff Manual respectively. Title Pages will be prepared in manuscript.

| Place | Date | Hour | Summary of Events and Information | Remarks and references to Appendices |
|---|---|---|---|---|
| BEHENCOURT | 25/10/16 | | On billets. Fine. Lt. Col. J.R. WINTERBOTTAM rejoined. Working party, 1 Officer and 100 O.R. of company left for ALLONVILLE | |
| " | 26/10/16 | | Wet. Lt. E.T. CORNISH joined from 4th Reserve Battn and was posted to D Coy. 2nd Lt N. STEEL to A Coy C Coy | |
| " | 27/10/16 | | In billets. Very wet. 2nd Lt A.H. EDMONDS joined from 4th Reserve Battn and was posted to C company | |
| " | 28/10/16 | | Fairly fine | |
| " | 29/10/16 | | 1 Officer and 50 O.R. of A company went to MILLENCOURT to take over billets and found covering party. | |
| " | 30/10/16 | | Heavy rain. Major COURT and 8 other officers reconnoitred line to MARTINPUICH | |
| " | 31/10/16 | | Brigade marched to MILLENCOURT | |

C.T. Clutterbuck
LT-COLONEL
COMDG 1/5th BN GLOUCESTER REGT.

145th Brigade.

48th Division.

-----

1/5th BATTALION

GLOUCESTERSHIRE REGIMENT

NOVEMBER 1 9 1 6

# WAR DIARY or INTELLIGENCE SUMMARY

Army Form C. 2118.

1/5 Gloucestershire Regt

Map Ref. France 57D. S.E. & N.E.

1 Nov. 1916.

| Place | Date | Hour | Summary of Events and Information | Remarks and references to Appendices |
|---|---|---|---|---|
| CONTALMAISON | 1.XI.16 | | Bn moved up to Dingle Camp at X 27 a 8.2, near laying wood between FRICOURT & CONTALMAISON. Lt Col COLLETT, RW GF NKLM to hospital. Major N. WATKIN Courtdick Command. | GN |
| Trenches N.W. of LE SARS | 2.XI.16 | | Bn relieved 11 Argyll & Sutherland Highlanders (15th Div.) in front line trenches N.W. of LE SARS. M15 a 16.4 M 16 a. Unit on left Canadian Infantry. Unit on right 8th Worc. 144 I Bde. Dispositions: Bn H.Q. 26 Avenue M27 a 6.7. A.Coy (Lt G.E. RATCLIFFE) 2 Platoons Scotland Trench M10 a 5.0 – M15 6 6 8. 2 Platoons Chalk Trench M16 A 2.7 – M15 6 66. B Coy (2t BINGHAM-NKKK) 1/2 Platoon Scotland Trench M15 6 6 8. to End of Sap M15 6 2.9. with post in Chalk Pit. 1/2 Platoon Ravine Trench M15 A 9 8 6 M15 a 5 6. 3 Platoons in Trench joining Scotland Trench & Ravine Trench M15 6 4.7 – M15 a 6.7. | GN |

Army Form C. 2118.

# WAR DIARY
## or
## INTELLIGENCE SUMMARY
(Erase heading not required.)

Maj. Ry 57 D.S.F. Fd. G.R.   1/5 Gloucestershire Regt

| Place | Date | Hour | Summary of Events and Information | Remarks and references to Appendices |
|---|---|---|---|---|
| Trenches N.W. LE SARS. | 2.xi.16 | | C. Coy. (Lt. K.E. CONDER) less 1 off & 100 O.R. away on working party. in reserve in Trench O.G.1 M.21.b.9.1 | G.A |
| LE SARS | 3.xi.16 | | D. Coy (Capt F.E. FRANCILLON) In support near junction of O.G.1. & Gilbert Alley M/15 c.7.5. Weather Fine Casualties nil | G.A |
| LE SARS | 4.xi.16 | | In trenches. Wet. Casualties 2 killed 8 O.R wounded. O.R | G.A |
| M.27.a.16. MARTIN PUICH | 5.xi.16 | | Relieved by 1/4 Oxford & Bucks L.I. & moved into support in 26 Avenue about. M.27.A.1.6. Casualties 8 O.R. 3 killed 8 wounded Relieved by 1/1 BUCKS B". O.B.K.L.I. & moved to MARTIN PUICH in dug outs Fine. Casualties Nil | G.A |
| MARTIN PUICH | 6.xi.16 | | Relieved by 1/4 R. BERKSHIRE Regt. moved to Dingle Camp X.27.a.3.2. Large night working on Gilbert alley. Casualties 2 wounded | G.A |
| X.27.a.8.2 | 7.xi.16 | | In Camp. Rain. Strength. 31 off 477 O.R. | G.A |

# WAR DIARY
## INTELLIGENCE SUMMARY

Army Form C. 2118.

Map Ref France 57D  1/5 Gloucestershire Regt

| Place | Date | Hour | Summary of Events and Information | Remarks and references to Appendices |
|---|---|---|---|---|
| X27a 8.2 | 8.xi.16 | | In Camp. Lot Lt C.S. NASON rejoined | GN |
| Y27a. 8.2 | 9.xi.16 | | In camp. wet. | GN |
| Shellwood X22c 2.7 | 10.xi.16 | | Moved to Shellu Wood Camp taking over from 1/8 R. Warwick Regt | GN |
| | | | 1951 Pte ELLIOT N Accidentally wounded. Fine. | |
| SHELTER WOOD | 11.xi.16 | | In Shellu Wood Camp. Fine | GB |
| SHELTER Wd. | 12.11.16 | | In camp wet. | Two |
| " | 13/11/16 | | In camp wet. | Two |
| " | 14/11/16 | 4 PM | Moved to trenches and relieved 6th R. WARWICKS. | |
|   |   |   | Dispositions:- |   |
|   |   |   | Battn. H.Q. 26th Avenue M27 a 67 |   |
|   |   |   | A Coy. (Lt G.E. RATCLIFF) in support in Sunken Road M16 c 42 |   |
|   |   |   | B - (Lt E.S. MASON) - reserve TANGLE ALLEY M 22 a 53 |   |
|   |   |   | C - (Lt E. CONDER) right front M16 D 76 to M16 B12 |   |
|   |   |   | D - (Capt F.E. FRANCILLON) left front M16 B13 to M16 A59 | Two |

Army Form C. 2118.

# WAR DIARY
## or
## INTELLIGENCE SUMMARY

*(Erase heading not required.)*

1/5 GLOSTER REGT

| Place | Date | Hour | Summary of Events and Information | Remarks and references to Appendices |
|---|---|---|---|---|
| Trenches | 14/11/16 | | Casualties 2 O.R. wounded 50 sent 31 off & 62 O.R. | nil |
| LE SARS | | | 2 Lts BOLLEID joined for duty. Continuous Heavy Fire | |
| | 15/11/16 | | Heavy Shelling. Casualties 2 O.R. killed | nil |
| | 16/11/16 | 9pm | Relieved C & A R. BERKS and moved — suffered at MARTINPUICH. B Coy did not move. A & D Coys in Grenadier PRO? TRENCH H53B | |
| | | | 2nd Lt HILL joined for duty | |
| MARTINPUICH | 17/11/16 | | Whole battalion out on working party 2 [?] ampt/O | nil |
| | 18/11/16 | | Relieved 4 R. BERKS in same line as on 14/11/16. Very mild Summer | |
| | | | A Coy right front | |
| | | | B — Left — | |
| | | | C — Support in Sunken Road | |
| | | | D — Reserve | |
| | | | B Coy heavily shelled during relief. Casualties 2/Lt HOWARD and | |
| | | | 2/Lt HILLER wounded 1 O.R. 1 killed 2 missing 26 wounded | |

Army Form C. 2118.

# WAR DIARY
## or
## INTELLIGENCE SUMMARY

*(Erase heading not required.)*

1/5 GLOSTER REGT

| Place | Date | Hour | Summary of Events and Information | Remarks and references to Appendices |
|---|---|---|---|---|
| Trenches LE SARS | 19/11/16 | | In General. W.O. Casualties O.R. 5 killed, 1 wounded. Lt. HAWKING went on leave. | |
| " | 20/11/16 | | Relieved by 8th WORCESTER Regt. and Moved to MIDDLE WOOD Ref X12 d44 (Sheet 57D S.E. 1:20,000) One company in RIDGE Trench. Very uncomfortable and wet. Casualties 10 O.R. 1 died of wounds | O.C. |
| MIDDLE WOOD CAMP | 21/11/16 | | On amn. Strength 32 Off. 651 O.R. | " |
| " | 22/11/16 | | Pte BOWNES shot by own gunner revolver and died of wounds | 3 P.U. |
| " | 23/11/16 | | In camp. Working party Casualties O.R. 1 died of wounds and 5 wounded | 3 P.U. |

**Army Form C. 2118.**

# WAR DIARY
## or
## INTELLIGENCE SUMMARY
1/5 GLOSTER REGT

*(Erase heading not required.)*

| Place | Date | Hour | Summary of Events and Information | Remarks and references to Appendices |
|---|---|---|---|---|
| MIDDLE WOOD CAMP | 24/11/16 | | Rain. Washing puttees | JWJ |
| | 25/11/16 | | In camp. Rain | JWJ |
| | 26/11/16 | | Moved to SCOTTS REDOUBT SOUTH (X 21 B 6 2) (taking over from 1/1 BUCKS BATTN. Capt H R SNOWDEN went on leave. | JWJ |
| | 27/11/16 | | In camp. Strength 26 Off 633 O.R. Fine | JWJ |
| | 28/11/16 | | In camp. Fine | BWJ |
| | 29/11/16 | | SCOTTS REDOUBT CAMP SOUTH. 10.30am Brigadier General WATT. Moved to trenches and relieved 1/4 OXFORDS + BUCKS Lt. in trenches Right Battalion area. Disposition. Bakn. H.Q. 26 lh Avenue. M24 A 67. C Coy (Lt. Condie's) Right front M11 & B 54 to M15 & B 56. D Coy (Capt FRAMPTION) left front M15 B 57 to N 15 A 56. B Coy (Lt MASON) Left Support in trenches M 15 B 58 D 31 to D 12. A Coy (2nd Lt BRETHER TON) Right Support OG 1. about M 22 A 12. 2nd lt MASON wounded slight. 1 O.R. wounded. Strength 26 Officers 623 O.R. | SJC |
| | 30/11/16 | | In trenches. Enemy quiet. Weather fine fog & frost. Casualties 2 OR wounded. | SJC |

E J Commick
Captain
1/5th Glos. Regt.
Adjutant
1/5th Glos. Regt.

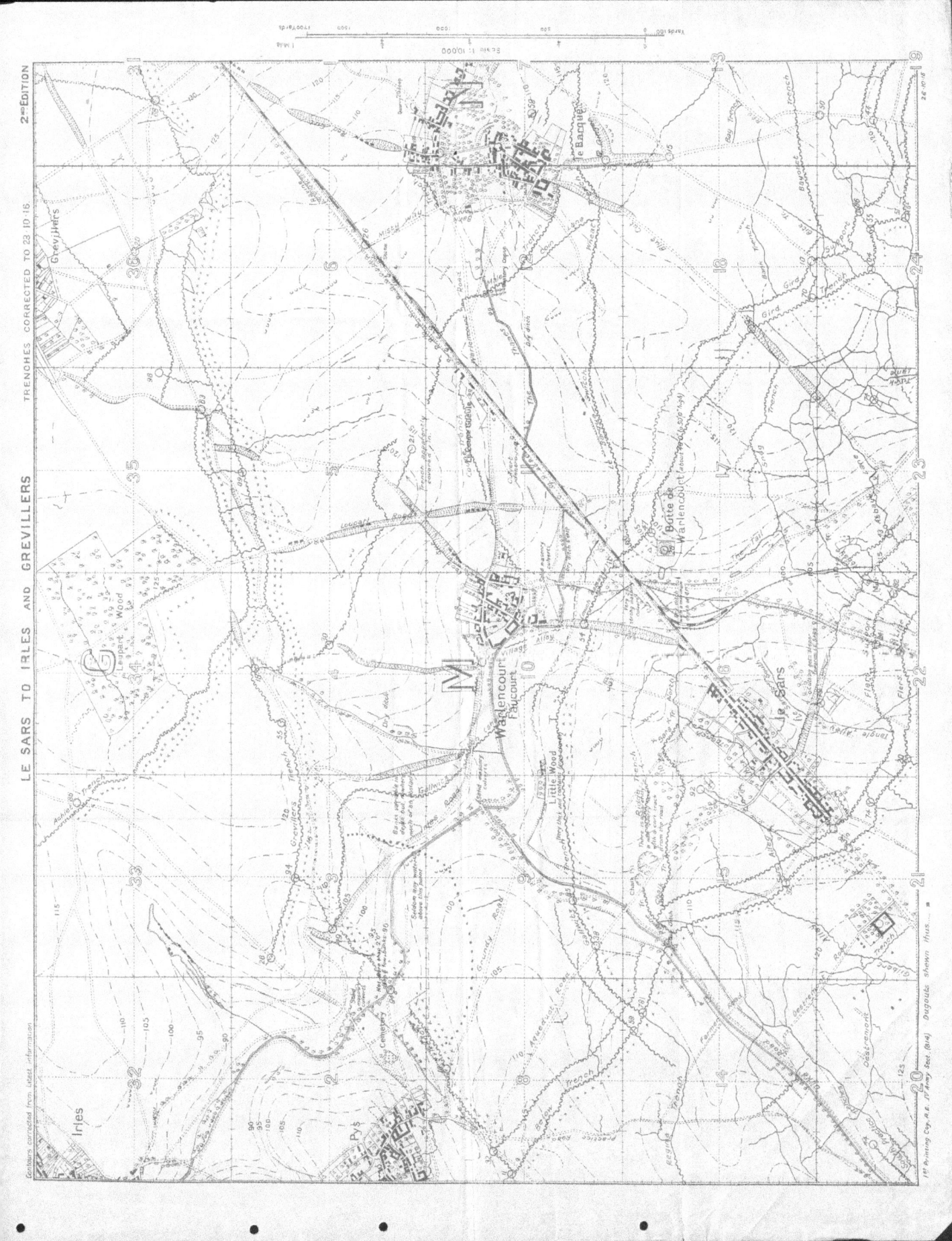

145th Brigade.

48th Division.

--------

1/5th BATTALION


GLOUCESTERSHIRE REGIMENT


DECEMBER 1 9 1 6

# WAR DIARY
## or
## INTELLIGENCE SUMMARY

(Erase heading not required.) 1/5 GLOUCESTERSHIRE Regt

| Place | Date | Hour | Summary of Events and Information | Remarks and references to Appendices |
|---|---|---|---|---|
| Trenches LE SARS | 1/12/16 | | Considerable shelling by enemy. Casualties 2 O.R. killed 3 wounded. 1 prisoner of 64th R.I.R taken by C company. Interchange company relief. B & D and A & C. | |
| " | 2/12/16 | | Heavily shelled in front. Casualties 4 killed 5 wounded all O.R. Major H.S.G. SCHOMBERG EAST SURREY REGT attached 1/4 OXFORD & BUCKS L.I. temporarily assumed command of Battalion. | |
| " | 3/12/16 | 10 P.M. | Relieved by 1/1 BUCKS BATTN. OXFORDS and BUCKS L.I. and moved to SHELTER WOOD CAMP NORTH. Casualties 1 killed 2 wounded. O.R. | |
| SHELTER WOOD CAMP North | 4/12/16 | | In camp. Rain | |
| " | 5/12/16 | | Rain | |

# WAR DIARY
## or
## INTELLIGENCE SUMMARY

*(Erase heading not required.)*

1/5 GLOSTER REGT

| Place | Date | Hour | Summary of Events and Information | Remarks and references to Appendices |
|---|---|---|---|---|
| SHELTER WOOD CAMP North | 6/12/16 | | In camp | RW |
| " | 7/12/16 | | In camp | RW |
| " | 8/12/16 | | Moved to MIDDLE WOOD CAMP relieved 1/4 OXFORD & BUCKS L.I. Two companies forward in RIDGE TRENCH and near BAZENTIN WOOD | RW |
| MIDDLE WOOD CAMP | 9/12/16 | | In camp | RW |
| " | 10/12/16 | | rain. Major L.G. PARKINSON 1/4 GLOSTER Regt assumed duties of 2nd in command. | RW |
| " | 11/12/16 | | In camp & wet | RW |

# WAR DIARY
## INTELLIGENCE SUMMARY

*(Erase heading not required.)*

1/5 GLOSTER REGT

| Place | Date | Hour | Summary of Events and Information | Remarks and references to Appendices |
|---|---|---|---|---|
| MIDDLE WOOD CAMP | 12/12/16 | | Battn moved to SCOTTS REDOUBT CAMP SOUTH. Rain and snow. | two |
| SCOTTS REDOUBT CAMP SOUTH | 13/12/16 | 3PM | Battalion moved to trenches near LE SARS and relieved 1/4 OXFORD and BUCKS L.I. on left of Divisional line. Dispositions:— Battn H.Q. 26th Avenue H.27.A.67 C Coy (2/LT A.T.L. GREAR) Right front 116 A 58 & M.15 B 57 D Coy (LT. CORNISH) Left front M.15 B 57 & M.15 A 56 A Coy (Capt. SNOWDEN) Right support O.G.1 about M.22 A 12 B Coy (2nd LT.  BINGHAM-HALL) Left support O.G.1 about M.15 D 51 (144 w. D.) Weather very cold the WORCESTERS Relieved by Division. Fine. Casualties 1 OR wounded | Ref. 57 & SW 1:20,000<br><br>two |

# WAR DIARY
## or
## INTELLIGENCE SUMMARY

*(Erase heading not required.)*

1/5 GLOSTER REGT

Instructions regarding War Diaries and Intelligence Summaries are contained in F.S. Regs., Part II. and the Staff Manual respectively. Title Pages will be prepared in manuscript.

| Place | Date | Hour | Summary of Events and Information | Remarks and references to Appendices |
|---|---|---|---|---|
| LE SARS Trenches | 14/12/16 | | Inter-company relief. A Coy relieved C and B relieved D Casualties. 1 O.R. wounded. Fine | nil |
| - | 15/12/16 | | Battalion were relieved by 6/7 R.SCOTTS FUSILIERS 15th Div and marched to VILLA CAMP XIIC63. 2nd LT BRETHERTON and 1 O.R. wounded Casualties | Two |
| VILLA CAMP | 16/12/16 | 10 AM | Battalion moved to BECOURT CAMP 'A' X26 c/F 2A. Nissen Huts to S.E. BECOURTS ERG rejoined 1/4 OXFORD & BUCKS L.I. Major L.G. Fine & cold. Major S PARKINSON assumed command of the Battalion | nil nil |
| BECOURT CAMP A | 17/12/16 | | In camp. Rain. Major H WATHEN COURT proceeded to Bn.H.Q to act as A.P.M. | nil |
| " | 18/12/16 | | In camp. Snow. Large working parties | nil |
| " | 19/12/16 | | In camp. Working parties | nil |
| " | 20/12/16 | | In camp. Rain | nil |

# WAR DIARY
## INTELLIGENCE SUMMARY

*(Erase heading not required.)* 1/5 GLOSTER REGT

| Place | Date | Hour | Summary of Events and Information | Remarks and references to Appendices |
|---|---|---|---|---|
| BECOURT CAMP A | 21/12/16 | | In camp. Rain. Bathing parties | |
| " | 22/12/16 | | In camp. Working parties | |
| " | 23/12/16 | | In camp. Draft of 280 O.R. joined | |
| " | 24/12/16 | | In camp. Working parties | |
| " | 25/12/16 | | Xmas Day. Cold and strong wind. Geese and plum pudding eaten at mid-day | |
| " | 26/12/16 | | In camp. Fine at first, rain later | |
| " | 27/12/16 | | In camp. Rain | |

# WAR DIARY
## or
## INTELLIGENCE SUMMARY

(Erase heading not required.)   1/5 GLOSTER Regt

| Place | Date | Hour | Summary of Events and Information | Remarks and references to Appendices |
|---|---|---|---|---|
| RECOURT CAMP A. | 28/12/16 | | Battalion moved with the Brigade to BRESLE via ALBERT and occupied huts vacated by 5th NORTHUMBERLAND FUSILIERS | |
| BRESLE | 29/12/16 | | Fatigues & cleaning up | |
| " | 30/12/16 | | Training. Major H. WATHEN COURT went to England | |
| " | 31/12/16 | | Church Parade. Strength 18 Officers 713 O.R. (104 O.R. away on musketry course | |

W Watkinson
Major
Comdg 1/5 Glos Regt

1/5th Bn Gloucestershire Regiment Vol 23

War Diary

Vol XXII

1st Jan 1917 to 31st Jan 1917

January 1917

Army Form C. 2118.

# WAR DIARY
## INTELLIGENCE SUMMARY
*(Erase heading not required.)*

Vol. XXII        1/5 GLOUCESTERSHIRE Reg.

Instructions regarding War Diaries and Intelligence Summaries are contained in F.S. Regs., Part II. and the Staff Manual respectively. Title Pages will be prepared in manuscript.

| Place | Date | Hour | Summary of Events and Information | Remarks and references to Appendices |
|---|---|---|---|---|
| BRESLE | 1/1/17 | | Training. Weather wet. | End |
| " | 2/1/17 | | Training. Lt Col. A.B. SKINNER 5th Cavalry assumed command of the Battalion | End |
| " | 3/1/17 | | do. Weather wet | End |
| " | 4/1/17 | | do and Baths. Wet | End |
| " | 5/1/17 | | Training. Honours. Major L.G. PARKINSON and Capt L.R.C. SUMNER Military Cross. 238 - (C.Q.M.S. HUXFORD J. - D.C.M. mentioned in Despatches - { Lt. Col. G.F. COLLETT  A.B. SKINNER | End |
| " | 6/1/17 | | Brigade inspected by Lt. Gen. Sir W.P. PULTENEY K.C.B. commanding III d Corps. Weather wet. | End |
| " | 7/1/17 | | Inspection of Billets by C.O. | End |

Army Form C. 2118.

# WAR DIARY
## or
## INTELLIGENCE SUMMARY
*(Erase heading not required.)*

Vol. XXII    1/5 GLOSTER REGT

| Place | Date | Hour | Summary of Events and Information | Remarks and references to Appendices |
|---|---|---|---|---|
| BRESLE | 8/1/17 | | C.O. Inspected companies. Rain. Transport Brigaded moved off to new area near OISEMONT | |
| " | 9/1/17 | 3.10 AM | Battalion moved to HEILLY and entrained for OISEMONT. | |
| | | 12 noon | reached OISEMONT detrained and marched to HERELESSART about 4 miles. Fine some snow. Good billets for all ranks. | |
| | | | Capt R.N.F. COOKE reported and took over | |
| HERELESSART | 10/1/17 | | Training was resumed. Capt R.N.F. COOKE resumed command of B company | |
| " | 11/1/17 | | Training. Col. Trevor. | |
| " | 12/1/17 | | Sports | |
| " | 13/1/17 | | Church Parade. Company training. | |
| " | 14/1/17 | | Church Parade in Factory. Sports. 2 m't B/M ARMSTRONG joined the Batt. for duty | |
| " | 15/1/17 | | Brigade Transport inspected by O.C. 145th Inf Bde. Horses. Battn headrs 0-1 in Farmhouse. Lecture by 1/4 R.BERKS. Lecture by C.O. | |

2449 Wt. W14957/M90 750,000 1/16 J.B.C. & A. Forms/C.2118/12.

Army Form C. 2118.

# WAR DIARY
## or
## INTELLIGENCE SUMMARY

(Erase heading not required.)

Vol XII

| Place | Date | Hour | Summary of Events and Information | Remarks and references to Appendices |
|---|---|---|---|---|
| MERELESSART | 16.1.17 | | Co Training. Kit Inspection. G.O.C. Division visited Batt. in Co Training Ground | N/A |
| " | 17.1.17 | | Co Training in Willet Grnd. Night Scheme for Scouts | N/A |
| " | 18.1.17 | | Co Training in Willet Grnd. Battalion Orderly | N/A |
| " | 19.1.17 | | Co Training. Practice in Attack Scheme | N/A |
| " | 20.1.17 | | Co Training. Do. Football match at Neuville, 15th Glos. R. v. 11 Arg & Batt. Brewing Tournament at Dieumont. | N/A |
| " | 21.1.17 | | Inter-Battalion Cross Country Run. | N/A |
| " | 22.1.17 | | Brigade Attack Scheme near Hallencourt. | N/A |
| " | 23.1.17 | | Divisional Tactical Scheme for Officers conducted by G.O.C. Division. Lecture by C.O. | N/A |
| " | 24.1.17 | | Brigade Attack Scheme near Hallencourt with aeroplane contact patrol. Batt. Concert | N/A |
| " | 25.1.17 | | Co Training. | N/A |
| " | 26.1.17 | | Co Training. Lecture by C.O. | N/A |
| " | 27.1.17 | | Battalion Attack Scheme. | N/A |
| " | 28.1.17 | | Church Parade | N/A |

Army Form C. 2118.

# WAR DIARY
## or
## INTELLIGENCE SUMMARY

(Erase heading not required.)

Vol XLII

| Place | Date | Hour | Summary of Events and Information | Remarks and references to Appendices |
|---|---|---|---|---|
| MERELESSART | 29.1.17 | 5 A.M. | Battalion moved to AIRAINES and entrained for CERISY GAILLY. | |
| | | 2.15 p.m. | Reached CERISY, detrained + marched to HAMEL. Occupied billets previously occupied by French. C.O. inspected billets. Fine; severe frost. | D.V.S |
| HAMEL | 30.1.17 | | Route march. | |
| | 31.1.17 | | Co. training. Inspection of Officers by Brigadier in bombing trench Fuzes. Revolver shooting by A + B Co. Officers + Lewis Gunners. | D.V.S |

A.B. Skinner
LT.-COLONEL,
COMDG. 1/5th BN. GLOUCESTER REGT.

CONFIDENTIAL

War Diary

of

1/5th Battalion Gloucestershire Regiment

From February 1st 1917 to February 28th 1917.

Army Form C. 2118.

# WAR DIARY
## or
## INTELLIGENCE SUMMARY
*(Erase heading not required.)*

Vol XXIII

| Place | Date | Hour | Summary of Events and Information | Remarks and references to Appendices |
|---|---|---|---|---|
| HAMEL | 1/2/17 | | Route march. Training from 11.30 – 12.30 | ditto |
| HAMEL | 2/2/17 | | Coy training 10.30 a.m. – 12.30 a.m. Route march 7.30 – 10.30 | ditto |
| | 3.2.17 | | Huns (6 huts) taken over from French Army. Very wet – frosty nearly | ditto |
| MARLY | 4.2.17 | | Church parade. Frosty weather. Snow | ditto |
| MARLY | 5.2.17 | | Coy Training | ditto |
| MARLY | 6.2.17 | | Coy Training. Physical drill + bayonet fighting class for N.C.O.s + officers | ditto |
| MARLY | 7.2.17 | | Took over from 1/7 WORCESTERS marching via CAPPY, HERBECOURT, | ditto |
| FLAUCOURT (BOYAU VAUDT) | | | | |
| SUPPORT Trenches S of BIACHES (LA MAISONETTE) | 8.2.17 | | Very frosty weather. Took over from the 1/7 WORCESTERS. Trenches very poor condition & whole except for points picketed by chunks of frozen earth – thrown down & even for men to walk if that rests in our Ghq. | ditto |
| 2nd Lines Trenches | 9.2.17 | | Still frosty. Enemy trolling quiet. A raft of "Granatenwerfers" in our front line, working rather annoying otherwise not important hits. | ditto |
| " | 10.2.17 | | | ditto |
| " | 11.2.17 | | On yesterday evening Enemy Plane driven off by 8 & 9 pm | ditto |

# WAR DIARY or INTELLIGENCE SUMMARY

Army Form C. 2118.

Vol XXIII

| Place | Date | Hour | Summary of Events and Information | Remarks and references to Appendices |
|---|---|---|---|---|
| In trenches | 12.2.17 | | Crest Pulpinantes entrances, no Bopo Matters & caged signal are nettles B in trenches. "D" Coy took no night from MUNSTERS | nil |
| Butrendon 20 SOPHIE TR | 13.2.17 | | 1ˢᵗ DIVISION. 10 men A.Coy went to MERRIGNOLLES. Relieved by 1/1 BUCKS BATT'N. Went back to SOPHIE TR behind HEBRZ COURT. 2 companies & HQRS. 4ᵗʰ coy at CROSSCOURT. "D" coy at —— | nil nil |
| SOPHIE TR | 14.2.17 | | General clean up of kit & box respirators inspection. Saints & mynls. Working parties by D & A coy. | nil |
| " | 15.2.17 | | Working parties found by D & B coys. | nil |
| " | 16.2.17 | | Inst. party went to them. Gunns primers where possible. | nil |
| SOPHIE TR MARLY CAMP | 17.2.17 | | Battn relieved by 1/8 WORCESTERS. Marched back to MARLY CAMP my sheet Poppy ment getting into stable | nil |
| MARLY | 18.2.17 | | Coy kit inspection. Footbath for men. | nil |
| " | 19.2.17 | | Specialists under spec. officers. | nil |
| " | 20.2.17 | | " Working in Camp. | nil |
| " | 21.2.17 | | " and training Bashins matching Games & Athletic sports | nil |

Army Form C. 2118.

# WAR DIARY
## or
## INTELLIGENCE SUMMARY

Vol: XXIII

(Erase heading not required.)

| Place | Date | Hour | Summary of Events and Information | Remarks and references to Appendices |
|---|---|---|---|---|
| MARLY | 22.2.17 | | Coy training. Lectures etc. | |
| " | 23.2.17 | | Lectures and arrangements to Parade for French General | |
| " | 23.2.17 | | Baths at EPPOY whole day | |

Army Form C. 2118.

# WAR DIARY
## or
## INTELLIGENCE SUMMARY
*(Erase heading not required.)*

Instructions regarding War Diaries and Intelligence Summaries are contained in F. S. Regs., Part II and the Staff Manual respectively. Title Pages will be prepared in manuscript.

| Place | Date | Hour | Summary of Events and Information | Remarks and references to Appendices |
|---|---|---|---|---|
| MARLY (SOPHIE TR) | 24.2.17 | | Battn. moved to SOPHIE trench at 10.30 a.m., taking over from 4th G.Loc | W.C. |
| SOPHIE TR FRONT LINE | 25.2.17 | | Took over front line, captains & right and left A. & B., C. & D. in support. Relief was completed A. Coy. D. in support. Relieved coys. from 7th machine line | G.W.C. |
| IN TRENCHES | 26.2.17 | | Good, bright, sunny day. Trenches gradually drying up. Western sector CHAMINADE, and CHAMINADE Rows was attempted and slightly improved W.N.C. Achilles, and slight. | |
| do do | 27.2.17 | | Another good day. relieved at night by BUCKS BATTALION | |
| SUPPORT | 28.2.17 | | Marched back to support near ancestor trench, in PRU COURT-BEACHES. Working parties all day found by A & C companies, D. & E companies finding parties for work under the Bucks. in ACHILLE & CHAMINADE. | W.C. |

A.W. Hutchison Lt. Major
Cmg. 1/5 Glos Regt.
1.3.17

CONFIDENTIAL

WAR DIARY

OF

1/5th Gloucestershire Regiment

From 1st March to 31st March 1917

Army Form C. 2118.

# WAR DIARY
## or
## INTELLIGENCE SUMMARY
*(Erase heading not required.)*

Volume XXIX.

Instructions regarding War Diaries and Intelligence Summaries are contained in F.S. Regs., Part II. and the Staff Manual respectively. Title Pages will be prepared in manuscript.

| Place | Date | Hour | Summary of Events and Information | Remarks and references to Appendices |
|---|---|---|---|---|
| SUPPORT ACHILLE WOOD | 1/3/17 | | In support. Weather good. Went back to front line again the evening. Bn. in right of left C in support. D reserve in ACHILLE WOOD. Weather fair. | JWC |
| O 5 a 89 Trenches | 2.3.17 | | Trenches still in a low state. Weather good. | JWC |
| Trenches CAPPY | 3.3.17 | | Battn relieved by 7th Worcesters took over from us with 2 companies in front. Coy and Coy went back to trenches in CAPPY. No casualties. Engineers dug back. Weather good. | JWC |
| CAPPY | 4.3.17 | | Day spent cleaning up & washing. Feet with the men. Soap feathers. Weather fair. | JWC |
| CAPPY | 5.3.17 | | Day spent in kit inspections, by Coy Commanders. Weather fair. Bths. | JWC |
| CAPPY | 6.3.17 | | Commanding Officers inspection in the morning. | JWC |
| CAPPY (ACHILLE WOOD) | 7.3.17 | | Battn relieved 1/6 GLOUCESTERS & 1/7 WORCESTERS. 2 companies at CAPPY to practise proposed raid. Weather very bad. | JWC |
| ACHILLE WOOD | 8.3.17 | | Weather improved. Fatigues during day working parties. Boche aeroplane brought down over our aerodrome balloons at ECLUSIER QUARRY. | JWC |
| ACHILLE WOOD | 9.3.17 | | Gas alarm at 10.30 pm from 1st Div. Wires again in awful condition. Discovered afterwards gas shells went the cause for the alarm. Weather fair. | JWC |
| ACHILLE WOOD | 10.3.17 | | Early this morning abt 4.30 am 1st IN BUCKS. Bey Hd. was unit for raid by steel gas shell & T.M. huts. Enemy at entrance to dug out. 17 casualties. Wind — | JWC |

2449 Wt. W14957/M90 750,000 1/16 J.B.C. & A. Forms/C.2118/12.

Army Form C. 2118.

# WAR DIARY
## or
## INTELLIGENCE SUMMARY
*(Erase heading not required.)*

Volume XXIV.

| Place | Date | Hour | Summary of Events and Information | Remarks and references to Appendices |
|---|---|---|---|---|
| ACHIEVE WOOD & TRENCHES | 11.3.17 | | Prepared air photo received. Button went out to the wound right section of Rifle Grant. Talking over from the Bucks. Trenches are much entrenched in C.17.A.A.IV.A.O.13 & POMMIERS. Wants much repaired in places, especially in C.17.A.IN.A.O.13 & POMM IE.125. Wealth very good very. In the evening many fires and extreme in front, but our wiring & our enemy patrol could be long delayed run. | June |
| Trenches | 12.3.17 | | | June |
| Trenches - CAPPY | 13.3.17 | | Relieved by 1/4 Glos. Our Scouts from many fires on the Eastern bank of PERONNE and after this no flame gushing from the place. A very quiet time in trenches. Rifles or W. Ens smelles. 3 inch trench mortar gunner Baker from Coin, Cup about its cleaning rifle adjustment generally cleaning up. | June |
| CAPPY | 14.3.17 | | C.Q.M.S. HUXFORD. & Sgt. JACKSON. D.F. were presented with D.C.M. midday mess by Lt. General PULTENEY at Div. H.Q. BATHS. Weather fine respectively. | June |
| CAPPY | 15.3.17 | | The above presentation took place today, not yesterday. Remainder of day after in bathing parade. | June |
| CAPPY | 16.3.17 | | Been carried out musically. Programme in evening for "C" Coy moved up to sector opposite LA MAISONETTE. In evening "D" Coy moved up to sector opposite Ly. "B" "A" Oxfords trenches opposite Lept Garden now in common army from 5 ow & raid as Sunken Road. at 2.30 a.m. Enemy opened a barrage fire on our trenches about an hour and not artillery opened but they did not well. The men - were much flower and to home | June |
| CAPPY | 17.3.17 | | | June |

Army Form C. 2118.

# WAR DIARY
## or
## INTELLIGENCE SUMMARY
(Erase heading not required.)

Volume XXIV

| Place | Date | Hour | Summary of Events and Information | Remarks and references to Appendices |
|---|---|---|---|---|
| [Frise?] (continued) | 17/3/17 | | an ENEMY GERMAN further A coy leading killed several Germans and then pushing rear into C coy behind behind & withdrew. A coy weakened the German outpost line. Found it [unoccupied?] and started movements. Patrols were immediately pushed forward thro' LA MAISONETTE [unoccupied?] to the & Frise [Mon?] to 3rd line & began surrounding. As soon as much lower than the enemy camp bagged patrol in to PRINCHES & the INDICNS on our right sentries. Patrols & Turk position [Pervoug?] further. By the evening our patrols had pushed on to PERONNE BIERPIGNY Road. During the evening PERONNE. We were pushed in to and battalion in [bivouac?] 2 weeks division with Corps to advance the enemy ahead to Peron it if. Plan attacked by him but B if we in sweep up | true |
| CAPPY | 18/3/17 | | 17.3.17. We were relieved by 1/4 GLOS. Weather good went back to CAPPY today. Weather fair | true |
| CAPPY | 19/3/17 | | Changed from HQ to CHATEAU. [...] weather [...] | true |
| CAPPY / PERONNE | 20/3/17 | | Went up to PERONNE today in ECLUSIER HALLE LA CROIX CONCE. [...] Town very much damaged having a house left standing. Battn. killed in hospital opposite Barracks. Very shortly night about 10 seen in windows. Burnt houses were still in fire. Weather fair. | true |
| PERONNE | 21/3/17 | | Working parties sent out to [Metropinh?] fires & clearing up streets of bricks & rubbish. During turn of [...] experience. Found Railway station badly knocked about. The Barracks [...] here also partially destroyed. Practically the whole was wall [...] but the place a [justice?] was quite unrecognisable as such. | true |

# WAR DIARY
## or
## INTELLIGENCE SUMMARY

*(Erase heading not required.)*

Army Form C. 2118.

Volume XXIV

| Place | Date | Hour | Summary of Events and Information | Remarks and references to Appendices |
|---|---|---|---|---|
| PERONNE CARTIGNY | 22/3/17 | | Battn. marched to via DOIGNT. COURCELLES to CARTIGNY and CATELET. 2 companies to HQD were billeted in CARTIGNY. 2 Companies in CATELET. Billets were placed. Batty. Hrs village HQrs were in CATELET. | J.W.C. |
| CARTIGNY | 23/3/17 | | Working parties today felling up [roads?] holes and ruts roads. Clearing trees from Nuvon road from DOIGNT - TERTRY. BENNETZ Jean Forest, Bosche to traces by Piece of wire fastens to branches, the other end to houses. Stak premier fraction lights, then [?] many trap. anneaux of grenades tied by wire together. Only no [?]. Fortification in the road being attached. Fruit trees. The whole concern was buried by the side of the road. There was heavy wind explosion [?] very small railway action Courtegne of [?] damage was done when an explosion occurred. Watch fire. Night falls of [?] in afternoon. | J.W.C. |
| CARTIGNY BOUVINCOURT | 24/3/17 | | Battn moved to BOUVINCOURT at 9 am this morning. B Coy going to BEAUVOIS. They are received [?] and French troops in the village. B Coy arrived of this trip Cmdrs inhabitants run around the village. There being evacues from various villages around where the enemy had destroyed. Leaving a village practically intact for us to live. There people. (All being men and girls from 15 - 20 years). Taken away to Germany. Weather good. | J.W.C. |
| BOUVINCOURT | 25/3/17 | | C and C apps moved to VRAIGNES, HANCOURT respectively, with instruction of POEUILLY. PLECHIN & BERNES. Any looks of the Bosch are seen. only a little sleeping indulged in by some. playful parties. the enemy. Weather sunny. | J.W.C. |
| " | 26/3/17 | | VRAIGNES. very little damaged and 1400 inhabitants evacues left. Whin [?] very long. Taken away as rate as possible to trek to BUSBY from surrounding villages. | J.W.C. |

Army Form C. 2118.

Volume XXIV

# WAR DIARY
## or
## INTELLIGENCE SUMMARY
(Erase heading not required.)

Instructions regarding War Diaries and Intelligence Summaries are contained in F. S. Regs., Part II. and the Staff Manual respectively. Title Pages will be prepared in manuscript.

| Place | Date | Hour | Summary of Events and Information | Remarks and references to Appendices |
|---|---|---|---|---|
| BOUZINCOURT CARTIGNY. | 28.3.17 | | March back to ERNOTIGNY. no billets were allotted to us, officers had to punt around to find billets for the men. Weather excellent. At PRONYERS + HANCOURT. 1 Killed 1 wounded remaining 7 wounded missing. Enemy country intensely shelled. Machines along VENDELLES and from BERNES by which masked about on top of second front line near minies. We got on my hill Beuret party instructions from Brigade Dermot he was taken down. | here |
| CARTIGNY | 29.3.17 | | C.E. Dutton in turn in Command and O[fficer] Comm[anding]. Still at CARTIGNY. moved from two H.Q.'s in Blunt in top of hill to Doulters Heath and to village. Nothing further. We were back with Brigade. Bucks take myself in absence to present arms. A.O.T.B. | here |
| " DOIGNT. | 29.3.17 | | Moved to DOIGNT. At 5:30 to honorable quarters in temporary Companies were billets in dug outs in DOIGNT WOOD. | here |
| DOIGNT | 30.3.17 | | Certain village. | here |
| DOIGNT TINCOURT | 31.3.17 | | Working parties gave to BUCKLEY working in newly. healthy new post. Battn. went to TINCOURT this afternoon at 1:30 pm. taking new from 8th WORC. Weather showery. | here |

A.B. Skinner Major
Comm[anding] 7/5 Bucks
1/4/17

April 1917

1/5th Batt. Gloucestershire Regiment

WAR DIARY

VOLUME XXV

95/26

269
10 sheets

Army Form C. 2118.

# WAR DIARY
## or
## INTELLIGENCE SUMMARY

(Erase heading not required.)

1/5 GLOSTER REGT.

| Place | Date | Hour | Summary of Events and Information | Remarks and references to Appendices |
|---|---|---|---|---|
| TINCOURT | 1.4.17 | — | Strength of Battalion. Fighting Strength 34 Offrs 853 O.R. Ration Strength 25 Offrs 883 O.R. Stood to at 6am & moved to K.8.6.2.3 as support to 144 Brigade during their attack on EPEHY. Battn not required & returned to billets at 8am. | |
| to Bivouac Camp K.7.b.2.9 | 2.4.17 | | Moved to Bivouac camp K.7.b.33. at 9.am – took over from 1/4 R. BERKS. Very cold & stormy. Men worked hard making Burdles to improve the Bivouacs. Patrols were sent by 8th WORCESTERS to RONSSOY to see if the place was held by the enemy. Battn 'Stood to' all day in case it was required to move up to RONSSOY. At 8pm news received that RONSSOY was reoccupied & Battn 'Stood down'. | |
| to EPEHY | 3.4.17 | | Moved up to EPEHY (via VILLERS FAUCON) in evening & took over from posts from 7th WORCESTERS. A Coy on right with 1/Warwn (& Lieut WAYLAND) in MALASSISE Fm. B. Coy on Left. D. Coy in Support. C. Coy in Reserve. Battn H.Q. in small shelter beside road at entrance to village. Posts very scattered & difficult to find. EPEHY heavily shelled during the night. Very wet & stormy. | |
| to VILLERS FAUCON | 4.4.17 | | Heavy fall of snow during night & early morning. Heavy shelling at intervals during day. Bttn relieved by 7 WARWICKS in evening & attack for RONSSOY – BASSE-BOULOGNE – LEMPIRE on next morning. | |

(Casualty)

Army Form C. 2118.

# WAR DIARY
## or
## INTELLIGENCE SUMMARY

*(Erase heading not required.)*

1/5 GLOSTER REGT

Instructions regarding War Diaries and Intelligence Summaries are contained in F.S. Regs., Part II. and the Staff Manual respectively. Title Pages will be prepared in manuscript.

| Place | Date | Hour | Summary of Events and Information | Remarks and references to Appendices |
|---|---|---|---|---|
| LEMPIRE | 5.4.17 | | Battn having moved for a short rest from EPEHY to VILLERS FAUCON, left the latter place at 2.45 a.m. The Brigade attacked the position as follows:- 1/4 R. BERKS (on right) — S 4 S.E. of RONSSOY — B-BOULOGNE; 1/4 OXFORDS (centre) — SW end of RONSSOY; 1/5 GLOSTERS (on left) — La Pannelle and B-BOULOGNE, with a detachment directed on MAYE Copse. Reserve 1/1 BUCKS. The following extracts from Battn Orders give details:- Forming up position was to W of RY embankment in F.8.a and c. 3) West WAGLANDS Station (A Coy) was still holding MALASSISE Farm, which was very heavily shelled during the day, took no part in the attack. Nos. Companies will move on the objective in the following order: C – D (less 2 Platoons in MAYE Copse) – A (less 1 Platoon holding MALASSISE Farm). B Coy will remain in Bn Reserve at F.8.c.2.4 (approx). | |

# WAR DIARY or INTELLIGENCE SUMMARY.

Army Form C. 2118.

1/5 GLOSTER REGT

Coys will move off in Arty formation, platoons in file, will extend half the Dn when leading 2 platoons arrive at F.14.a east. When in position Coys will have 2 platoons in each line in 2 ranks – interval 10-15 yds between men; distance 10 yds between ranks of platoons; distance 50 yds between waves.

"B." D. Coy will detail 2 platoons, under Lieut CORNISH (2 guns 145 MGC attached) to take up position on road F.8.d facing MAYE Copse. This det-m-t will attack MAYE Copse at Zero hour, & held it to form a defensive flank.

4.7. Objective 4/5 GLOSTERS F.15.d.6.3. to F.15.c.8.2.
No.7. Position of Bn. H.Q. F.8.c.2.4.

One Section per Company carried bombs and 20 rifle grenades.

There had been a heavy fall of snow & as it was a bright night it is thought our movement to the Ry embankment, up the valley between the railways, was spotted by the enemy. The enemy shelled the ground in F.7.d immediately after the Batt. had passed. A very heavy barrage was put down by the enemy which fortunately was always just behind the rear Coy & inflicted practically no casualties. The enemy was holding the N.W. end of LEMPIRE strongly with machine guns and as became evident after the retirement of the enemy were in some strength on N edge of LEMPIRE in small rifle pits.

The position was assaulted in rising fine style by the leading companies, and a position taken up, held, on N.E. side of village by Sam ?????. The enemy did not put up a fight at MAYE Copse, though it was held. Nine prisoners were captured and 2 machine guns. A few of the enemy were killed. During the day our own

Army Form C. 2118.

# WAR DIARY
## or
## INTELLIGENCE SUMMARY.
(Erase heading not required.)

1/5 GLOSTER REGT.

| Place | Date | Hour | Summary of Events and Information | Remarks and references to Appendices |
|---|---|---|---|---|
| VILLERS FAUCON | 5.4.17 | | new positions were heavily shelled by the enemy. The attacks made by 1/4 R. BERKS & 1/4 OXFORDS met with equal success. Our casualties were 15 killed and 40 wounded (2 subsequently died of wounds). Capt. CONDER was slightly wounded. Subsequently 1 D.C.M. and 1 military medals were given to men of the Battalion for this fight. | |
| | | | The Battn. was relieved during the evening by the 1/1 BUCKS and marched back to VILLERS FAUCON. | |
| to Bivouac E 29 b. 8.7 nr St EMELIE | 6.4.17 | | The Battn. moved during the day and erected a bivouac camp near St EMELIE. Weather very wet and stormy. | |
| to HAMEL | 7.4.17 | | Battn. employed clearing up St EMELIE. Relieved by 1/6 GLOSTERS & returned HAMEL - 2 casualties on way caused by enemy long range shelling. | |
| do | 8.4.17 | | Bivouac. Working parties renewed clearing up. Weather stormy with snow storms. | |

Army Form C. 2118.

# WAR DIARY
## or
## INTELLIGENCE SUMMARY.

(Erase heading not required.)

1/5 GLOSTER REGT

| Place | Date | Hour | Summary of Events and Information | Remarks and references to Appendices |
|---|---|---|---|---|
| HAMEL | 9.4.17 | | Working parties etc. | |
| " | 10.4.17 | | | |
| " | 11.4.17 | | | |
| " | 12.4.17 | | | |
| to LEMPIRE positions | 13.4.17 | | Batt took over left sub. sector in front of LEMPIRE and BASSE-BOULOGNE. Weather very wet & stormy. | |
| " | 14.4.17 | | Batt took over left sub. sector in front of LEMPIRE and BASSE-BOULOGNE. Weather very wet & stormy. | |
| to Camp S. of STE EMELIE | 15.4.17 | | Relieved by 1/1 BUCKS. Batt returned to Burrows Camp fields R/ embankment. | |
| | 16.4.17 | | Batt moved at 10 pm to vicinity of ESCLAINVILLERS wood to be ready in support during attack by 1/4 BERKS on GILLEMONT Farm and 1/1 BUCKS on TOMBOIS Farm & the KNOLL. Weather very wet & stormy, heavy rain. Heavy snow all night — men out in open fields. Attack on GILLEMONT which was strongly held did not progress. The 1/1 Bucks got in (at TomBois but Companies on the right were hung up by enemy | |

Army Form C. 2118.

# WAR DIARY
## or
## INTELLIGENCE SUMMARY.
(Erase heading not required.)

1/5 GLOSTER REGT

| Place | Date | Hour | Summary of Events and Information | Remarks and references to Appendices |
|---|---|---|---|---|
| | 17.4.17 | | were on the right. O.C. 1/1 BUCKS then ordered forward 'B' Coy (this Coy had moved straight to LEMPIRE from camp) to move straight down road & attack right of the farm. This movement was now well covered not by B. Coy under Capt HOLLING-TON. The Coy got through the wire & moved up a sunken road, were about 8 Germans were killed. No 5 Platoon under 2/Lieut GRUBB being particularly good work. At 11am A. Coy were ordered to move up to LEMPIRE - later 3 platoons of A. Coy were moved forward to TOMBOIS Farm. At 5 am Battn H.Q. and C & D Coys returned from ESCAUMVILLERS took to Camp, soaked through. At about 6am Major BAKER ordered a 1st Lieut- patrol to be sent to PETIT PRIEL Farm from our B. Coy. to find out if the position was held by two or by the enemy. A patrol of 1 NCO (Cpl BUTT) & 8 men moved out. They were unable to return- the farm on the place was being heavily shelled by own guns. When the shelling stopped they pushed forward & reoccupied the position. Remained there all day, until relieved by a patrol sent forward by the Bn on our left. (photo? 1-3) 4 pm. Corporal BUTT received the Military Medal for this particularly fine bit of work. Sergt COOPEY received The Mil-Medal for ?? | |

Army Form C. 2118.

# WAR DIARY
## or
## INTELLIGENCE SUMMARY.
*(Erase heading not required.)*

1/5 GLOSTER REGT.

| Place | Date | Hour | Summary of Events and Information | Remarks and references to Appendices |
|---|---|---|---|---|
| LEMPIRE To TOMBOIS Farm to Camp Resting | 18.4.17 | | Leading regularly during the attack on the Farm (TOMBOIS). 2 Lieut GRUBIS and 2 recommended for the Military Cross. | |
| | 19.4.17 | | Relieves 1/1 BUCKS in newly captured positions at 9pm. Enemy put up Barrage during relief — believed that enemy tapping our telephone wires & & greater precautions to be taken when speaking. 1/5 GLOSTERS took over TOMBOIS Farm positions — very safe relief — relief complete by 3.4 am. | |
| Camp | 20.   " 21     " 22     " 23     " | | Batt'n in camp — carrying parties & company parades slowly. Inter Coy Football matches | |
| | 24.4.17 | | All ranks had breakfast at 3.30 am instead of at 4 am. Smaller moved at 5 am to TEMPLEUX Wood to be in readiness in case of enemy counter attack on GILLEMONT Farm. At 5pm HQrs A+B Coys returned to Camp C+D Coys remained in TEMPLEUX Wood. Weather fortunately fine. | |
| To TOMBOIS Farm Positions | 25.4.17 | | Coys moved from camp from 1.15 am onwards) from TEMPLEUX Wood at 2 am & all were in position at N end of RONNSOY Wood at 3 am — acting in support of 1/4 GLOSTERS A+B Coys were ordered to support 1/4 GLOSTERS | |

Army Form C. 2118.

# WAR DIARY
## or
## INTELLIGENCE SUMMARY.
(Erase heading not required.)

1/5 GLOSTER REGT

| Place | Date | Hour | Summary of Events and Information | Remarks and references to Appendices |
|---|---|---|---|---|
| TOM BOIS Farm positions | | | TOM BOIS Farm positions and C md. to support 1/7 WORCESTERS in GILLEMONT Farm positions. H'Qrs remained during day in RONNSOY wood. At relief time (9pm) Wrd Coy joined A&B in new positions near TOM BOIS farm and relieved 1/4 GLOSTERS. H'Qrs moved to LEMPIRE, with C Coy remaining near Shepherds Knoll in the "Brasserie" in Battn Reserve in cellars in LEMPIRE. | |
| To Camp near St EMELIE | 26.4.17 | | Relieved by 1/1 BUCKS. A B & D Coys moved to camp near R'y embankment St EMELIE. H'Qrs remained near LEMPIRE workhouse. C Coy occupied posts in "Brasserie" line. | |
| To TOM BOIS farm positions. | 27.4.17 | | Took over line from 1/1 BUCKS | |
| To TINCOURT | 28.4.17 | | | |
| | 29.4.17 | | In TOM BOIS farm positions. Relieved by 1/6 GLOSTERS & returned to camp in TINCOURT - 7½ mile march. We have Ex-troop at a half way house & came back in fine style. | LEMPIRE - BASSE - BOULOGNE. Guiry heavily shelled during the morning. |
| | 30.4.17 | | Camp - quiet day - One working party provided for 2 hours in afternoon. | Strength of Battn. Fighting Strength Offrs 37 OR 750. Ration Strength Offrs 25 OR 615 |

Army Form C. 2118.

# WAR DIARY
## or
## INTELLIGENCE SUMMARY.
*(Erase heading not required.)*

1/5 GLOSTER REGT

| Place | Date | Hour | Summary of Events and Information | Remarks and references to Appendices |
|---|---|---|---|---|
| | | | Summary for month | |
| | | | Honours & Rewards | |
| | | | 28.3.17. A/C C. HAYDEN | |
| | | | Mid³ M.M. Pte T.J. SESSIONS | |
| | | | 4.4.17. A/C A.E. THORNE | |
| | | | Mid³ M.M. Sergt H.C. BARNES | |
| | | | A.T. TACKSON | |
| | | | " G.W. HYISS | |
| | | | " 40 E.T. RYDER | |
| | | | Cpl W.J. CHANDLER. | |
| | | | 14.4.17. Corp H. CAUDLE | |
| | | | Mid³ M.M. A/Cpl W. EXELL | |
| | | | L/Cpl F. PRINGLE | |
| | | | 25.4.17 Sergt A. COOPEY | |
| | | | Mid³ M.M. Cpl R. BUTT. | |
| | | | 21.4.17 Dvr E.H.G. FARMER | |
| | | | D.C.M. | |
| | | | Military Crosses | |
| | | | 5.4.17. 2/Lieut H. M°L. MILLAR | |
| | | | 8.4.17 Capt E. CONDER | Admissions to |
| | | | 12.4.17 2/Lieut F.S. HILL. | Hospital during |
| | | | | month 57. |
| | | | Casualties | |
| | | | 4.4.17  1 OR wounded | |
| | | | 5  —  15 — Killed 40 OR wounded. | |
| | | | | (2 died subsequently) |
| | | | 13 —  1 OR Killed 1 OR wounded | |
| | | | 15  1  —  1  — | |
| | | | 17 —  1  3  — 1 missing | |
| | | | 19  —  —  4  1 | |
| | | | 25  1  —  2  — | |
| | | | 26  —  1  4  1 | |
| | | | 27  —  —  3  — | |
| | | | Total. 24 OR Killed | |
| | | | 59 — wounded. | |

R.B. Thurnam Lt Col
Commdt 1/5 Gloster

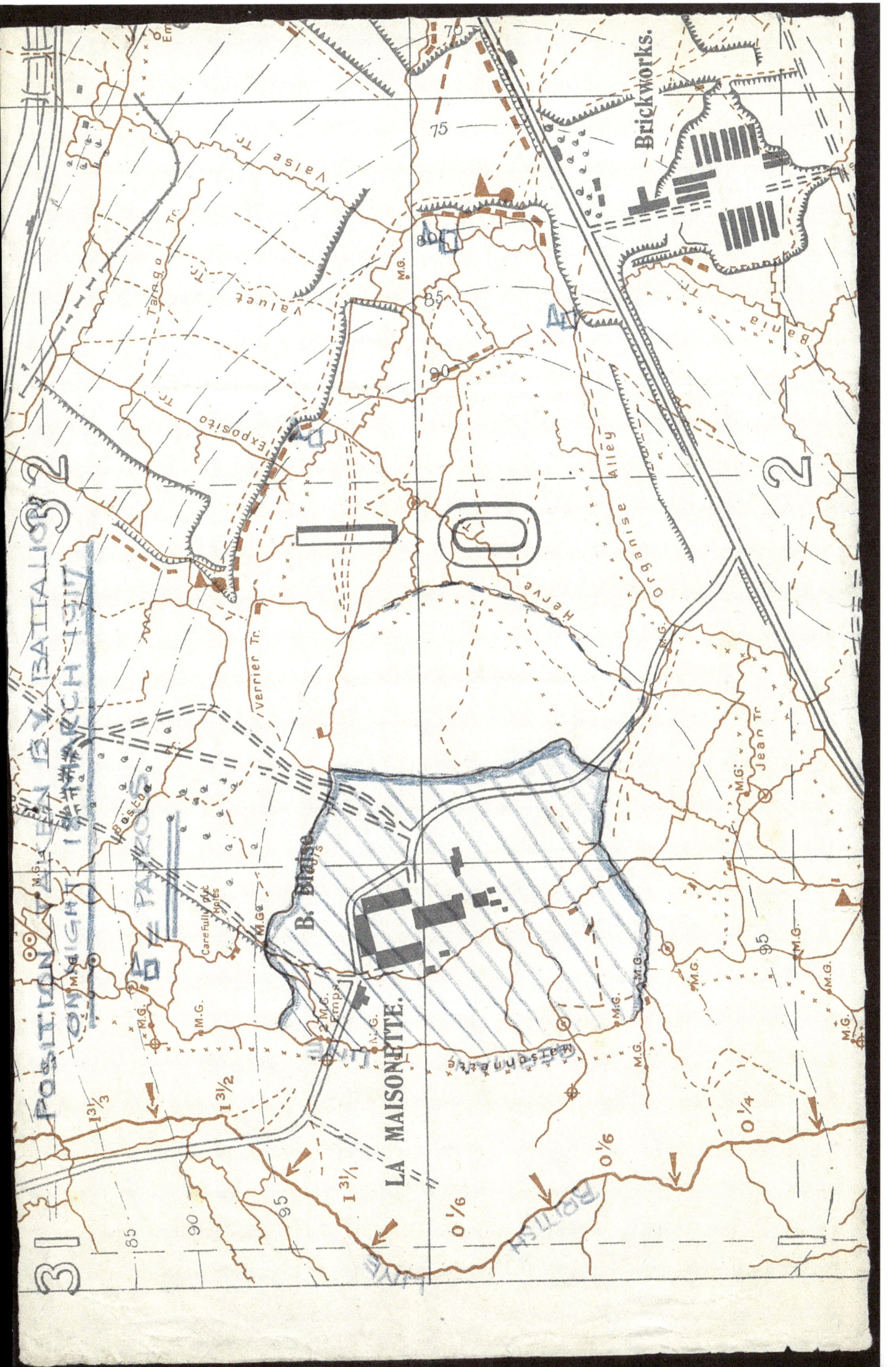

1/5th Bn. Gloucestershire Regt. Vol 27
May 1917

War Diary

Vol. XXVI

Army Form C. 2118.

# WAR DIARY
## or
## INTELLIGENCE SUMMARY.
(Erase heading not required.)

| Place | Date | Hour | Summary of Events and Information | Remarks and references to Appendices |
|---|---|---|---|---|
| CARTIGNY | 1.5.17 | - | Strength of Battn - Fighting Strength Officers 37. OR 750. Rations - - 25. - 815. | Apl |
| " | 2.5.17 | | Marched from Camp TINCOURT to Past Billets in CARTIGNY. | |
| Camp LEMESNIL | 3.5.17 | | March to W H LEMESNIL and pitched camp in new site. Busy day getting settled down. | |
| " | 4.5.17 | | Paraded in morning - Squad drill - weather fine & hot. | |
| " | 5.5.17 | | do do do | |
| " | 6.5.17 | | do do working party. | |
| " | 7.5.17 | | Church parade. O.R.'s v. knotty. | |
| " | 8.5.17 | | Company parades. weather fine, wind. working party men | |
| " | 9.5.17 | | " " " " " " and all day. working party " | |
| " | 10.5.17 | | " " " fine & hot. Officers' Riding School in camp. " | |
| " | 11.5.17 | | " " " Scheme for Coy Commanders Officers Riding School. Pioneers completed large wooden shanty for Sergeants Mess. In evening Pioneers completed Bath & Mess huts for Battn Mess almost completed. | |
| " | " | | Orders to move to COMBLES. | |
| Camp COMBLES | 12.5.17 | | Very hot day. March to COMBLES via PERONNE - CLERY. Corps Commander (Gen'l ...) congratulated Battn on very good work done whilst in II Corps during this trying march. Came o'clock march - A great march. Steel helmets - very hot sun on Packs at beginning of march | |

Army Form C. 2118.

# WAR DIARY
## or
## INTELLIGENCE SUMMARY.
(Erase heading not required.)

Instructions regarding War Diaries and Intelligence Summaries are contained in F. S. Regs., Part II. and the Staff Manual respectively. Title pages will be prepared in manuscript.

| Place | Date | Hour | Summary of Events and Information | Remarks and references to Appendices |
|---|---|---|---|---|
| Camp BANCOURT | 13.5.17 | | Batt. marched to BANCOURT. starting at 4 a.m. The Band played a very short distance out. A single man fell out. Found Anzac Cps. R.V. | ARJ |
| Support line BEAUMETZ | 14.5.17 | | Quiet men. Took over Right Batt. Support line from 5th Bde. Regt 33rd Bth. H.Drs H.Qrs 2 Coys in S of BEAUMETZ. 1 Coy. CAMBRAI 1 Coy S of DOIGNIES. 1 Coy N of DEMI-COURT. | A.R.J |
| " | 15.5.17 | | Quiet day. | |
| " | 16.5.17 | | " Weather wet, rectd. | |
| " | 17.5.17 | | " | ARJ |
| DEMICOURT | 18.5.17 | | Relieved 1/1 Bucks in Front line posts. A.C.D. Coys front line posts. A Coy 3rd Bucks. R.J. | ARJ |
| " | 19.5.17 | | Good patrol work by Lieut BINGHAM. HALL B. Coy. & 2/Lieut LAKE C. Coy. | R.H |
| " | 20.5.17 | | A party of D. Coy under 2/Lieut LATROBE carried out a very successful raid. Struck an enemy post containing 4 men. 4 Men 3 were killed 1 captured (severely wounded) Our casualties were 1 O.R. killed 6 O.R. wounded. mostly by fire from another enemy post slightly in rear of the post raided. A party of C. Coy under Lieut RATCLIFF also went out to raid but found no occupied enemy posts. Enemy artillery fairly active all day - also some minenwerfer flies figures | ARJ |
| " | 21.5.17 | | C. Coy raiding party prepared to go out during the night but was cancelled owing to special R.E. operation. Wired hereinen were also cancelled. Enemy artillery as before. | ARJ |

Army Form C. 2118.

# WAR DIARY
or
# INTELLIGENCE SUMMARY.
(Erase heading not required.)

Instructions regarding War Diaries and Intelligence Summaries are contained in F. S. Regs., Part II, and the Staff Manual respectively. Title pages will be prepared in manuscript.

| Place | Date | Hour | Summary of Events and Information | Remarks and references to Appendices |
|---|---|---|---|---|
| DEMICOURT to Wd HERMIES | 22.5.17 | | Enemy shelling ER & depot Reliefs by 4th B'de Cos during night. 2nd D Coy Reserve N of HERMIES, A & B Coys Support N/W of HERMIES respectively. Special R.E. operation again postponed. | CWS |
| Bivouacs | 23.5.17 | | Quiet day. | CWS |
| " | 24.5.17 | | do | |
| " | 25.5.17 | | do | |
| | 26.5.17 | | Two 6" Hy Batteries & one 60 pounder Battery shoot to H'qrs C'd Coy Bivouacs were very heavily shelled during morning from 2.30 - 3 pm necessitating removal of men to canal bank. A Coy Partners N of HERMIES heavily shelled during morning - 4 casualties all slight. Hdqrs A & D Coys moved to camp at S corner of VELU Wood at 9 pm. | AE CWS |
| Camp VELU Wood | 27.5.17 | | Camp lightly shelled during daylight. During afternoon moved into cover of Wood. B Coy returned from E of HERMIES. | CWS |
| " | 28.5.17 | | Quiet day. | CWS |
| To Front line HERMIES | 29.5.17 | | Quiet day. Relieved 4/1 B'de Cos Battn in Right Sub Sector E of HERMIES. | CWS |
| do | 30.5.17 | | Quiet day. Working parties during night went first on bypaths, later on R.3 b of HERMIES - HAVRINCOURT Road. At this place enemy had a large number of groundtrip wires & work could not be carried out. | CWS |
| do | 31.5.17 | | | |

Army Form C. 2118.

# WAR DIARY
## or
## INTELLIGENCE SUMMARY.
*(Erase heading not required.)*

| Place | Date | Hour | Summary of Events and Information | Remarks and references to Appendices |
|---|---|---|---|---|
| | | | Enemy shelled the main road railway line intermittently throughout the night and fired at large numbers of flares - working party did not cease work until about 3 am (6/6) when it became darker & to 6 & work was started on other jobs. Pte Bamberger & NCOs were wounded. 3 men billet. | R.R. |
| | | | The following attended schools - Those marked + having very good reports: IV Army School - 2/Lt Corlett 48 Div Gunnery School - 2/Lt Whiteside +, Cpl Tolley, L/C Hodges, L/C Chandler, L/C Kerr IV Army School - Lieut Hawkins +, CSM Barley + 46 Div Gas Course - L/C Outen IV Army Signal School P.E. Fry + Pte Trinder + | |
| | | | Casualties during month | |
| | | | Honours & Awards. Military Cross - Lieut Swift. 1. D.C.M. Lieut Lotham, Lieut F.E. Ralph, Cpl Barley, Sergt C. Jackson Mentions in Dispatches | |
| | | | Strength of Battn. Fighting Strength 34 Officers 741 OR Ration 25 " 625 - | |

A.B.R—— Lt Col
Comdg 1/5 Staffords
3/6/17

JUNE 1917.

1/5th Bn. Gloucestershire Regiment

War Diary

VOL. XXVII

Army Form C. 2118.

# WAR DIARY
## or
## INTELLIGENCE SUMMARY.
(Erase heading not required.)

1/5 GLOUCESTER

| Place | Date | Hour | Summary of Events and Information | Remarks and references to Appendices |
|---|---|---|---|---|
| HERMIES | 1.6.17 | | A cold day in front line trenches. "C" Coy. B⁰ Reserve. B Coy in support. normal wire reserve. Enemy shelled HERMIES & GUERNIES and the Company lines during the day. | |
| | | No.2 ptn. | Lt. RATCLIFFE No.2 platoon of "D" Coy. made a reconnoissance raid on Canal du Nord when within 30 yards of raid. Enemy fired drum fire signal rockets (greenish) & at the same time opened fire from the trenches and two M.G. opened fire in the same direction and another M.G. from the same direction (not identified.) | MA10 |
| | 2.6.17 | | Enemy shelled front line, one of our men being slightly wounded. A Patrol of "C" Coy. (Lt. SMITH) (2nd Bn Bucks) went to M. Bank line (M 7.c.) 4.40 am was discharged at 12.10 am (could not so after enemy). All HERMES DEMICOURT turned of from SPOIL HEAP searching trenches in NOYEUX & pk - | |
| | | 11 p.m. | A/3 STEEL "D" Coy. crossed the R. Canal du Nord. one is broken over canal) in HERMIES to HAVRINCOURT wood there being "firing" Patrol returned mountain ditch. Spoil Heap all quiet & firm of men. | |
| | 3.6.17 | 3:35 a.m. | S/L GRUBB and ? R. and J. were sent to investigate making a descend at Patrol was held up and by one machine gun and again by own barrage. Beyond seeing a room in HAVRINCOURT from the SPOIL HEAP everything was quiet and patrol returned. | MA11 |
| | 3.6.17 | | Enemy shelled HERMIES, west of HERMIES and the FACTORY. Battalion relieved by Bucks Bn B⁰ HQ's G. Sunken Road BEAUMETZ. B Coy. (Capt. McDOWELL) ? E Sunken Rd./ B⁰ HQ METZ. C Coy. (Capt. CONDER.) D Coy (Capt. FRANKLIN) J 24.4.9.5 Right Reserve Coy A Coy (Capt. ROLLINGTON) J 22.6.99 Left Reserve Coy | MA11 |

Army Form C. 2118.

# WAR DIARY
## or
## INTELLIGENCE SUMMARY.
(Erase heading not required.)

1/5 GLOUCESTER REGT.

Instructions regarding War Diaries and Intelligence Summaries are contained in F. S. Regs., Part II. and the Staff Manual respectively. Title pages will be prepared in manuscript.

| Place | Date | Hour | Summary of Events and Information | Remarks and references to Appendices |
|---|---|---|---|---|
| BEAUMETZ | 4.6.17 | | Quiet day. Bombing training B and C Coys. | WD/40 |
| " | 5.6.17 | | Box respirator and tube helmet Inspection. | WD/40 |
| " | 6.6.17 | | Rifle grenade and Lewis Gun Training B and C Coys. B Coy relieved "D Coy" in Rifle Reserve by C " " A " Self " | WD/40 |
| " | 7.6.17 | | Quiet day. D Coy (Capt FRANCILLON) moved up to E "SUNKEN ROAD SOUTH of HERMIES" in S.S.6.d. to act as Brigade Reserve whilst Buckle Bn marked enemy post on West bank of CANAL about N.28.d.4.9. | WD/40 |
| " | 8.6.17 | | Inspection of rifles Box respirators and Helmets A Coy 200 rapid loading working and bombing practice. Baths in afternoon at VELU A and D Coys. | WD/40 |
| HERMIES | 9.6.17 | | Relieved Bucks Bn during night in Right Subsector Bn Hdqrs HERMIES. B Coy (Capt MACDOWELL) Front Line PMS Right C Coy (Capt CONDER) " " Left D Coy (Capt FRANCILLON) East of HERMIES. J.30.b A Coy (Capt HULLINGTON) Bn Reserve. J.23.d. Patrol of 1 Officer 1 O.R. went out at 11.30pm and patrolled along DEMICOURT - SENSÉE HEAP road towards SPOIL HEAP returned without incident. Enterprise patrol 1 N.C.O 2 O.R. worked down left Coy front got before dawn close without any result. | WD/40 |

Army Form C. 2118.

# WAR DIARY
or
# INTELLIGENCE SUMMARY.
(Erase heading not required.)

1/5 GLOUCESTER REGT

Instructions regarding War Diaries and Intelligence Summaries are contained in F. S. Regs., Part II. and the Staff Manual respectively. Title pages will be prepared in manuscript.

| Place | Date | Hour | Summary of Events and Information | Remarks and references to Appendices |
|---|---|---|---|---|
| HERMIES | 10.6.17 | 12.15 am | Slight hostile shelling of HERMIES and the factory during the day. Lt BINGHAM HALE and 10 O.R. went out from left of Right Coy. When 50 yards out several T.M's fell in valley west of SPOIL HEAP followed by an artillery barrage behind left Coy front line posts. Probably to prevent 2nd party in front of our posts. Patrol heard a party in front retiring and went afterwards followed on from about 150 yds away. Patrol returned without further incident. Patrol A 1 NCO and 6 O.R. from left Coy went out at 1.15 am. towards SPOIL HEAP, arriving in sight of enemies wire. Patrol moved parallel to wire for a short distance and returned having seen nothing. | Nil. |
|  | 11.6.17 |  | Enemy shelled HERMIES and the FACTORY everyday. Also Right Coy front posts. Patrol of 1 NCO & 6 O.R. from Left Coy examined 90 yards of enemies wire on North west front of the SPOIL HEAP. Enemy fired grenadinewerfers and rifle grenades during night at Right Coy front posts & Henry Trench. Lt Col A.B. SKINNER proceeded to England on leave. MAJOR D.S. WARD took command of Bn. | Nil. |
|  | 12.6.17 |  | Enemy shelled HERMIES and front line slightly. Patrol of 1 Officer & 2 O.R. reconnoitred HERMIES - GRAINCOURT road. 1 Officer 2 O.R. went out to select site for new post to command S.W. of SPOIL HEAP but returned without doing so owing to bone visibility and no own artillery fire. A Coy (Capt HOLLINGTON) relieved C Coy (Capt CONDER) B Coy (Capt MACDOWELL) relieved by D Coy (Capt FRANCILLON) | Nil. |

Army Form C. 2118.

# WAR DIARY
## or
## INTELLIGENCE SUMMARY.
(Erase heading not required.)

1/5 GLOUCESTER REGT.

Instructions regarding War Diaries and Intelligence Summaries are contained in F. S. Regs., Part II. and the Staff Manual respectively. Title pages will be prepared in manuscript.

| Place | Date | Hour | Summary of Events and Information | Remarks and references to Appendices |
|---|---|---|---|---|
| HERMIES. | 13.6.17 | | Enemy shelled Post in Right Company heavily. Sine Patrols 1NCO and 2 OR and 1NCO. 6 OR. went out from Right & Left Coys respectively. Each located enemy working parties. LT RATCLIFF proceeded to England on leave. | Appx. |
| " | 14.6.17 | | 2/LT BRUTON & 1 OR. went out to locate M.G. on other side of Canal. One patrol from SPOIL HEAP and another from HAVRINCOURT. Patrol returned unable to locate MG in question. 2/LT BINGHAM HALL & 1 OR. went to locate enemy PO's S of SPOIL HEAP. 1 examined wires. | Appx. |
| " | 15.6.17 | | Bn relieved by Bucks B" Battn & proceeded to Camp at VELU WOOD. LT J.P. WINTERBOTHAM & BRIGADE for instruction 2/LT B.V. BRUTON assumed duties of Adjutant. CAPT. SUMNER returned from FLIXECOURT. To army school. | Appx. |
| VELU WOOD. | 16.6.17 | | Batn in HAPLINCOURT. | |
| " | 17.6.17 | | Inspection of Rifle gas helmets, etc. Church Parade 11 am and afternoon Inspection of Bn by G.O.C. & 2nd Div. | Appx. |
| " | 18.6.17 | | Physical drills, Rifle exercises, Bayonet fighting & rifle bombing. Bayonet training for Officers. | Appx. |

Army Form C. 2118.

# WAR DIARY
## or
## INTELLIGENCE SUMMARY.
*(Erase heading not required.)*

1/5 GLOUCESTER Regt

| Place | Date | Hour | Summary of Events and Information | Remarks and references to Appendices |
|---|---|---|---|---|
| VELU WOOD | 19.6.17 | | Training, inclusion Rapid wiring | WW |
| " | 20/6/17 | | Inspection by G.O.C. 145 Bde. | WW |
| " | 21/6/17 | | Bn relieved Bucks Bn in front line posns. A Coy (Capt HOLLINGTON) Right front Posn. B Coy (Capt MACDOWELL) Left " " C Coy (Capt PRANCILLON) Forward Reserve C Coy (Capt CONDER) Bn Reserve. 2 LT RUBINSTEIN and 18 O.R. went out to inspect enemy wire in front of SPOIL HEAP. Defensive patrols went out just before dawn. | WW |
| HERMIES | 22/6/17 | | 2 LT BINGHAM HALL & 8 O.R. went to reconnoitre enemy posts in K.14.d. have returned without information. 1 NCO 6 O.R. went out to look for enemy working parties. | WW |
| " | 23/6/17 | | 1 NCO 8 O.R. went out from left coy to reconnoitre enemy working in K.14.b. and returned at 2 a.m. having located a digging party. CAPT PRANCILLON (D Coy) proceeded to Seaside Camp on leave. LT HAWKING took over command of D. Coy. | WW |

Army Form C. 2118.

# WAR DIARY
## or
## INTELLIGENCE SUMMARY.
(Erase heading not required.)

1/6 GLOUCESTER. REGT.

| Place | Date | Hour | Summary of Events and Information | Remarks and references to Appendices |
|---|---|---|---|---|
| HERMIES | 24/6/17 | | Company relief. C Coy (Capt COMBER) Right front posts<br>D Coy (Lt HAWKINS) Left do.<br>B Coy (Capt MACDOWELL) Forward Reserve<br>A Coy (Capt HOLLINGTON) Bn Reserve<br><br>2/Lt AK STANLEY & 12 OR went to ascertain if enemy were working at N corner of SPOILHEAP and found wiring in progress.<br>LT COL SKINNER returned from leave to ENGLAND. | Nil. |
| | 25.6.17 | | Enemy shelled Right Front Coy.<br>2/LT BINGHAM HALL. 10 OR went out to locate enemy post South of SPOIL HEAP.<br>2/LT RUBINSTEIN 10 OR went to reconnoitre track for approach to this post.<br>MAJOR D.J. WARD to ENGLAND on leave and for course at ALDERSHOT. 2/LT CRUICKSHANKS returned from England to attend<br>MAJOR RENDALE, CAPT DAVIES & Army School awaiting for instruction— | Nil. |
| | 26.7.16 | | Two platoons under 2/LT BINGHAM HALL and 2/LT RUBINSTEIN covered by bombard went proceeded to raid post South of SPOIL HEAP.<br>2/LT BINGHAM HALL and 1 platoon formed raiding party, the remaining platoon forming a covering party. 300 yards in rear and slightly to the North of the raiding party. After one minute bombardment of post raiding party went in and found post unoccupied. Raiding party then with drew and covering party proceeded to reconnoitre SPOIL HEAP finding this occupied party withdrew.<br>MAJOR N.H.WALLER rejoined form. Div Hqs. | Nil. |

Army Form C. 2118.

# WAR DIARY
## or
## INTELLIGENCE SUMMARY.

(Erase heading not required.)

1/5 GLOUCESTER REGT

| Place | Date | Hour | Summary of Events and Information | Remarks and references to Appendices |
|---|---|---|---|---|
| HERMIES | 27.6.17 | | Bn. relieved by BUCKS Bn. Adjnt. 'A' and 'B' Coy to SUNKEN ROAD BERTINCOURT D Coy (Capt HAWKINS) Right and C Coy (Capt CONDER) Left. Reserve line. | Wthr |
| BEAUMETZ | 28.6.17 | | Quiet day | Wthr |
| " | 29.6.17 | | Coy. inspections etc. | Wthr |
| " | 30.6.17 | | Bn. relieved BUCKS Bn in Front Line. <br> A Coy - (Capt. HOLLINGTON). Right front post <br> B " - (Capt MACDOWELL) Left do <br> D " - (Lt HAWKINS.) Forward Reserve <br> C " - (Capt CONDER) Bn Reserve <br> Casualties during month : killed in action 2, wounded 13, wounded (8 Wightal party), 1 since died. Major D. Ward - Military Cross. Sgt. Smoulding. D.C.M. Cpl Tolley M.M. 1gt. Cushings French Medaille Militaire. The following obtained good reports at courses. Lt Abery, Schofl Capt. Simmens + Sgt. Mussleth IV Army School 216 King's R. Gas School Fighting strength 33 offrs 708 OR Rations " 22 offrs 655 OR | |

R.B. Skinner Lt Col.
Comdg 1/5 Gloucesters

CONFIDENTIAL

# War Diary

— of —

1/5th Battalion Gloster Regiment

VOLUME XXVIII

From 1st July 1917 to 31st July 1917

20 August 1917

Army Form C. 2118.

# WAR DIARY
## or
## INTELLIGENCE SUMMARY.
*(Erase heading not required.)*

9/5 GLOUCESTER Regt

Instructions regarding War Diaries and Intelligence Summaries are contained in F. S. Regs., Part II. and the Staff Manual respectively. Title pages will be prepared in manuscript.

| Place | Date | Hour | Summary of Events and Information | Remarks and references to Appendices |
|---|---|---|---|---|
| HERMIES | 1/7/17 | 12.15 am | 2 O.R. and 10 O.R. went to examine enemy posts on N.W side of BOIS HEAR but found it unoccupied. | |
| " | | 12.30 am | One N.C.O. and 6 O.R. reconnoitred old enemy post at K.20.C.37 and found it unoccupied. | AWW |
| | 2/7/17 | | Battalion relieved by 1st NORTHUMBERLAND FUSILIERS and marched to camp near FREMICOURT at 1.26.a.1.8 Ref 57C 1/40,000. the remainder of night | AWW |
| FREMICOURT | 3/7/17 | | Battalion moved at 7 pm to BIHUCOURT and camped for the night. Lt RATCLIFF rejoined from leave. | AWW |
| BIHUCOURT | 4/7/17 | 5 pm | Battalion moved to BELLACOURT via ACHIET LE GRAND, BLAINZEVILLE and RANSART | AWW |
| BELLACOURT | 5/7/17 | | Platoon Training | AWW |
| " | 6/7/17 | | Company Training. Lt Col A.B. SKINNER relinquished command and warned to proceed to England, INDIA. Lt Col W. ADAM 1/7 WORCESTER Regt 2/Lt STEEL posted to Enfield for Course | AWW |

Army Form C. 2118.

# WAR DIARY
## or
## INTELLIGENCE SUMMARY.
(Erase heading not required.)

1/5 GLOUCESTER R.

Instructions regarding War Diaries and Intelligence Summaries are contained in F. S. Regs., Part II. and the Staff Manual respectively. Title pages will be prepared in manuscript.

| Place | Date | Hour | Summary of Events and Information | Remarks and references to Appendices |
|---|---|---|---|---|
| BELLACOURT | 7/7/17 | | Company Training | MM |
| | 8/7/17 | | Church Parade. 3 Officers W.O. & 61 O.R. RIVIERE. 2/LT BRETHERTON rejoined and was posted to "D" Coy. MAJOR M.H. WALLER proceeded to XVIII Corps at or selecting on following scheme | MM |
| | 9/7/17 | | Brigade exercises. Attack on HAMELON FARM & LADINIFER WOOD. 2/LT CORNISH proceeded to England on leave | MM |
| | 10/7/17 | | Range Practices. Ratt. LT.W. HAWKING transferred to "B" Coy. 188 O.R. Reinforcements arrived. | MM |
| | 11/7/17 | | Battalion Training. 2/LT WAGLAND proceeded to England on leave. | MM |
| | 12/7/17 | | Company Training | MM |

Army Form C. 2118.

# WAR DIARY
## or
## INTELLIGENCE SUMMARY

*(Erase heading not required.)*

1/5 GLOUCESTER Regt

| Place | Date | Hour | Summary of Events and Information | Remarks and references to Appendices |
|---|---|---|---|---|
| BELLACOURT | 13/7/17 | | S.G.M.C. lectured to all officers at BAILLEULVAL on forthcoming operations. Company Training. | WMW |
| " | 14/7/17 | | Battalion training. Lectures to officers on forthcoming operations. | WMW |
| " | 15/7/17 | | 3 officers went Battalion lectures. Instructions on forthcoming Church Parade | WMW |
| " | 16/7/17 | | Company Training. Lectures to officers on forthcoming operations | WMW |
| " | 17/7/17 | | Brigade exercise at BIENVILLERS and DOUCHY starting 2 a.m. returning to billets 7:30 pm | WMW |
| " | 18/7/17 | | Range practice. Lectures to N.C.O's on forthcoming operations | WMW |

Army Form C. 2118.

# WAR DIARY
## or
## INTELLIGENCE SUMMARY
*(Erase heading not required.)*

1/5 Gloucester Regt

Instructions regarding War Diaries and Intelligence Summaries are contained in F. S. Regs., Part II. and the Staff Manual respectively. Title Pages will be prepared in manuscript.

| Place | Date | Hour | Summary of Events and Information | Remarks and references to Appendices |
|---|---|---|---|---|
| BELLACOURT | 19/7/17 | | Company Route marches. Baths | MAH |
| " | 20/7/17 | 2pm | Battalion moved to POMMIER and took over billets from 1/6th R. WARWICKS. 1/5 STEEL rejoined from leave. | MAH |
| POMMIER | 21/7/17 | | Inspection | MAH |
| " | 22/7/17 | 2am | Entrained at MONDICOURT | MAH |
| | | 11.30am | Detrained at GODESVAERVELDE | |
| | | 2.0pm | moved to HOUTKERQUE, arriving about 5pm | |
| HOUTKERQUE | 23/7/17 | | Company training | MAH |
| " | 24/7/17 | | Brigade route march | MAH |

2449 Wt. W14957/M90 750,000 1/16 J.B.C. & A. Forms/C.2118/12.

Army Form C. 2118.

# WAR DIARY
## or
## INTELLIGENCE SUMMARY

(Erase heading not required.)

1/5 GLOUCESTER Regt

| Place | Date | Hour | Summary of Events and Information | Remarks and references to Appendices |
|---|---|---|---|---|
| DUNKERQUE | 25/7/17 | | Company Training. R.G.E. inspected Bavieres Pier. LT CORNISH returned from leave. | WW |
| " | 26/7/17 | | Company Training. R.G.E. inspected mens huts. | WW |
| " | 27/7/17 | | Battalion Route march. Battalion XV under Capt SUMNER departed (6 SHROPSHIRES and others by 11 points to 8. | WW |
| " | 28/7/17 | | Company Training. R.G.E. inspected No 8 Platoon in fighting order. 2"LT WAGLAND returned from leave. 2"LT BAMBERGER rejoined from hospital and was posted to A Coy 2"LT L.E. de RIDDER joined and was posted to C. Coy | WW |
| " | 29/7/17 | | Wet day. | WW |

Army Form C. 2118.

# WAR DIARY

## INTELLIGENCE SUMMARY

1/5 GLOUCESTERSHIRE REGT.

(Erase heading not required.)

| Place | Date | Hour | Summary of Events and Information | Remarks and references to Appendices |
|---|---|---|---|---|
| ST JAN TER BIEZEN | 3/4/17 | | Courses (contd) | |
| | | | 14/7/17 2/Lt BROWNE W.R. + 2 O.R. to XVIII Corps School | |
| | | | 10-4-17. Major D.J. WARD to Senior Officers Course Aldershot | |
| | | | 18-4-17 2.O.R. Bombing + T.M. School | |
| | | | 3.O.R. XIX Corps Signalling | |
| | | | 2/Lt R.F. McDOWALL + 10.O.R. G.H.Q Small Arms School | Spw |

J Allen Lt Col
Comm 1/5 Batt Glo. Rgt.

Army Form C. 2118.

# WAR DIARY
## or
## INTELLIGENCE SUMMARY

(Erase heading not required.)

1/5 GLOUCESTER Regt.

Instructions regarding War Diaries and Intelligence Summaries are contained in F. S. Regs., Part II. and the Staff Manual respectively. Title Pages will be prepared in manuscript.

| Place | Date | Hour | Summary of Events and Information | Remarks and references to Appendices |
|---|---|---|---|---|
| HOUTKERQUE | 30/7/17 | | Coys. Individual training. - Box respirator drill etc. Lectures to NCO's on map reading and compass. | MTW |
| ST. JAN TER BIEZEN | 31/7/17 | 11. A.m. | Battalion moved to ST JAN TER BIEZEN and took over camp from 1/7th R. WARWICKS. On Eve of Z Day of Battle. N. W. of YPRES. 48th Div. in reserve to XVIII Corps. | |
| | | | Strength. | |
| | | | Fighting Strength 1—7—17    Officers 33    O.R. 706 | |
| | | | do    31—7—17    34    942 | |
| | | | Ration Strength 1—7—17    22    644 | |
| | | | do    31—7—17    30    859 | |
| | | | Casualties. 1 O.R. died of wounds 3—7—17. | |
| | | | Courses 2—7—17. 9 O.R. Corps Snipers School ROVES. | |
| | | | 3—7—17. 1 O.R. V Army School of Infantry (as Instructor). | Two |

2449 Wt. W14957/M90 750,000 1/16 J.B.C. & A. Forms/C.2118/12.

1/5th Bn. Gloucester Regiment

War Diary Vol 30.

August 1914.

VOLUME XXIX

Army Form C. 2118.

# WAR DIARY
## or
## INTELLIGENCE SUMMARY

(Erase heading not required.)

1/5 GLOUCESTERSHIRE REGT

| Place | Date | Hour | Summary of Events and Information | Remarks and references to Appendices |
|---|---|---|---|---|
| SI JAN TER BIEZEN | 1/8/17 | | Heavy rain all night and morning. | |

# WAR DIARY or INTELLIGENCE SUMMARY

Army Form C. 2118.

**1/5 Bn Gloucestershire Regt.**

| Place | Date | Hour | Summary of Events and Information | Remarks and references to Appendices |
|---|---|---|---|---|
| ST JAN TER BIEZEN | 1.8.17 | | Heavy rain all night and morning. Mostly wet. Company training. Five about by Crows for Bn. | |
| TER BIEZEN | 2.8.17 | | 2/Lt HAWKINS on leave to England | |
| " | 3.8.17 | | Company route march. | |
| VLAMERTINGHE | 4.8.17 | | Bn moved to camp at VLAMERTINGHE but too much room | |
| YPRES | 5.8.17 | | Bn arrived W of YPRES and took over trenches in C.II.d and C.II.c from 17th SHERWOODS and 13th K.R.R.S. C company on right (CAPT CORDER) A Company left (CAPT HORLINGTON) D company right support (LT CORNEY) B Company left support (LT RATCLIFFE). Hostile shelling very heavy and continuous. A good many casualties. | 2 P.A.M |
| " | 6.8.17 | | Hostile shelling continued & also casualties. Patrol consisting of 2nd Lt GULLICK, 2/MAJOR & 1/h.O.R.C moved out at 11.25 P.M. to reconnoitre the EAST bank of STEENBEEK. So enemy was found. Patrol was not fired on returned at 11.45 P.M. | 2.P.C.1 |

Army Form C. 2118.

# WAR DIARY
or
## INTELLIGENCE SUMMARY.

*(Erase heading not required.)*

Instructions regarding War Diaries and Intelligence Summaries are contained in F. S. Regs., Part II. and the Staff Manual respectively. Title pages will be prepared in manuscript.

1/5th Sussex [?] Regt.

| Place | Date | Hour | Summary of Events and Information | Remarks and references to Appendices |
|---|---|---|---|---|
| YPRES | 7.8.17 | | Relieved by 1/1 Bucks & moved to Cons. Tank. & quiet day shelling during relief. Covered by a counter attack on the outposts in number. Many dead lying out in the Canal. Some few still during to night. CAPT FRANCILLON & 2nd LT REMNANT Sim wounded in knee. | APPX |
| VLAMERTINGHE | 8.8.17 | | Relieved by 1/1 ROYAL WARWICKS & marched back to JAMBRE camp hirs Vlamertinghe. | APPX |
| " | 9.8.17 | | In resting & inspections by Company Commanders. 2/Lt BRUTON arrived to take over Adjutants duties. 2/Lt CORNISH to 5 ARMY SCHOOL. | APPX |
| " | 10.8.17 | | Company route march. | APPX |
| " | 11.8.17 | | Company training. Hostile aeroplane flew & dropped [?] | APPX |

# WAR DIARY
## or
## INTELLIGENCE SUMMARY. 1/4 Bn. Warwickshire Regt.

*(Erase heading not required.)*

Army Form C. 2118.

| Place | Date | Hour | Summary of Events and Information | Remarks and references to Appendices |
|---|---|---|---|---|
| VLAMERTINGHE | 12.8.17 | | Brigade practised over ground similar to that over which we were to attack. A.C.O's & officers only | XX1 |
| " | 13.8.17 | | Do — with the Bn. | XX11 |
| " | 14.8.17 | | Do | XX111 |
| YPRES | 15.8.17 | | Bn. moved up to ST JULIEN and deployed for attack in GREEN LINE. C Company on right. A Coy on left forming 1st & 2nd waves. B Coy in right forming 3rd & 4th waves in artillery formation. | LR11 |
| ST JULIEN | 16.8.17 | 4.45 a.m. | ZERO hour 4.45 A.M. We attacked (inclusive) enemy strong points namely "BORDER HOUSE", Gun Pitts in S. side of ST JULIEN — WINNIPEG — some found. Machine guns in JANET FARM and in hedges in rear prevented any further advance. A line containing A.M.G.m C12C.35.65 was still held by the enemy. M.G's were do. and went. Rifle grenades and A.G. covered everywhere. By this time the barrage had left us behind & many casualties had occurred. | |

Army Form C. 2118.

# WAR DIARY
## or
## INTELLIGENCE SUMMARY.

*(Erase heading not required.)*

1/5 Bn Gloucestershire Regt

| Place | Date | Hour | Summary of Events and Information | Remarks and references to Appendices |
|---|---|---|---|---|
| ST JULIEN | 16.8.17 | | The Bn started digging in on its forward position. Was shelled with R.G. all the time. During the day the enemy airmen were very active caused us some casualties | App 1 |
| | 17.8.17 | | During the night the 8th WARWICKS took up a line of P.O.P's about 100 yds in advance of our posts and (proceeded) We remained in our outpost till the enemy when and came and (proceeded) on to DANNBRE hot meal at REIGERSBERG Camp Our casualties were: 1 officer killed 8 officers wounded 20 O.R. killed — many wounded | App 1 |
| VLAMERTINGE | 18.8.17 | | Rested and reorganized. CAPT HAWKINS + A Company (B.H. been blown in during attack). CAPT MACDOWELL B Cy. LT RATCLIFF & 2/LT DEATON C Cy. 2/LT BINGHAM-HALL D Cy. These were the only officers exclusive of HQ who returned from attack. Many men of Cos had to be made up | App 1 |

Army Form C. 2118.

# WAR DIARY
## or
## INTELLIGENCE SUMMARY  1/5 Bn Gloucestershire Regt
(Erase heading not required.)

| Place | Date | Hour | Summary of Events and Information | Remarks and references to Appendices |
|---|---|---|---|---|
| VLAMERTINGHE | 19.8.17 | | Cleaned up and reorganized. Church Parade. | KRCO |
| " | 20.8.17 | | Company training. 20 men frauds sent on leave. | RRCO |
| " | 21.8.17 | | - Do - Church arranged to be replaced by an equal number | RRCO |
| " | 22.8.17 | | Also MAJOR WALLER to assist C.O. and 3 Company commders proceeded to HAZEBROUCK for demonstration in attack in strong point. Company training. Indic plateoon hing of war competition | RRCO |
| " | 23.8.17 | | - Do - | RRCO |
| " | 24.8.17 | | - Do - | RRCO RRCO |
| " | 25.8.17 | | - Do - | RRCO |
| " | 26.8.17 | | Bn. moved to REIGERSBURG Camp. | RRCO |
| REIGERSBURG | 27.8.17 | | Moved up at 4.25 P.M. in reserve. Bad weather | |

Army Form C. 2118.

# WAR DIARY or INTELLIGENCE SUMMARY

(Erase heading not required.)

1/5 Bn. Gloucestershire Regt.

| Place | Date | Hour | Summary of Events and Information | Remarks and references to Appendices |
|---|---|---|---|---|
| REIGERSBURG (continued) | 27.8.17 | | Our position of assembly was that vacated by 1/4 Royal BERKS. ie GUN PITS, JEW HILL, W. of JANET FARM. 2 Coys on Right, B. Coy on Left. C. & A. Coys in reserve. Formed up in section in artillery formation with few casualties. On arrival at position of assembly found it already occupied by BERKS. & WARWICKS. so at 6.30 P.M. moved back to W. bank of STEENBEEK. At 10 P.M. orders were received to side slip to the left to HILLOCK FARM, which was done by B.C. & D. Coys. Orders A Company being in KITCHENER WOOD line. At 3 A.M. B & D Coys were ordered to move back to O.G.1. which was done. | APP1 |
| ST. JULIEN | 28.8.17 | | Bn. relieved by 1/10 LONDON Regiment. About 30 casualties shown by 58th Division & moved to REIGERSBURG Camp. | APP2 |
| DAMBRE CAMP | 29.8.17 | | Moved back to DAMBRE camp. A Company in Lorries. Col. ADAM went on leave | APP3 |

**Army Form C. 2118.**

# WAR DIARY or INTELLIGENCE SUMMARY

(Erase heading not required.)

1/5 Gloucestershire Regt

| Place | Date | Hour | Summary of Events and Information | Remarks and references to Appendices |
|---|---|---|---|---|
| ST JANSTER-BIEZEN | 30.8.17 | | Bn. moved back to ROAD CAMP, St JANSTER-BIEZEN. | XRCS |
| " | 31.8.17 | | Organization - 130 reinforcements arrived.<br><br>Total Casualties O.R. 69 killed 249 wounded 15 Missing.<br>Capt Conder, 2nd Winterbotham, 2nd Wayland wounded 1/8/17.<br>2nd Lieut Gullick wounded 2/8/17.<br>2nd Lieut Steel killed 16/8/17.<br>2nd Lieut Bamberger Missing 16/8/17.<br>Capt Hollington, Lieut Corbish, 2nd Pyralt, Lake, Bretherton La Trobe wounded 16/8/17.<br>Capt McDowall wounded 29/8/17.<br><br>               O.      O.R.<br>Fighting Strength  1/8/17  34  940  31/8/17  22  778<br>Ration Strength  1/8/17  29  875  31/8/17  19  623.<br><br>2nd Fowler to Lewis Gun School, 10 R.S Army School, 6 O.R NCO's Training Class, 12 Reinf to 6th Warwickshire<br>Leave<br>Lt-Col Adam, Capt Hawkins, Capt Trauellor, Capt Foster, 2nd Rubenstein | XRCS |

M.H. Walker  
Lt Colonel,  
Comdg. 1/5th BN. GLOUCESTER REGT.

1/5th Bn: Gloucestershire Regt. Vol 31

WAR DIARY.

VOLUME XXIX

SEPTEMBER 1917

Army Form C. 2118.

# WAR DIARY
## or
## INTELLIGENCE SUMMARY

(Erase heading not required.)

| Place | Date | Hour | Summary of Events and Information | Remarks and references to Appendices |
|---|---|---|---|---|
| ROADS CAMP | 1.9.17 | | Co + Platoon Training | |
| ST JAN TER BIEZEN | 2.9.17 | | Brigade Church Parade. Presentation of medals by G.O.C. Brigade. | |
| | 3.9.17 | | Co Training | |
| | 4.9.17 | | Route march by Cos. All Officers except H.Q. Officers proceeded to XVIIIth Corps School, VOLKERINCKHOVE (on Course of Lectures). | |
| | 5.9.17 | | } Co + Platoon Training | |
| | 6.9.17 | | } | |
| | 7.9.17 | | Musketry Practices on new Brigade range Thirito Camp. Co + Platoon Training. Officers returned from Corps School. | |
| | 8.9.17 | | Co Training. Platoon Exercise. | |
| | 9.9.17 | | Brigade Church Parade. Roman Catholic Divine Service. | |
| | 10.9.17 | | Route march by Cos., including a Platoon Exercise. | |
| | 11.9.17 | | Musketry on Range. Co + Platoon Training. | |
| | 12.9.17 | | } Co Exercises. Deployment + attacks on Strong Points. | |
| | 13.9.17 | | } | |
| | | | G.H. | |

Army Form C. 2118.

# WAR DIARY
## or
## INTELLIGENCE SUMMARY

*(Erase heading not required.)*

Instructions regarding War Diaries and Intelligence Summaries are contained in F. S. Regs., Part II. and the Staff Manual respectively. Title Pages will be prepared in manuscript.

| Place | Date | Hour | Summary of Events and Information | Remarks and references to Appendices |
|---|---|---|---|---|
| ROADS CAMP (cont.) | 14.9.17 | | Route march by Cos + Practice Deployment from Column of Route. Inspection of A.C. by C.O. Baths at new Camp Baths. | |
| " | 15.9.17 | | Musketry on Range. Live Bowling + Grenade firing. Musketry Competition with Lewis + Vickers Target in afternoon. 5 teams, one from each Co. + 1 from H.Q. details. Won by C Co. | |
| " | 16.9.17 | | Battalion moved to LIQUES area for Divisional Training, but as at ABEELE. Detrained at AUDRICQUES. Marched 14 miles + billeted H.Q. + C Co. at ALEMBON. A + B Co. at SANGHEM. D Co. at LE VENTU. | |
| LIQUES AREA | 17.9.17 | | Inspections. D Co. moved to Billets in ALEMBON. | |
| " | 18.9.17 | | Practice by Cos of 48th Div. F.119. | |
| " | 19.9.17 | | Brigade Scheme in C Area | |
| " | 20.9.17 | | Co Parades for Physical Drill + Practice of F.119 (Field Firing) | |
| " | 21.9.17 | | Brigade Scheme | |
| " | 22.9.17 | | Field Firing at GUEMY. | |

Army Form C. 2118.

# WAR DIARY
or
## INTELLIGENCE SUMMARY.
(Erase heading not required.)

| Place | Date | Hour | Summary of Events and Information | Remarks and references to Appendices |
|---|---|---|---|---|
| LICQUES AREA (cont.) | 23.9.17 | | Church Parade at SANGHEM. Kit Inspection. | |
| | 24.9.17 | | Field Firing at GUEMY. Divisional Field Firing Competition. Won by D Co. 1/5 Glos. Regt. Battalion moved to BONNINGUES. | |
| BONNINGUES | 25.9.17 | | Battalion moved to REIGERSBURG Camp. Entrained at WATTEN and detrained at REIGERSBURG. | |
| REIGERSBURG | 26.9.17 | | Moved at 8 p.m. to CANAL BANK in reserve to 58th Divisional attack on AVIATIK Farm. A Co. moved up to CALIFORNIA DRIVE. | |
| CANAL BANK | 27.9.17 | | Battalion relieved 2nd and 10th LONDON Regt. in the line. C Co. right front, D C° left front, B C° in support, A C° in reserve. | |
| | 28.9.17 | | In front line. Very heavy enemy shelling. LT. COL. W. ADAM gassed. | |
| | 29.9.17 | | Battalion relieved by 1/4 R. BERKS + moved to support Battalion Positions to have CHEDDAR VILLA. MAJOR A.B. LEO D-BAKER took over command. | |
| | 30.9.17 | | Battalion relieved by 1/4 OXFORDS + moved to CANAL BANK | |

Army Form C. 2118.

# WAR DIARY
## or
## INTELLIGENCE SUMMARY.

(Erase heading not required.)

Instructions regarding War Diaries and Intelligence Summaries are contained in F. S. Regs., Part II. and the Staff Manual respectively. Title pages will be prepared in manuscript.

| Place | Date | Hour | Summary of Events and Information | Remarks and references to Appendices |
|---|---|---|---|---|
| | | | Honours awarded:- | |
| | | | CAPT. G.E. RATCLIFF } | |
| | | | 2nd LT K.A. ROBERTSON } MILITARY CROSS | |
| | | | " A.J. DEATON } | |
| | | | 240038 C.S.M. SMITH V.G. } D.C.M. | |
| | | | 240276 L/CORP. MILLICHAP, P.J } | |
| | | | 203244 SERG. PULLIN J. } | |
| | | | 203706 " HODGES J.T. } | |
| | | | 210773 CORP. STREET C.H. } MILITARY MEDAL. | |
| | | | 240750 L/CORP. COOK, C } | |
| | | | 203696 PTE CLEE M. } | |
| | | | | |
| | | | OFFICERS JOINED DURING MONTH | |
| | | | 2nd LT E.G. TOWNSEND | |
| | | | " H. TILL | |
| | | | " E.A.R. JOSEPHS | |
| | | | " H.S.A. MOORE | |
| | | | " R.E. SHEARS | |
| | | | " C.W.E. RAWLINGS | |
| | | | " C.L. POMEROY | |
| | | | " C.L. OVENDEN | |
| | | | " R.F. TAYLOR | |
| | | | " H.C. PARSONS | |
| | | | " S. BRYANT | |
| | | | " H.A. COOKE | |
| | | | " O.V. DAVIES | |
| | | | ATTACHED to replace CASUALTIES:- | |
| | | | 2nd LT HAYES | |
| | | | " B. TWELVETREES | |
| | | | " C.M. PHINN | |

# WAR DIARY
## or
## INTELLIGENCE SUMMARY.

*(Erase heading not required.)*

Army Form C. 2118.

| Place | Date | Hour | Summary of Events and Information | Remarks and references to Appendices |
|---|---|---|---|---|
| | | | FIGHTING STRENGTH  1.9.17  22 OFF.  776 O.R.      31.9.17  34 OFF. 880 O.R. <br> RATION STRENGTH  16 "  630 "                            17 "  731 " <br><br> CASUALTIES. <br> KILLED  10 O.R. <br> DIED OF WOUNDS  2nd LT C.W.E. RAWLINGS <br> WOUNDED  CAPT C.A. HAWKINS <br> " 2nd LT H.S.A. MOORE <br> " E.G. TOWNSEND <br> " C.W. PHINN (1st Bucks att.) <br> 74 O.R. <br> Do (Slight, at duty) 1 O.R. <br><br> COURSES. <br> 2nd LT F.J. CLIFTON  Small Arms School  G.H.Q.  3-12.9.17. <br> " V.B. BINGHAM-HALL  P.T. & Bayonet Fighting  16.9.17. <br> " R.E. SHEARS  XVIII Corps L.G. School  21.9.17. <br><br> P.B. Lloyd Baker <br> MAJOR Lt.Colonel <br> COMDG. 1/5th BN. GLOUCESTER REGT. | |

1/5TH BN. GLOUCESTERSHIRE REGT.

# WAR DIARY

VOL: XXI

OCTOBER 1917

Army Form C. 2118.

# WAR DIARY
## or
## INTELLIGENCE SUMMARY.
(Erase heading not required.)

**W. GLOUCESTER REGT**

| Place | Date | Hour | Summary of Events and Information | Remarks and references to Appendices |
|---|---|---|---|---|
| CANAL BANK | Oct 17 1 | | Btn in reserve. Resting, cleaning up etc. | |
| " | 2 | | D - - - at 2130 p.m. moved to REIGERSBURG camp. | |
| REIGERSBURG | 3 | | Btn in reserve. Inspections etc. | |
| | 4 | | Moved to CALIFORNIA DRIVE HQrs at CHEDDAR VILLA in reserve to 143 Bde. Started at 6.0 a.m. At 3.30 p.m. gun? having moved up to position of closer support at ARBRE received orders to attack at 5.0 p.m. Attack formation and objectives. A Coy in reserve at ALBATROSS with Btn H.Q. B coy, C coy and D coy from right to left attacking ADLER Fm, INCH HOUSES and VACHER Fm respectively. The coys formed up just S. of WINCHESTER Farm the morning of the hour, at 5.0 p.m. attacked. Owing to the barrage being too far ahead and hung over the line our men advanced only 200 yds, where the fraction was established. Casualties were 5 O.R. for the total was 2 Officers killed & wounded and 135 O.R. Btn HQrs moved to ARBRE with A Coy. | |
| | 5 | | Btn close support. | |
| | 6 | | Relieved by 2nd R. WARWICKS at 2.0 a.m. & moved to REIGERSBURG. | |

Army Form C. 2118.

# WAR DIARY
## or
## INTELLIGENCE SUMMARY.
(Erase heading not required.)

1/5 Gloucester Regt

| Place | Date | Hour | Summary of Events and Information | Remarks and references to Appendices |
|---|---|---|---|---|
| REIGERSBURG | 7-10-17 | | Bn in Bivouacs. reorganisation etc. Major D.J. WARD rejoined from Senior Officers' School ALDERSHOT | |
| | 8-10-17 | | Moved to DAMBRE camp to huts at 2.30 p.m. Large parties of Bn for carrying parties etc left befor hand. Very heavy rain. | |
| DAMBRE Camp | 9-10-17 | | In reserve. Another stretch of heavy fatigues and kit inspection etc. | Casualties for period O.R. 1 killed, 11 wounded |
| | 10.10.17 | | At DAMBRE CAMP – carrying parties, shell out - do - | B/11 |
| | 11.10.17 | | – do – Parties returned - inspections - kit cuttings - | B/11 |
| | 12.10.17 | | At 5.45 p.m Battalion moved to ROAD CAMP – STANSTER BIEZEN arriving 7 p.m. heavy rain throughout march. Echelon B & reinforcements arrived from HOOT MERNS | |
| STANSTER BIEZEN | 13.10.17 | | at ROAD CAMP - heavy rain - cold winds | B/11 |
| | 14.10.17 | | Marched to HOPOUTRE (being camp) at 6.30 a.m. entrained by 10.25 a.m. detrained at LISNY YELLOWTEL 5.30 p.m. marched to CAMBLAIN L'ABBE arriving at 2.30 a.m. 15/9/17. 2/Lt COOKE + 100 men acted as detraining party of 5th Brigade | B/11 |
| CAMBLAIN L'ABBE | 15.10.17 | | cleaning up - inspections under OC Companies arrangements | B/11 |
| | 16.10.17 | | Company Kommand parade 11 pm. At 3 pm Bn attended Brigade Parade at CAMBLAIN L'ABBE for presentation of Medals by Brigadier General D.M. WATTS D.S.O. The following were announced | B/11 |

Army Form C. 2118.

1/5 GLOUCESTER REGT

# WAR DIARY
## or
## INTELLIGENCE SUMMARY.
*(Erase heading not required.)*

Instructions regarding War Diaries and Intelligence Summaries are contained in F.S. Regs., Part II. and the Staff Manual respectively. Title pages will be prepared in manuscript.

| Place | Date | Hour | Summary of Events and Information | Remarks and references to Appendices |
|---|---|---|---|---|
| CAUDRON L'ABBÉ | 16.10.17 | | Chas decorated. 240276 L/Cpl MILLICHAP RJ D.C.M. 203696 Pte CLEE M. M.M. | |
| | 17.10.17 | | Company Games. Lt Col ADAM reports Rowntreelinst (KH?) Major AB LLOYD BORER under him | |
| | 18.10.17 | | Moved to VILLERS au BOIS taking over huts from 2nd CANADIAN BATTN. | |
| VILLERS au BOIS | 19.10.17 | | Company Training - Platoon training & night patrolling | |
| | 20.10.17 | | do Draft in range | |
| | 21.10.17 | | Church service in hut. Half draft take over trenches in range (Coy/pm Officer in) | |
| | 22.10.17 | | Platoon training - night patrolling. repairs wiring. Lecture by Major ANDERSON Experimental Dept 1st ARMY | |
| | 23.10.17 | | Company training - Range - Officers taken on Lewis Gun | |
| | 24.10.17 | | Platoon training - repairs wiring - Range Patrolling | |
| | 25.10.17 | | - do - | |
| | 26.10.17 | | Platoon Training. Battalion Drill. Patrolling in evening. A Co cleaning trenches Reinforcements sent forward | |
| WINNIPEG CAMP | 27.10.17 | | Platoon Training. Range Practices. Patrolling in evening. Concert at CANADIAN THEATRE Working party at night in front line | |
| | 28.10.17 | | BRIGADE PARADE. Presentation of medals by G.O.C. Church Parade with 1/4 R. BERKS. Association Football Match. 1/5 GLOS. Officers beat 1/4 R. BERKS. Officers 2-1. Working party at night in forward area | |

Army Form C. 2118.

# WAR DIARY
## or
## INTELLIGENCE SUMMARY.

*(Erase heading not required.)*

Instructions regarding War Diaries and Intelligence Summaries are contained in F. S. Regs., Part II. and the Staff Manual respectively. Title pages will be prepared in manuscript.

| Place | Date | Hour | Summary of Events and Information | Remarks and references to Appendices |
|---|---|---|---|---|
| VILLERS-AU-BOIS (cont) | 29.10.17 | | Autumn Training, musketry, Range Practice. Lecture on Artillery to Officers, NCOs by 2nd Lt C.D.WHITE. Athletics in evening. | RNR |
| | 30.10.17 | | Route march by Cos. Partly trained men working. | RNR |
| | 31.10.17 | | Filling in trenches. Fitting Equipment. Kit Inspection. Partly Trained men, musketry. Lecture by O.C. to Officers & NCOs. | RNR |

CASUALTIES

2nd Lt. B. TWELVETREES  Killed  4.10.17
" H. TILL  "  4.10.17
a/CAPT. E.F. FOWLER  Wounded 4.10.17
2nd LT. K.A. ROBERTSON  "    "
" W.R. BROWNE  "    "
" O.V. DAVIES  "    "

O.R.
K. W. M. GASSED
20 105  7  26

FIGHTING STRENGTH

|         | OFF. | O.R. |
|---------|------|------|
| 1.10.17 | 27   | 754  |
| 31.10.17| 30   | 709  |

RATION STRENGTH

|         | OFF. | O.R. |
|---------|------|------|
| 1.10.17 | 24   | 724  |
| 31.10.17| 28   | 651  |

Army Form C. 2118.

# WAR DIARY
## or
## INTELLIGENCE SUMMARY.
(Erase heading not required.)

| Place | Date | Hour | Summary of Events and Information | Remarks and references to Appendices |
|---|---|---|---|---|
| | | | COURSES. | |
| | | | 1 O.R. School of Cookery. | |
| | | | 1 O.R. School of Musketry, ENGLAND. | |
| | | | 1 O.R. V Army Infantry School. | |
| | | | 2nd Lt A.J. DEATON Do. | |
| | | | 1 O.R. XVIIIth Corps L.G. School. | |
| | | | 1 O.R. Small Arms School G.H.Q. | |
| | | | 2nd Lt J.H.O'LEARY Transport Course. | |
| | | | " C.L. OVENDEN V Army Sniping School. | |
| | | | 2 O.R. 1st Army Musketry Camp | |
| | | | 1 O.R. 1st Army Signal School | |
| | | | 3 O.R. V Corps Gas School. | |
| | | | 2nd Lt R.R.E. ELCOCK } V Corps Infantry School | |
| | | | H.G. POWELL } Do. | |
| | | | & O.R. | |
| | | | SERG. PULLIN E. to ENGLAND for Commission. | |
| | | | HONOURS & AWARDS. | |
| | | | 2nd Lt E.A.R. JOSEPHS M.C. | |
| | | | 240715 C.S.M. W. MIDDLECOTE D.C.M. | |
| | | | 240562 L/CORP M. JORDAN M.M. | |

LT-COLONEL,
COMMD. 1/5th BN. GLOUCESTER REGT.

WO 95/2763

5 PARTS

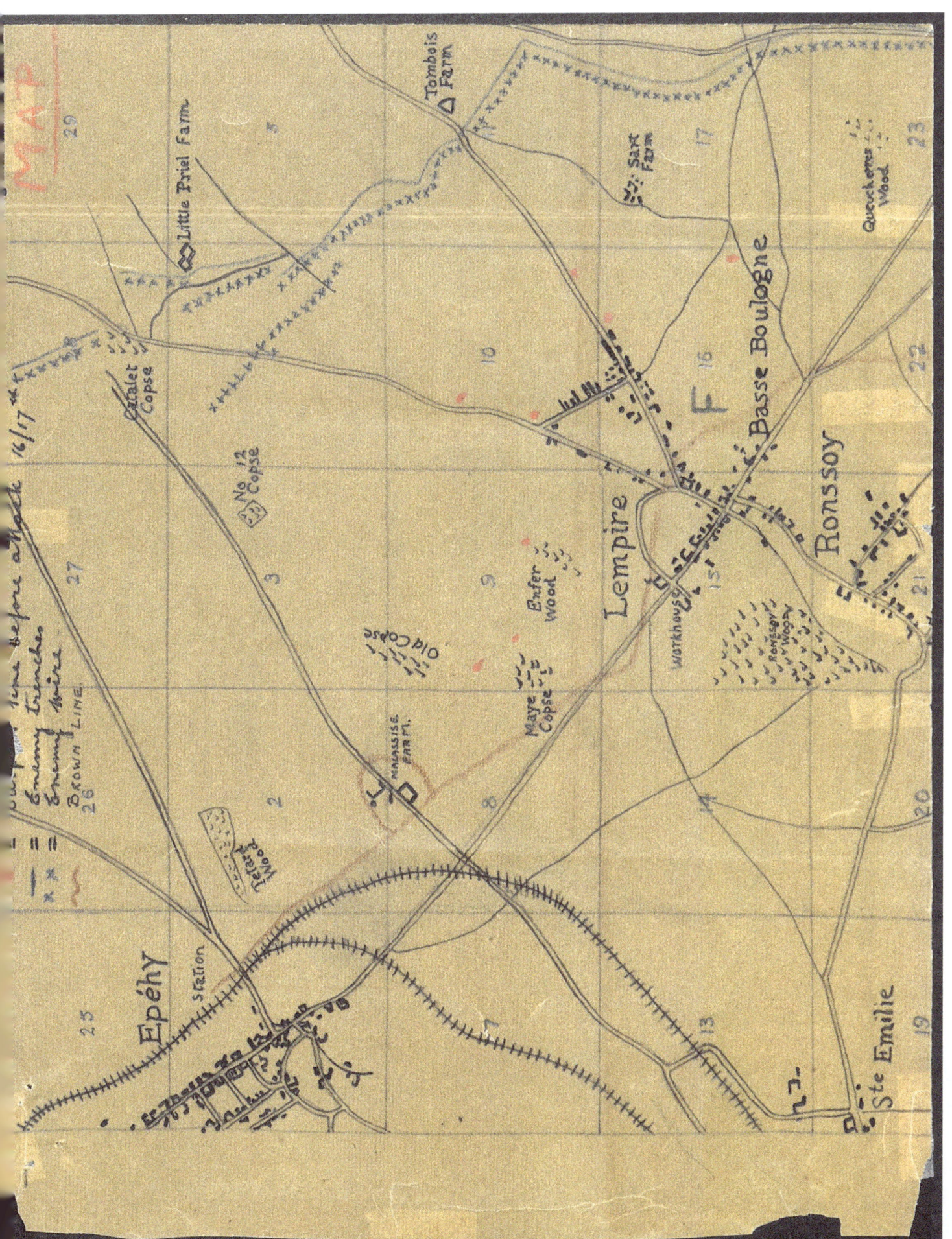

WO 95/2763
5 PARTS

WO 95/2763
5 PARTS

HINDENBERG LINE

28

26

25

30

Malakoff Fme

WO95/2763

5 PARTS

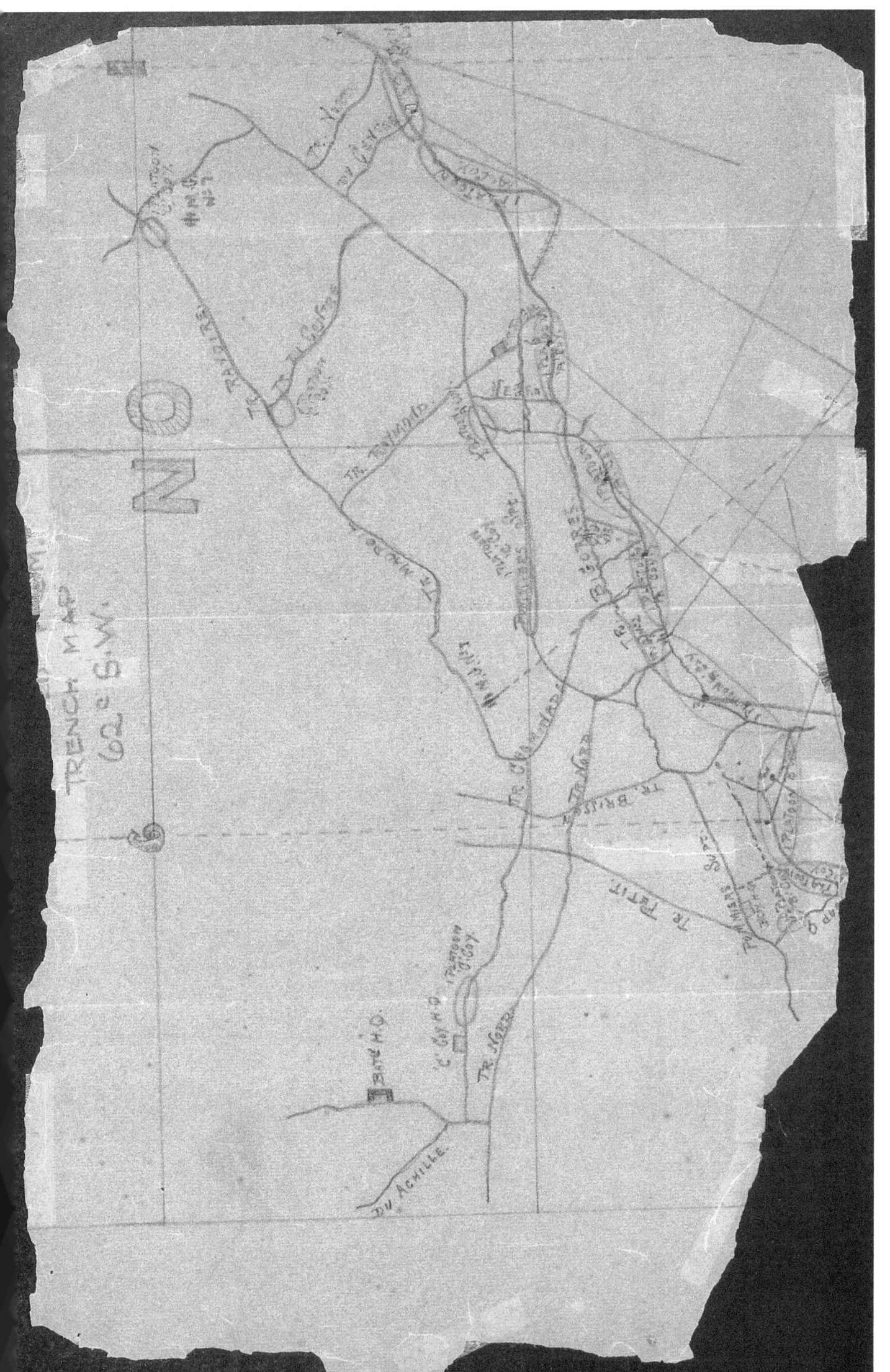

www.ingramcontent.com/pod-product-compliance
Lightning Source LLC
Chambersburg PA
CBHW080922230426
43668CB00014B/2178